BRITAIN IN THE WORLD TODAY

BRITAIN'S MOMENT
IN THE MIDDLE EAST
1914–1956

BRITAIN'S MOMENT IN
THE MIDDLE EAST
1914–1956

Elizabeth Monroe

THE JOHNS HOPKINS PRESS : BALTIMORE

Published in Great Britain by
Chatto & Windus Ltd
42 William IV Street
London W.C.2

Library of Congress Catalog Card Number: 63-18821

TO
HUMPHREY

CONTENTS

MAPS

ACKNOWLEDGEMENTS

MY thanks go, in the first place, to all the friends in the Middle East who have helped me with information, advice and hospitality during twenty-five years of intermittent work and travel in their countries. I likewise thank many friends in Britain, France and the United States who share with me an interest in Middle Eastern affairs. They include, in particular, the board and staff of *The Economist* newspaper, to which I owe most of my opportunities for travel.

More immediately, I thank the Warden and Fellows of St. Antony's College, and the Principal and Fellows of St Anne's College, Oxford, for shelter and encouragement during the years in which I worked on this book. I also thank the Leverhulme Trust for support of the project. The book took shape at a series of the Friday seminars at St Antony's Centre of Middle Eastern Studies, and I am grateful to members of the 1961 vintage of that seminar for lively comment and suggestions. Particularly do I thank Albert Hourani and Sir Reader Bullard for giving me generous amounts of their time and thought.

I am indebted to Christopher Sykes for getting me his brother's permission to use Sir Mark Sykes's papers; to the Librarian of New College, Oxford, for access to Lord Milner's papers; to Richard Hill of the School of Oriental Studies at Durham University for help with Sir Reginald Wingate's papers, and to Elie Kedourie for some suggestions about these; to William Yale, now of Boston University, for information about the circumstances in which he made his reports to the State Department forty-five years ago; to the Controller of Her Majesty's Stationery Office for permission to quote material that is Crown copyright; to the Chartwell Trust for permission to quote from Sir Winston Churchill's works; to Colonel Pierre Rondot and David Wynne-Morgan for permission to quote from their writings; to Leonard Stein for guidance about certain events of 1917; to Stephen Longrigg for his long memory about some of the early negotiations for oil concessions, and to Mrs. Clara

Boyle and C. J. Edmonds for permission to quote from private letters.

For help with research, I thank Ann Williams, librarian of the Middle East Centre at St. Antony's; also the College Librarian, the Librarian of the Foreign Office, and the library staffs of Chatham House and the London Library. Especially, I thank the staff of the Chatham House Press Library for indefatigable delving into its unmatched store of material. I also acknowledge bibliographical help from the libraries of the Middle East Institute in Washington and the *Centre d'Etudes de Politique Etrangère* in Paris.

I am indebted to the following publishers and newspapers for permission to quote from the books or articles published by them that are listed in the references on pp. 221–226:

In Britain: Messrs. Allen & Unwin, Edward Arnold, Benn, Cape, Cassell, Collins, Constable, the Cresset Press, Hamish Hamilton, Harrap, Heinemann, Hodder & Stoughton, Hutchinson, Macmillan, John Murray, the Oxford University Press, Nicholson & Watson, Vallentine Mitchell; and to Messrs. A. P. Watt for securing permission from the owner of the copyright to quote from the *Life of Lord Salisbury*.

The Economist, The Observer, The Sunday Times, The Times.

In the United States: Messrs. John Day, the Cornell University Press, Houghton Mifflin.

The New York Herald Tribune.

Lastly, I thank Daphne Johnstone, Daphne Hitchcock and Ann Liley for help with decipherment and typing, and Margaret Linell and Erica Newton for work on the index.

Oxford, 1963.   E. M.

INTRODUCTION

FORTY years is a common measure of time in Middle Eastern history and fable, and for almost exactly that period—from the British capture of Baghdad and Jerusalem in 1917 until the Suez crisis of 1956—Great Britain was the paramount power in most of the Middle East. This book is about the establishment of that power, the uses to which it was put, and the reasons for its decline after 1945.

Forty years is only a moment in the life of a region with a recorded history of four millennia. Britain's time of dominance will seem short in the eyes of later centuries. But to those who took part in it, the moment seemed long enough for the performance of services useful both to Britain and to certain Middle Eastern peoples. These British citizens saw their service in terms of their local work: harnessing the Nile, training armies and policemen, teaching tree-planting to halt soil erosion, trying to reconcile Arabs to Jewish settlement, introducing Kurdish highlanders to central government or, if they belonged to the *corps d'élite*, administering the Sudan. But the basic motive behind all their effort was to keep the route to India orderly and secure. Only after 1945 did it become obvious that they were also helping to hold the Soviet gateway to Africa, and to safeguard the east-west passage of quantities of oil that were becoming indispensable to western Europe.

The present generation is apt to underrate the enormous role played by India in the British scale of values before the Indian Independence Act of 1947. It had a Secretary of State to itself in the British Cabinet, and was an empire in its own right. In the report that inaugurated the Committee of Imperial Defence in 1904, India ranks next after the Royal Navy as a component of British strength:

> The British Empire is pre-eminently a great Naval, Indian and Colonial power.[1]

The order of precedence is justified. In the first decade of this century, approximately half the British army was stationed in India, and in addition the Indian army, in which all but the most junior officers were British, numbered nearly a quarter of a million men, with an almost inexhaustible reserve of manpower at its back. Long before India made its great contribution to British victory in the two World Wars, this huge, pivotable force could be used, and had been used, as far east as China and as far west as Egypt, the Sudan and Ethiopia to uphold British influence and trade; its importance was paramount to the last:

> With the loss of India and Burma the keystone of the arch of our Commonwealth Defence was lost [wrote Lord Alan-brooke, till 1946 Chief of the Imperial General Staff]. Without the central strategic reserve of Indian troops able to operate either east or west, we were left impotent. . . .[2]

India also provided a valuable range of training grounds for army service in almost every climate—mountain, jungle, desert, everything except Flanders damp and mud. India as a commercial asset accounted in 1913 for nearly ten per cent of total British trade, and was by far the United Kingdom's best customer; this last place it had lost by 1938 to Australia and the Union of South Africa, but in 1946—the last full year of the old relationship—India was back again at the head of the list.

The Government of India made policy in its own right, including foreign policy; it was not bound to refer matters to London. During the nineteenth century, it forged south Asia into a single unit for defence purposes by means of annexations, alliances and the exercise of influence, and extended that unit into the Middle East. It formed a great shield that included Aden (annexed in 1839 as a guarantee against Egyptian expansion) and the Arab principalities of the whole coast of Arabia, where, by a series of agreements that began while Napoleon was in Egypt, it won promises to keep other foreigners out. India handled relations with the Ottoman province of lower Mesopotamia (where its representatives long used the Indian title of 'resident', instead of consul); it dealt with Afghanistan. In Persia, after fifty years of tussle and overlap with London, the two governments reached in 1860 a gentlemen's agreement whereby all British consular and diplomatic posts in the south and east of the country were staffed from India, while London handled Teheran and the remaining consulates, including Tabriz, Isfahan and Shiraz. One result of these arrangements was that, for years, the men at both ends tended to look on the Middle East not as a single region but as a desert with two edges, one belonging to the Mediterranean and the other to the Indian Ocean. The distinction survived until the great leap forward in communications brought about by the Second World War, after which regular bus and air services and the multiplication of oil pipelines narrowed the desert gap.

Britain's long-standing preference for the ocean route to India, for its greater cheapness as well as freedom from interference, is well known because of Palmerston's notorious opposition to the cutting of the Suez Canal. But in fact, the short route caused anxiety to statesmen from a much earlier date. The House of Commons first debated its security in 1791, in connexion with an ultimatum to Russia that Pitt had issued in foreboding about Catherine the Great's expansionist policy on the Black Sea. He failed to carry a majority large enough to maintain his stand, and told a friend "with the tears in his eyes" that

> they cannot be made to comprehend a case in which the most valuable interests of the country are at stake.[3]

Almost simultaneously, in Egypt, a pioneer of the short route named George Baldwin was appointed Consul-General at Alexandria, only to see his functions suspended in 1793 as too expensive at £2,000 a year. Not until Napoleon made his thrust at Egypt in 1798, and laid plans for a treaty with Persia in 1807, was full British and Indian attention given to the danger of letting the short route fall under the dominance of France or Russia.

But which route? There was a choice of two—one overland from Alexandria to Suez and thence via the Red Sea, the other across the north Syrian desert, and down the Euphrates to the Persian Gulf. To an age that knows in retrospect the value later placed on the Suez route by all British governments, it is startling to recall for how long the two competed for favour as the quickest and safest way east. Though steam vessels from India were reaching Suez by 1830, and plying regularly by 1834, two iron river steamers were in 1836 hauled across the desert to the upper Euphrates at British public expense. But this expedition, commanded by a tireless enthusiast called Colonel Francis Chesney, was a failure from the standpoint of speed; one vessel was lost by night in a hurricane and the other was too slow, even downstream, to be worth duplicating. Yet competition with Suez continued, even though the Egyptian route was always secure, and the Euphrates one often tampered with by Arabs in spite of protection by gunboats from

India. (In the end, the overland route proved the more practical only for the electric telegraph, opened in 1865 via both Mesopotamia and Persia.)

The explanation of an apparent anomaly is political. Mehmet Ali, the Albanian who had secured himself the viceroyalty of Egypt, had expansionist ambitions, and in 1834 fulfilled them by seizing Syria from his Turkish overlord; by his agreement with the Turks of 1833, he bestrode both routes in a way that was never to recur until the three years during which Nasser's United Arab Republic included Syria—from 1958 to 1961. The British had not always been hostile to Mehmet Ali; in 1819, the Government of India had solicited the help of his son, Ibrahim Pasha, in putting down the Persian Gulf pirates, while Ibrahim was stamping out a rebellion in eastern Arabia on behalf of the Sultan; further, many British advocates of the Suez route—particularly shipowners and merchants —would have liked the British Government to come to terms with Mehmet Ali. When the representative of a new British steamline, the P. & O., held conversations with him in 1840, he said in effect (as Nasser was to say over a hundred years later) that he had no interest in stopping traffic that brought him in a useful income:

> It is very bad policy on the part of your government to fight with me; this is your high road to India, and I shall always promote it.[4]

There were British politicians, too, who thought that Mehmet Ali was the man to back, reckoning that as he had challenged and defeated the Sultan, Turkey was bound to disintegrate. But Palmerston disagreed, and had good reasons for doing so. One was the predilection that Mehmet Ali had always shown for French help and advice, and the risk, therefore, that France would be in a position to block both British routes. Another was a recent and profitable British commercial agreement with the Turks. But far the most important was that, if Mehmet Ali's successes led to a break-up of the Ottoman Empire, its subdivision was bound to work out to the advantage not only of France but of Russia. By the eighteen-thirties the Russians were a menace to the route not only at the Black Sea straits but farther east, through a newly formed friendship with Persia. Hence the well-known Palmerstonian axiom that "Turkey is as good a guardian of the route to India as any Arab would be"—a ground for British support of the Ottoman Empire that was to last until 1914; here, too, was a first hint of the British preference for "good old Turks", and Mesopotamians, over

Egyptians with their long-standing affiliations with Mediterranean civilizations and French culture.

After 1840, when Palmerston, by a masterly settlement, simultaneously contrived to confine Mehmet Ali to Egypt and deprive Russia of some advantages at the Straits, the French threat to the short routes receded, but that of Russia increased steadily both in Europe and Asia. There were three methods of meeting it—by war, by partition of territory, or by supporting buffer states, and the British on occasion used each of the three.

Resort to war was rare; apart from the Crimean War in 1854, it happened only twice, and at second-hand—once in 1856-7 with Persia (which at the time amounted to a Russian battering-ram) and once in 1878-80 with Afghanistan, to try and counter the influence of Russian agents. There would have been war over Russia's exacting peace terms to Turkey after the Russo-Turkish war of 1877 had the Queen and the British man-in-the-street had their way. (... "Oh! if the Queen were a man, she would give those Russians *such* a beating . . .") But British statesmen preferred Disraeli's "peace with honour", and in 1878 came away from the great scene of barter at the Congress of Berlin with useful gains. Though forced to accept Russian expansion in the Balkans and at the east end of the Black Sea, they had undone the Czar's worst annexations, fended him off from Constantinople, and secured "a tolerable settlement for the Porte"; they had also secured the same for Britain, for they had acquired a lease of Cyprus for two purposes—to help with the future defence of Turkey-in-Asia, and to serve as "the key to western Asia" and a new staging post on the route to India.

The British avoided the method of partition for as long as they could. Acquisition of an island was feasible; acquisition of territory on the mainland was out of the question because it would entail compensation to other powers, because of anxiety to avoid frontiers close to powers with large land armies, and because, after British experience in the Indian Mutiny in 1857, Britain was chary of taking on the management of more orientals. The British desire and technique was to create friendly buffer states by means of influence, exercised through trade treaties, loans, friendly advice, and pressure by ambassadors or gunboats if necessary. By these means, successive British governments hoped to influence Middle East governments in the right direction, by which they meant towards a pro-British foreign policy, as well as towards liberal reform at home. London was forever lecturing the Turks, and extracting promises from the

Sultan to be good to his Christian minorities and to reform his administration; even a Viceroy of India (where the Government knew far more than Whitehall about the difficulty of influencing Asians for any length of time) wrote in 1878 of Afghanistan that

> The best arrangement for Indian interests would be, *me judice*, the creation of a Western Afghan Khanate, including Merv, Maimena, Balkh, Kandahar and Herat, under some prince of our own selection, who will be dependent on our support.[5]

In Persia, because of the greater power of persuasion and menace possessed by Russia in the north over Britain in the south, no British statesmen pressed similar plans for regeneration until 1919.

Until the end of the eighteen-sixties, the system worked well enough in Turkey, but by degrees it was defeated through a combination of Turkish evasiveness, and Turkish resentment at erosion of Turkish territory and at too many sermons. As the British ambassador reported to London in 1885,

> We alone of the Great Powers adhere to the old system of acting *Schoolmaster*.[6]

Primacy of influence was therefore lost at Constantinople, though no one else obtained it until a unified Germany entered the competition, free from all taint of objection to Armenian massacres or seizure of pieces of Ottoman territory.

In Egypt, too, the mid-Victorian goal was a friendly, regenerated and liberal government—a target that became more important after the Suez Canal was opened in 1869. British objection to this French venture soon faded because of the usefulness of the waterway, and the security of the Canal had become a British interest when Disraeli purchased the Khedive's shares in the Company in 1875. But in Egypt, as in Turkey, the goal of regeneration under a friendly prince was never reached; Western influence, exercised by France even more than Britain, led to a rake's progress on the part of Mehmet Ali's descendants, and, in 1876, to Anglo-French Dual Control of Egypt's rickety finances. Rulers who are run by foreigners soon lose the respect of their people, and Egyptian discontent with the ineptitude of a ruling house and ruling class of Turks produced a nationalist reaction. The leader of the nationalist movement, Arabi Pasha, was of pure Egyptian origin and was the prototype of many twentieth-century colonels to follow: his aims were an end to rule by self-interested aristocrats, and an end to dependence on foreigners. The British occupation to which his rebellion gave rise was not a deep-laid plot of long-standing; Gladstone's Liberal government that ordered occupation had shown some sympathy for Arabi's "truly national" aspirations; it wanted no more Indias and no "egg of a North African empire"; its aim was to restore Egypt's finances, and to preserve a system of parity with France that had stood both powers in good stead in dealing with Turkey and Russia.

Occupation, singlehanded, was the work of a moment, provoked by the accidental coincidence of several events—loss of European life during riots in the course of Arabi's rebellion; quarrels over Ireland in the cabinet, sharpened by the perpetration of the Phoenix Park murders in Dublin, with their suggestion of the dangers of unbridled nationalism; a change of government in France that brought in a ministry which preferred to conserve all energies for *revanche* against Germany. The crowning argument was of course the safety of the Canal.

But occupation had tremendous drawbacks. It constituted, in Lord Salisbury's words, an "intolerable hamper" on relations with France, Turkey and Russia, and gave Germany gratuitous chances to play on these antagonisms. Soon, everyone except Jingoes and land-grabbers wanted to get out; in 1887, a Conservative government agreed with the Turks to evacuation within three years subject to a right of re-entry to "remove danger" of invasion or internal disorder. Out of distaste for this clause, France and Russia succeeded in stopping Turkish ratification of the agreement, which is mentioned here because of its likeness to the proviso for "reactivation" of the Canal Zone base that Eden successfully negotiated with Nasser in 1954.

Once in, it was difficult to get out, and soon two compelling motives for staying began to appear. First, regeneration of the Khedive's government was not a matter of months or a year or two, as had been hoped, because no one had foreseen what Baring, later Lord Cromer, called the "utter incapacity of the ruling class"; administration on the lines of that in the princely states of India therefore began. Secondly, loss of British influence at Constantinople reduced the chances of blocking Russia in the Balkans, and Egypt began to look like an alternative bastion for the route to India. Finally, at the end of the eighties, an acquisition that was by most people's standards a poor second to dominance at Constantinople turned out to be serving a second purpose.

For the last two decades of the nineteenth century, the balanced

B

mind of Lord Salisbury dominated British overseas policy as
thoroughly as Palmerston had done at an earlier stage. In 1889,
an instinct that his daughter and biographer labels "the call of the
Nile" became

> a central episode in his calculated prevision of events . . . from
> this date, the necessity of safeguarding the Nile valley from the
> intrusion of other white powers begins to appear in his corre-
> spondence as a separate and dominating factor in his policy.[7]

Why so necessary? In a splendid book written in 1961, *Africa and
the Victorians*, subtitled *The Official Mind of Imperialism*, Professor John Gallagher and Ronald Robinson answer the question
from contemporary records. Britain's dominant motive during the
scramble for Africa was preservation of the long and the short
routes to India. In this interest, wars were fought in South Africa
and the Sudan, rich territories in west Africa were bargained away
and poor ones in north-east Africa prized beyond their economic
worth; the whole pattern stemmed from the occupation of Egypt:

> The Mediterranean and Indian interest, like a driving wheel in
> some vast machine, was now engaging the lesser wheels of
> eastern-central Africa and connecting them one by one to its own
> workings. At the turn of Salisbury's strategy, these once remote
> and petty interests in the Sudan, Uganda and the northern hinter-
> lands of Zanzibar were changing into safeguards of Britain's
> world power.[8]

In Africa, security by influence gave place to security by occupation and barter in a way that was not possible in territories closer
to Russia. Therefore farther north, in Turkey, Persia and Afghanistan, despots and their dilapidated governments were propped up
no matter how unsatisfactory their behaviour. Russia had discovered, from about the time of the Crimean War, that a show
of might on the Asian steppes was a good way of exercising pressure
on London. And so, as an alternative to pressure at the Straits, it
kept pushing its spearhead forward towards the bounds watched by
the Government of India: to Khiva in 1864; to Bokhara in 1865;
to Tashkent and Samarkand in 1867; to Merv in 1884. The moves
nearly always interlocked with events in Europe, and sometimes
with events in the Middle East. For instance, Disraeli's dispatch of
Indian troops to Malta during the Turkish crisis of 1877 prompted
Russian interference in Afghanistan. And in 1885, the scare caused

in Britain by Russia's seizure of Penjdeh in Afghanistan immobi-
lized troops for lack of which there could be no response to the
public outcry for an expedition to avenge Gordon's death at
Khartoum. This task successive governments were secretly glad to
postpone until Egypt was better able to re-occupy its former
province of the Sudan. The dervishes, Salisbury wrote to Cromer,
were as good an agent as any for "keeping the bed warm"; they
were left to do so until Cromer and Kitchener were ready for the
re-conquest in 1898—in time to oust the French from the small
outpost that French troops had in that year reached and occupied
at Fashoda on the White Nile.

The Franco-Russian alliance of 1894, British military deficiencies
revealed by the Boer War, the German concession for the Baghdad
Railroad won in 1903, the growing German naval challenge—these
and other changes in Europe threatened the pattern of power in the
Mediterranean and Middle East, and, to meet the danger, Britain
was constrained to adopt a course till then avoided—partition of
Middle Eastern interests with rivals. By an agreement of 1904, it
exchanged with France a free hand for itself in Egypt against a free
hand for France in Morocco. (As part of this bargain the British
won French consent—never before obtainable—to waiving, until
the end of the British occupation of Egypt, international supervision
of free passage through the Suez Canal, as laid down in the International Suez Canal Convention of 1888; Britain did not adhere to
this convention until it got its way in 1904.) In 1907, under pressure of mounting tension in Europe, a second partition took place.
The British Government—by now a Liberal Government—agreed
with Russia to divide Persia into two spheres of influence, separated
by a no-man's-land. Both these bargains, made as if local opinion
counted for nothing, at once became black marks against the British
name among Egyptian and Persian nationalists—blacker than
against the name of France or Russia because more was expected
of British liberalism.

Yet liberal instincts were only too often cut short by the exigen-
cies of British Middle Eastern policy. Given the need for Ottoman
stability in Asia, British action on behalf of minorities rightly
struggling to be free had to stop at the Bosphorus. In 1840, there
could be no official support for Lebanese Christian aspirations to be
a second Greece. In 1860, the nearest approach to British succour
took place, when, after widespread massacres, a group of powers—
Britain among them—intervened with the Sultan on behalf of the

Lebanese Christians. But France was the chief agent through whom they obtained a special régime, for it was the French who were authorized to land a force in fulfilment of their ancient ties with the Christians of the Levant. In 1882, Gladstone snuffed out Arabi's Egyptian nationalism; in the 'nineties he could do nothing material for the Armenians. Sympathy there might be for the Persian Constitutionalists of 1905–6, or the Young Turk revolutionaries against the misrule of Abdul Hamid in 1908, but in Persia sympathy did not stand in the way of the agreement with Russia, while in Turkey, it was offset by a new set of British misgivings:

> If, when things are going well in Turkey [wrote Sir Edward Grey in 1908] we are engaged in suppressing by force and shooting a rising in Egypt of people who demand a constitution, the position will be very awkward.[9]

When the Young Turks in their turn became oppressors, and Arab secret societies were working for some form of Arab autonomy, or decentralization of Turkish authority, representative Arabs made advances to the British both in Cairo and in India. The most celebrated of these encounters was that between Kitchener and the Amir Abdullah, a son of the Sharif of Mecca, in Cairo in April 1914. To the displeasure of the Turkish Government, Abdullah, when staying with the Khedive, paid an official call on the British Agent and Consul-General. He followed it up with a request to Kitchener's assistant, Ronald Storrs, for a gift of arms to his father. He was given no encouragement, because such plans "pre-supposed a break-up of Turkish authority". The sequel to his visit belongs to the body of this book.

The purpose of this introduction is not to compress the whole course of events into a few pages, but to direct attention to incidents and trends that illuminate the story to follow. Many patterns will recur—the need to adapt great power policies to interests lying far outside the area; the continuity of British policy by successive governments, however liberal or anti-imperialist their complexion; the dichotomy between London and the Government of India; the better British accord with Turk and Arab than with Egyptian; the confirmed optimism that caused British statesmen to underrate the unpopularity to which they exposed rulers whom they supported and advised; finally, after a lull, the resumption of Russian pressure. During that lull, which began with the collapse of Czarist Russia before the end of the First World War, the British greatly extended their own commitments in the Middle East. They did so to maintain the tranquillity that they had long thought vital to their interests, and that had previously been maintained, however shakily, by the Ottoman Empire.

ACCIDENT AND DESIGN IN WAR: 1914–18

ON October 27, 1914, the German battle-cruiser *Goeben*, lying off the northern mouth of the Bosphorus, handed some orders to three Turkish destroyers. Two days later, she bombarded Russian ports in the Black Sea in their company, and tumbled the Turks into the First World War. The deed, done without notice because the Turkish cabinet was divided on the issue of war or peace, was a major diplomatic defeat for Britain and its Entente allies.

The Entente powers, working in ignorance of the alliance against Russia that the Turkish war party had signed with Germany at the beginning of August, reckoned that they had done "everything conceivable", as Lord Grey was later to write, to keep the Turks neutral. They wanted this chiefly because they needed their whole strength to fight Germany, but also in order to keep the Black Sea Straits open to the Russian grain trade, and to keep Russia solvent and supplied. By British standards two other motives were just as important: the one, fear that war with the only independent Moslem power, and with the Caliph of Islam, would overtax India's loyalty and disturb Egypt; the other, fear of a military threat to the Suez Canal at a time of need for the quick passage of Indian troops to France.

But Grey's phrase makes no allowance for a big limitation to the inducements that Britain, France and Russia were able to offer. These propositions, coming from a trio of foreign offices, amounted only to the highest common factor in three separate and self-interested policies, and were no match for Germany's single-minded offers. Germany could afford to be generous at the expense of Egypt or Greece, and could agree to waive the judicial and financial privileges enjoyed by foreigners—the Capitulations—against which the Turks had been battling for two generations; the Entente powers, for reasons dear to one or other of them, could not. The offers that they could jointly make were trifles by Turkish standards —for instance, to guarantee the integrity of Ottoman territory "during the present war"; such a promise was of small account to Young Turks who had lately experienced the worthlessness of a

similar great-power guarantee in the Balkan war. Turks with long
memories also reflected that whereas the Germans had never taken
advantage of their weakness to seize Turkish property, the French
had taken Algeria and Tunisia, the British Egypt and Cyprus, and
the Russians the Crimea and parts of the Caucasus.

A crowning reason for Turkish mistrust was provided by Britain
alone. On the outbreak of war with Germany, all British eyes were
fixed on the rival strengths of the battle-fleets in the North Sea,
and to improve the balance there the British Admiralty had im-
pounded for cash two Turkish cruisers that had been built in
British shipyards, and were ready for delivery. They were the apple
of Turkey's eye, having been bought partly by public subscription,
and their loss was a blow to Turkish pride. To make matters worse,
a British naval blunder allowed the Germans to exploit it. Through
spiritless reading of some conflicting Admiralty instructions, the
British Commander-in-Chief in the Mediterranean allowed the
German cruisers *Goeben* and *Breslau* to slip out of Messina and
away to the Dardanelles. The impounding of the Turkish ships,
though psychologically unfortunate, had been the lesser of two
evils; the error whereby two German substitutes appeared off Constantinople was a plain disaster. There they lay, just offshore, for all
to see—bounty from the Kaiser to offset the ships that Britain had
withheld. Before long the Turks, to evade complications about
belligerent warships in neutral waters, announced that they had
bought the two cruisers, and gave them Turkish names. But, purchase or no purchase, the ships remained under German command,
and on October 29 the German admiral in the *Goeben* pushed
matters to the conclusion already described. The Kaiser had forced
a huge adjustment in the whole pattern of British thinking about
the Middle East.

For a century, foreign thrusts towards India had been parried by
a policy of keeping the Ottoman Empire whole, and using Turkish
Arabia, Persia and Afghanistan as a glacis which Britain did not
want to occupy, but could not afford to see occupied by an enemy.
With the entry of the Young Turks into the war, the first became
enemy territory and the road to the other two lay open to subversive
agents. The change was fundamental, and produced a quick succession of political and military reflexes.

The military moves were reinforcements for Egypt, an expedition to secure the head of the Persian Gulf, and a naval bombardment of the Dardanelles forts. This last venture was worse than

useless; ordered in hopes of setting up a Turkish reaction against German influence, it merely angered the Turks, and is an early example of the futility of using nineteenth-century techniques on twentieth-century nationalism; its chief result was to show the Germans where Turkey's defences needed strengthening. Precautions in Egypt were due to fear of German influence in the Turkish army and Turkish proximity to the Suez Canal. The force for Mesopotamia was urged from two quarters; one was the Government of India, which wanted to prevent eastward penetration by German agents, and to preserve the friendly sheiks of Kuwait and Mohammerah from Turkish pressure or attack; the other was the Admiralty, because 25,000 tons of oil per month were by this time being exported from the new oilfields in south Persia. As early as October 2, 1914, precautionary troop and fleet movements were agreed upon by London and Simla, and a force was dispatched to loiter in the Persian Gulf and to land at the entrance to the Shatt-el-Arab should war be declared; it did so within a week of the attack on the Russian ports. It took out insurance against Moslem uneasiness by carrying with it a series of proclamations from the Viceroy about the inviolability of the Holy Cities of Arabia and Mesopotamia, and by the end of November it was in occupation of the port of Basra and telling the river-bank Arabs that it had no quarrel with them. It achieved all its immediate purposes. Though German agents scored great successes in central Persia, where they worsted the British from 1914 till 1916, they never penetrated beyond that area with enough stamina to do harm.

Simultaneously, in the Eastern Mediterranean, the British made sure of two Turkish territories that they held under special arrangements. Cyprus—a leasehold since 1878—they annexed out of hand on the day that they went to war with Turkey. Egypt presented them with more of a problem. One complication was its indeterminate international status and the illogic of their own position there—under promise to go, but forever arranging to stay. Another was the Ottoman affiliations of its ruler and ruling class; the Egyptian royal house was of Albanian descent, and the upper ranks of society were largely Turkish. The three choices before Britain were annexation to the British Empire, declaration of a protectorate, and mere deposition of the Khedive (who had fled to Turkey) followed by the institution of a regency.

In retrospect, it is easy to see that the third would have been the best course—less humiliating to Egyptians, more palatable to allies, and making no difference to the British military grip on the country. Sensitive observers thought so at the time. But sensitivity to Egyptian opinion has never been a British strong suit, and in London a majority of the Cabinet favoured annexation. By contrast the Residency in Cairo wanted a protectorate, in order to be true to past assurances that Egypt was on the way to self-government, and in tribute to the co-operation it was getting from the Egyptian ministry in power. Happily it had its way and annexation was rejected; for even the declaration of a protectorate, which was finally made on December 18, 1914, had international consequences that were not foreseen by Englishmen, who looked upon it merely as a change of form. The Russians commented that they had heard the news "with particular pleasure", and the Czar minuted "excellent" in the margin of the dispatch. By their standards the change was one of substance, and a precedent for other expansionist bookings-in-advance.

In London, the overwhelming load of immediate Cabinet business did not prevent some Ministers from mentioning future possibilities in the Middle East. Staid minds continued to dwell on the good old Turk as the best hope of law and order in those parts, but roving ones advanced other ideas. At a Cabinet meeting on November 9 Lloyd George referred to the "ultimate destiny of Palestine", and after it Herbert Samuel spoke to Grey about the possible formation of a Jewish state, and the need for British influence in its formation because "proximity to the Suez Canal would render its good will a matter of importance to the British Empire". Winston Churchill favoured an attack on the Gallipoli peninsula as the best way of defending Egypt, and Lord Kitchener entered into a brisk correspondence with the Commander-in-Chief in Egypt, Sir John Maxwell, about achieving the same end by an attack on Alexandretta, where the Baghdad railway ran near to the coast, and which seemed to Maxwell "the safest and most fruitful" way to embarrass the Turks.

Pundits familiar with Egypt and Arabia also began to discuss the idea of stirring up the Arabs to revolt. "I was talking to Crewe the other day at the Turf Club," wrote Lord Cromer in October to his former Oriental Secretary, Harry Boyle, "and he agreed with me that a few officers who could speak Arabic, if sent into Arabia, could raise the whole country against the Turks." Ronald Storrs, Boyle's successor in Cairo, had the same idea, and Sir Reginald Wingate, the Governor-General in the Sudan, established a contact

with the Sharif of Mecca through a religious dignitary in Omdur-
man.

The action that was to count for most was taken by Kitchener.
War Minister now, but till lately High Commissioner in Egypt,
and before that Commander-in-Chief in India and one-time lieu-
tenant in charge of a so-called archaeological survey of Palestine,
he was the embodiment of the long-standing military dream of
land control on the route to India. While in Egypt, he had heard
from various informants of Arab discontent with the Young Turks;
as has been mentioned, he was approached by one or two influential
Arabs, including the Amir Abdullah, a son of the Sharif of Mecca,
about Britain's attitude to Arab aspirations. So as not to disturb
Anglo-Turkish relations, he had at the time given guarded replies.
In September 1914 his memory of the encounter with Abdullah
was jogged by a private letter from Storrs. He thereupon wrote with
his own hand the famous message of September 24, 1914, telling
Storrs to send a "secret and carefully chosen messenger" to
Abdullah inquiring whether the Arabs would be "with us or
against us" should Turkey be forced into the war. This he followed
in November with two further messages, one to Abdullah and one
to his father. The second and more flowery said:

> Till now we have defended and befriended Islam in the person
> of the Turks. Henceforward it shall be that of the noble Arab.
> It may be that an Arab of true race will assume the Khalifate
> at Mecca or Medina, and so good may come by the help of God
> out of all the evil which is now occurring. It would be well if
> your Highness could convey to your followers and devotees who
> are found throughout the world in every country the good tidings
> of the freedom of the Arabs and the rising of the sun over
> Arabia.[1]

Kitchener did not live to see the sunrise; he was drowned in
the *Hampshire* on the very day in June 1916 that the standard of
Arab revolt was finally raised. But in 1914, all such projects were
dreams for lack of men and means to implement them, and because
everyone agreed that all available resources must be bent on beating
Germany in France. In any case, mistrust between the allies in the
first months of the war led to the dropping of several schemes for
assaulting Turkey that might well have improved the general chance
of winning. For instance, in August, a Greek offer to place all
naval and military resources at the disposal of the Entente was

refused because of Russian objections, and the idea of attacking Alexandretta was more than once discarded because of French susceptibilities about Syria. In Britain, all responsible statesmen and officials recognized the necessity for close co-operation with the French, and saw that it would be unsuitable to take advantage of France's ordeal in Europe in order to poach a preserve in Syria that had been a recognized French interest since the days of Louis XIV—indeed, since the Crusades. By the turn of the year, however, stalemate in France, and Turkish successes in the Caucasus had rendered everyone less selective (though not less mistrustful) and just as the British War Council was beginning seriously to consider sideshows, the Russians asked for a diversion to draw off Turkish pressure from their Caucasus front. They got it, but not at the point they would have chosen, for the outcome was the Dardanelles campaign.

Apart from French susceptibilities about Syria, the main reason for choosing the Dardanelles, rather than one of the softer spots on the Syrian coast, was the greater advantage to be gained in Europe. If successful, the campaign would cut Turkey off from Germany, and cut the Turkish army in two; it would also win the Entente some badly needed Balkan allies, put Constantinople under their control, open the Straits route to Russia and (a motive added by private commentators to those which found their way into minutes) it would serve to keep the Russians in their place in the Eastern Mediterranean. In the beginning, it was also chosen because it was to be a purely naval operation. In fact it achieved none of these ends; it did, on the other hand, excite Italian appetite and bring Italy into the war against its former allies. By the end of 1915, it had produced the humiliation of a withdrawal, suffered simultaneously with a defeat outside Baghdad brought on by the over-confidence of those in charge of the force in lower Mesopotamia, which overran its strength.

But before these disasters happened, British invasion of Turkish soil at both ends of the Ottoman Empire had suggested to both the Russians and the French that the one ally that had no land frontier with Germany was stealing marches on them in the Middle East. Another bombardment of the Dardanelles forts, this time initially successful, brought matters to a head, and on March 4, 1915, Russia lodged its claim to Constantinople and the Straits. To the British and French, this proposition was a bombshell. Although the Russians had earlier asked how they stood over Constantinople, they had given their allies to understand that they would be content with its neutralization. And although the British idea that influence at Constantinople was a vital interest had diminished since the decision to remain in Egypt, cession of what Grey called "the biggest prize of the entire war" was a black prospect. Asquith invited the opposition leaders to attend the War Council. Here, fear that the Russian public was losing its zest for the war, coupled with gratitude for Russian chivalry in attacking at the time of the Marne, and a wish to induce Russia to withdraw its objections to Balkan allies, caused the meeting to swallow its misgivings, and to agree to what Churchill dubbed a "convulsive gesture of self-preservation". Imagination quails at the effect this decision would have had on the 1919 settlement in the Middle East if Russia had ended the First World War in as high fettle as it ended the Second.

France, though equally downcast by this turn of events, was immediately ready with its own claim: Syria running as far east as Damascus and including Palestine. The British Government, though long aware that the Ottoman Empire was shaky, had made no set plans for its eventual break-up, partly out of the British habit of shoring up Turkey, and partly because the effect of a change upon Egypt was rated "awkward". The only stipulations with which it was immediately ready were that the Moslem Holy Places must in any event remain in Moslem hands, and that the zone of Central Persia which had been labelled neutral in the Anglo-Russian agreement of 1907 should be added to the British sphere of influence; the undistributed middle had since become a proven oil area.

So long as the fate of the Dardanelles campaign hung in the balance, the British Cabinet was in no hurry to be specific about further requirements. In any case it was divided. Asquith and Grey were against acquiring any more territory; Herbert Samuel was circulating a memorandum on the future of Palestine; Lloyd George supported this, and Winston Churchill wanted to stake a claim to "Mesopotamia, with or without Alexandretta". To clear its collective mind, it set up, in April 1915, a committee on British desiderata in Asiatic Turkey, under the chairmanship of a Foreign Office official, Sir Maurice de Bunsen. The main advantage of the de Bunsen Committee was that it caused members of the Foreign Office, War Office and India Office, Admiralty and Board of Trade to sit down together and thrash out a programme, with the help of the secretary to the Committee of Imperial Defence, Maurice Hankey, and his new assistant, Sir Mark Sykes. Its findings, which were ready at the end of June 1915, have not yet been published apart from one short excerpt on Palestine that appeared in a White Paper issued during the Palestine Conference of 1939. But from this, and from references to the report in Mark Sykes's private papers, it is clear that the committee set out various choices, depending on whether or not an independent Turkey survived with or without Constantinople, and whether the victors preferred to divide the spoils by partition or by means of spheres of influence. In either event, it assigned Palestine to the British sphere, but reported that "Palestine must be recognized as a country whose destiny must be the subject of special negotiations, in which both belligerents and neutrals are alike interested".

In contrast to the British, the French were in a hurry for definitions. Their strength was being sapped by the ordeal on the western front and they reckoned that the passage of time was doing them no good. But not until October 1915 did the British Cabinet agree to talks. It was brought to change its mind by military failure in Gallipoli and Mesopotamia, by its desire to allay French mistrust of its motives so as to free all energies for the struggle in France, and in order to define and restrict French claims to Palestine; at this stage, French claims to "Syria" covered a greater Syria that extended from the Taurus Mountains in the north to the Egyptian border in the south. Other inducements to hurry were the successes that the Russians were scoring in the Caucasus, and the stage that British officials had reached in cautious development of Kitchener's idea of detaching the Arabs from the Turks. The Sharif of Mecca had referred in some of his messages to the future of Syria, and the Cabinet decided that the time had come to pursue its dealings with him in agreement with France. The man chosen to conduct this delicate negotiation was Mark Sykes, who had shortly before been dispatched by Kitchener on a grand tour; he had carried the de Bunsen report in his baggage, was Francophile, and had come back from Cairo critical of its anti-French "Fashoda outlook" and full of the risks of quarrelling with France.

Because of the controversies that were later to arise over conflicting promises and imperfect liaison, it is as well to be clear that at this stage the exchange of messages with Mecca in which Kitchener had taken a personal part was being maintained through more than one channel—by Wingate from Khartoum and by McMahon from Cairo; but this piece of duplication was immaterial, for these two men acted in unison. Both were responsible to the Foreign Office, and Wingate's private papers show that both were in constant touch with that office and with one another about what they were saying to the Sharif. McMahon was cautious by nature and, though he had ample experience of India, had none of the Arabs or of Europe; he was not of a temperament to deviate from Whitehall's instructions. Wingate, though he had been immured in the Sudan for much of his working life, had, as its Governor-General and as Sirdar of the Egyptian army since 1899, been responsible for intelligence about Arabia; he was a Kitchener disciple, and shared with some of 'K's' former subordinates in Cairo a dream of Arab unity under British guidance. But he had also made in the course of his duties several good friends in high office in London, with whom he corresponded voluminously, and he too was made aware that Britain could not disregard the French. He also wrote constantly to Cairo where, though he found McMahon unresponsive, he was in close touch with an old friend, Colonel Gilbert Clayton, the director of civil and military intelligence. Clayton was a father-figure; everyone went to him for balanced advice; Storrs had consulted him about the propriety of jogging Kitchener's elbow; as well as writing often to Wingate, he was in daily touch with McMahon's staff. The ring of consultation was complete, and bad liaison was not the reason for the misunderstandings that ensued; in November 1915 Wingate wrote privately to Lord Hardinge, the Viceroy of India, that

> it is very satisfactory to feel that we are now all more or less of one mind.[2]

But even if all were agreed, a basic difficulty remained—the problem of reconciling the conflicting requirements that the Foreign Office had to handle in the winter and spring of 1916. The war situation in Europe demanded that every consideration be given to French susceptibilities; at the same time there was pressure from the soldiers in Gallipoli for a diversion in Arabia, so that it was desirable to keep alive the Sharif's interest in leading a revolt. Everyone knew of the grand ideas that he had first expressed in his initial letter, dated July 14, 1915, about 'the independence of the Arab countries', but it was difficult to be specific with him about the Levant while negotiations were in progress with the French. In this dilemma, the solution adopted was to be vague with Mecca; the Wingate papers suggest that the imprecision of the McMahon letters—so often put down to carelessness, or guile, or the flowery style of McMahon's oriental secretary Ronald Storrs—was intentional.

By the end of October 1915, McMahon's correspondence with the Sharif had reached a stage at which the latter (who, warned Wingate, was "somewhat nervous") was upbraiding McMahon for cold and guarded language, and seemed in need of a stimulant. Therefore McMahon on October 24 dispatched the assurance to him that later became a major subject of Anglo-Arab controversy. This told the Sharif that, subject to three reservations, Britain was "prepared to recognize and support the independence of the Arabs" within the very wide limits that he had demanded. The reservations excluded from this undertaking: first, coastal areas "lying to the west of the districts of Damascus, Homs, Hama and Aleppo" which, said McMahon, were "not purely Arab"; second, regions affected by "our existing treaties with Arab chiefs" (which meant the Persian Gulf area of Arabia); and third, regions in which "the interests of her ally France" limited Great Britain's freedom to act alone. The first reservation used a word for 'district' (*vilayet*) which equally meant 'province', and this ambiguity was later to cause trouble; the third represented Foreign Office anxieties, for, three days before McMahon's letter of October 24 was dispatched, Grey had suggested to the French ambassador in London that they should discuss the frontiers of Syria, and, by inference, of other Arab areas. A month later, Mark Sykes settled to this task with his French opposite number, Georges Picot.

Sykes, who had been in Cairo during his grand tour, of course knew that letters were being exchanged with Mecca. He and Picot worked in this knowledge throughout the winter; they went to Petrograd in March 1916 to confer on the portions of their agreement that affected Russia, and on April 16 the whole, still in draft, was communicated to McMahon in Cairo. Plenty of people besides McMahon and his staff must have seen both the letters to Mecca and the Sykes-Picot draft before the agreement with France was given final form in letters exchanged with Paris in May. Yet the Sykes-Picot agreement spelt out old-fashioned spheres of influence in the Arab areas. The conclusion that must be drawn is that, *at the time*, the statesmen and officials concerned reckoned that, since they had been non-committal with the Sharif, there was no conflict between the two documents.

Many books have been written about the discrepancies between the two undertakings. Less has been said about where they tallied.

Both allowed for purely British control in southern Mesopotamia, and purely French control in the long coastal zone of what is now Lebanon and Syria. Both provided for the independence of the Arab peoples (in the plural); Grey's letter of May 16 that put the finishing touch to the Sykes-Picot agreement added "provided that the co-operation of the Arabs is secured, and that the Arabs fulfil the conditions and obtain the towns of Homs, Hama, Damascus and Aleppo". Both took for granted an Arab Arabia. The sweeping assurance about independence was, however, subject to reservations that were not identical in both, though these were loosely enough worded to be open to the same interpretation. The McMahon letter specified that its assurances applied only to regions wherein Britain was free to act without detriment to France; otherwise it said nothing about the French; it "understood" that the Arabs had decided to seek only British assistance. The Sykes-Picot agreement specified the areas in which the assistance was to be British, and in which French—roughly, Gaza to Kirkuk for Britain, Damascus to Mosul for France. This division by lines running east and west was against natural boundaries and communications, but tallied with the strategic and financial interests of the two European states involved; Kitchener wanted France to have Mosul for the classic Indian army reason that nowhere must Britain run the risk of sharing an Asian frontier with Russia.

The undertakings differed on three main points. By the Sykes-Picot agreement only, Britain was to be accorded outright a small enclave containing the ports of Haifa and Acre. Secondly, the two documents differed about arrangements for the interior of Syria; the Sharif was given to understand that this would be wholly independent, and the French that as they would be the sole supplier of "advisers or foreign functionaries" they would have a measure of supervision over it. Lastly, about Palestine, the Sykes-Picot document was specific; it was to have an international administration

> the form of which is to be decided upon after consultation with Russia, and subsequently in consultation with the other allies, and the representatives of the Shareef of Mecca.[3]

The McMahon letter, by contrast, was unclear about Palestine, for the ambiguous reference to areas west of "the *vilayet*" of Damascus might have included Palestine, or it might not.

The first of these discrepancies is unimportant because it fell to

the ground in the course of time. The second was the least honest
item in the transaction. For the Sharif, though warned about French
interests, was not told the extent to which they were being met.
Had he known, he would certainly have protested, and might never
have joined the allies. For the Arabs of the Ottoman Empire,
though appreciative of French learning and culture as exported to
them over the centuries, were mistrustful of French political ambitions because, through links with the Arabs of Tunis, they had
heard that French advice soon led to French control.

As to Palestine, it is galling to think how easily McMahon could
have devised some form of words intimating to the Sharif that
several faiths held that land in reverence, and that there must be
multilateral agreement about it. There is more than one indication that the British intended to leave latitude for agreement, and
therefore to exclude Palestine from the area of Arab independence;
one pointer is the provision made in the Sykes-Picot agreement for
consulting the Sharif. Another is a curious incident in March 1916
—little known because it came to nothing; in that month, Grey
consulted the French and Russians about offering the Jews "an
arrangement in regard to Palestine" which the three allies

> might hope to use . . . in such a way as to bring over to our side
> the Jewish forces in America, the East and elsewhere which are
> now largely, if not preponderantly, hostile to us.[4]

The very conception of such a proposal suggests that the future of
Palestine was still reckoned to be an open question.

Some of the men concerned in the negotiations later averred that
the Sharif knew that the McMahon letter was meant to exclude
Palestine. But it did not say so. It therefore led to controversy,
though not immediately. But whether or no the Sharif understood,
Christian scruples were not officially explained to him until a surge
of discomfiture followed the disclosure of all the secret agreements
by the Bolsheviks in November 1917. Then, D. G. Hogarth of the
Arab Bureau in Cairo was sent to Jidda to explain matters. He
gave the explanation; he also gave an assurance that, in Palestine,
no one people would be subject to another; he reported the Sharif
to be unperturbed:

> He declared himself to be quite in sympathy with both inter-
> national control in Palestine and the encouragement of Jews to
> settle there, and he volunteered the remark that the course of the

war must inevitably modify in certain points the agreements of the allies with himself. He asked only to be informed frankly and fully of such proposed modifications and the reasons for their necessity should it arise.[5]

The Sharif also resisted Turkish attempts to win him back by making capital out of the Bolshevik evidence. It was only after Zionist arrivals had begun to reveal political ambitions, and after the Sharif's son Feisal had been turned out of Damascus in 1920, that a grievance based on McMahon's imprecision about Palestine became a major issue between the Arabs and Britain.

By modern standards, the difference of greatest significance between the McMahon letter and the Sykes-Picot agreement is one of spirit. Yet at the time of their signature it did not seem so great. 1916 was the last year of an old familiar world of intact empires, letters from Nicky to Georgie, secret agreements secretly arrived at, and treatment of whole populations as chattels. It was also the last year of freedom from criticism by anti-imperialist allies. The current situation on the battlefronts is part of the context. The Sharif had not fired a shot; no one knew how far his writ ran, except that it did not extend over Ibn Saud; the Turks were still attacking the Suez Canal, threatening Aden, and holding a British force besieged in Kut. In the event, still remote, of Turkish collapse, no one was sure of Arab capacity for management and some provision was needed for preserving law and order in Arab lands. The Sykes-Picot arrangement was not an unnatural one for the purpose; indeed, for its date, it contained a substantial puff of the wind of change that was bringing in the kind of nationalism that the Sharif hoped to dominate. Where the British were at fault was in being so flowery with him and so vague about the singular and plural of "people". The Arabic language is apt to carry away its users, and, though they had refused to accord the Sharif the title he fancied, which was "King of the Arabs", they often used wording that came close to it. For instance, their anniversary message at the end of the first year of his revolt referred to "Your Majesty and the Arab Nation".

Another major reason for unawareness of the discrepancies that have been described was that, in the relevant months, the differences that preoccupied British minds were not between Cairo and London, but between these two and the Government of India. The Viceroy was perturbed by the admiration for Turkey that prevailed not only among Indian Moslems, but among non-Moslem Indian nationalists brimming with admiration for the Young Turks. He was averse first to blockade of the Hejaz, and later to encouraging the Sharif's revolt because he recoiled at the thought of dividing Islam, or stirring up trouble for the Caliph, or exposing the Pilgrimage to hazards. He argued that the Sharif would be regarded as a rebel in both India and Afghanistan, and that the risk of attaching blame to Britain for embroiling the Moslem Holy Places, or the Hejaz, in the war ought not to be run. London, Cairo and Khartoum recognized the risk involved but were in favour of taking it, and their view prevailed. But it did so in a climate of intense irritation owing to the number of authorities—civil and military, at home and abroad—to be consulted every time a step was taken; Mark Sykes, when compiling reports for the Cabinet in the second half of 1916, in one moment of exasperation listed eighteen, including London, Cairo, Khartoum, Aden, Mesopotamia and India. Disagreement continued even after the Sharif's revolt had started and the Pilgrimage had been successfully weathered in September 1916 (with the sacred carpet conveyed from Egypt in a British warship, but the prayers at Mecca said in the name of Sultan Mehmed V of Turkey). How far were the Sharif's doings to be published? London and Cairo favoured publicity; the Government of India was against it.

Bad communications contributed to the confusion. For instance, the McMahon letter of October 24, 1915 did not dovetail with a treaty of independence signed six weeks later with Ibn Saud by Sir Percy Cox, the Chief Political Officer with the force at Basra; and the Sykes-Picot agreement was communicated to Cairo but not to Basra; in May 1917, Mark Sykes apologized to Cox for the omission: "I was assured that you had had a copy of it as far back as ten months ago." All through 1916 and 1917, the "western Arabians" in London and Cairo were enraged with Government of India men for being surly and unco-operative about the Sharif's revolt, while the people at the Government of India end were aghast at the free rein being given to nationalism by the Arabophiles in Cairo—a versatile group of men whose virtues included Hogarth's scholarship, Storr's wit and brilliance, Cornwallis's steady head and Clayton's equable leadership, but of whom T. E. Lawrence is the remembered name. The flaws in the British front did not escape the Arabs. At one point, on mention of the British government, the Sharif remarked: "I see five governments", and at another

Ibn Saud told Percy Cox that "although you yourself probably appreciate my fears", maybe the representative of the British government who was conducting negotiations with the Sharif did not. The Arab tribes were not the only people in the peninsula who were united, yet not at one.

Thus by the time the Asquith government fell at the end of 1916, though there had been much fumbling, and some issuing of promises not wholly compatible with each other, most of the undertakings could have been made to fit into a pattern and to be tolerable to the people they affected, if they had been worked with goodwill. The biggest exception was the promise of Constantinople to an alien people. Asquith's and Grey's personal preference for taking on no new territory had been set aside, largely through inability to withstand the cut-and-dried ambitions first of Russia, and consequently of France. Claims lodged by these two allies had given British imperialists, and soldiers schooled in plans for defending India, occasion to make a bid to keep Mesopotamia. But the Turks still held Gallipoli, Baghdad, Medina and Sinai, and were skirmishing close to Aden. There was reason to fear that they could count on the winter snows in the Caucasus to hold the Grand Duke Nicholas while they transferred seasoned troops south to deal with the Sharif's untrained army, and to take Mecca.

In the Middle East, the year 1917 is a watershed.

Elsewhere, it was the worst year of the war—one of continuing ordeal, huge casualties in Flanders, unrestricted submarine warfare, failure at Salonika and the collapse of Russia. But locally it is the year of liberation from the promise of Constantinople, of the capture of Baghdad in March and Jerusalem in December, and of the attainment of positions from which to leap into the breaches left in Asia by the defection of Russia. The dynamo that produced the necessary vigour was Lloyd George. He is greatly criticized for the impulsiveness with which he took political decisions in the Middle East, and the mistakes to which these led, but he must be credited with breaking stalemates and pushing on with campaigns relatively cheap in human life and valuable in terms of British power. For this we have the word of Maurice Hankey, now secretary to the cabinet:

The new Prime Minister never lost sight of the advantages he might hope to derive at the eventual peace conference from the acquisition of the territory of our enemies. He wanted assets

to bargain with against those of the enemy . . . Among the
assets which seemed to the Prime Minister to be obtainable from
our enemies without too great a drain on our resources were
German East Africa which was still holding out, Palestine,
perhaps Syria, and Mesopotamia. This is an aspect of the matter
often lost sight of by those who inveighed against the "sideshows".[6]

But against the advantages must be offset some political plunges
that brought little profit, even in the short run, and that soon proved
a drain on British power and reputation. For 1917 is also the year
in which the British climbed on to the shoulders of the Zionists
in order to get a British Palestine, issued the Balfour Declaration,
began to set aside the Sykes-Picot agreement, and to make promises
that were incompatible beyond remedy.

The prospect of a British capture of the Holy Land appealed to
Lloyd George as a man of religious upbringing, a romantic and
a citizen of the British Empire. His friend, C. P. Scott of the
Manchester Guardian, has recorded talks in the spring of 1917 in
the course of which Lloyd George said that Britain "could take
care of the Holy Places better than anyone else"; that a French
Palestine was "not to be thought of"; that he was "altogether
opposed" to a condominium with France, and that "once we were
in military possession it would make a great difference". Within
days of taking office as Prime Minister he had given new impulse
to plans for an advance from Egypt.

This campaign was not an immediate success. General Murray
was repulsed before Gaza in March and again at his second try in
April. But before the failure, Lloyd George had instructed Mark
Sykes to join the expedition as chief political officer. On April 3,
with Curzon, he saw Sykes on the eve of his departure and instructed him to make every effort for a British Palestine, to give no
pledges to the Arabs, and to do nothing to prejudice the Zionist
movement. These instructions were welcome to Sykes personally;
he was a Kitchener disciple, and had been averse to the item in
the Foreign Office brief for his talks with Picot that had prescribed
international management for Palestine. He was also, from some
moment in 1916, pro-Zionist. On his way through Paris to Cairo,
he was honest with Picot about a departure from their agreement.
He had written to him of Jewish ambitions in February, seeing "no
great difficulties in the way" provided "a just understanding

could be come to with the Arabs", and on April 5 he broached the idea of British suzerainty by international consent. The French were not pleased. Sykes gave as one of his reasons for the change "the importance of meeting Zionist demands".

The Zionist contribution to this decision is fully described in Leonard Stein's impressive *The Balfour Declaration*. Though Herbert Samuel had left the cabinet, the loss to the Zionists was more than offset by the long-standing friendships of other ministers with Zionists or gentile champions of Zionism—Lloyd George's with C. P. Scott,

> while Balfour had at his side, as assistant Foreign Secretary, Lord Robert Cecil, who after meeting Weizmann in 1915 had become, in his own words, 'a Zionist by passionate conviction'.[7]

Stein goes on to describe the conversion of Lord Milner, and the pro-Zionism of several younger men whom Lloyd George had installed in huts in the garden of No. 10 Downing Street to serve as a brains trust, attached to the War Cabinet with the privilege of direct access to ministers. This team was nicknamed "the garden suburb"; the ability of its members was great; they were Philip Kerr, then editor of *The Round Table*, Leo Amery, William Ormsby-Gore (back from McMahon's staff in Cairo) and Mark Sykes; they worked unencumbered by departmental duties and with time to think—a boon that helps to account for the great influence that some of them exercised on overburdened Ministers. They were well-placed for putting the Zionist aim back on to the Cabinet agenda whenever the overwhelming pressure of war business crowded it out.

They handled a huge range of imperial business, for they prepared summaries for the Cabinet of events all over the world, as well as memoranda on the unity of policy. Sykes was responsible for the Middle East. Amery, who was secretary of an interdepartmental committee on territorial changes outside Europe that set to work early in 1917 under Curzon's chairmanship, tells in his memoirs how

> my draft also urged the special importance of securing continuity of territory both in East Africa and between Egypt and India. All this was adopted without alteration.[8]

His idea of controlling a chain of aerodromes in the Middle East was at first "greeted with derisive laughter", but when the

Imperial War Cabinet's sub-committee on peace terms put the final polish on its report, "I got its substance". All this came naturally to a man who thought Germany's claim for colonies "artificial, and not like our own overseas policy, deep-rooted in the instincts of the nation".

In April 1917, the United States came into the war. This great event was a huge and immediate asset in terms of naval warfare and the blockade, but took some time to make itself felt on land, and at once revealed itself as in some ways a diplomatic liability. Balfour went to Washington towards the end of the month to acquaint the Americans with British war aims. In the Middle East, these were the complete destruction of Turkey, with the possibility of leaving the Turks a piece of Asia Minor; Armenia, Syria and Arabia were to be detached. The secret treaties had to be divulged to President Wilson. As Balfour later told his niece and biographer:

> "I was bound to tell him. But it was a very delicate business, for of course they *were* secret. The way I got over it was to tell him about them *as* a secret, as man to man. I told him personally."⁹

Wilson's intimate adviser, Colonel House, found them "all bad", and told Balfour so. Among the details that had to be divulged were the British claim to Mesopotamia and "an area which is contiguous to Egypt" and the French and Italian claims in Anatolia. Balfour spoke of an international Palestine; both now and later, he personally favoured Anglo-American control. Almost simultaneously, Italian demand for a fair share of Asia Minor was being handled by Lloyd George at the French Alpine village of St. Jean-de-Maurienne, and when these talks were formalized into a diplomatic agreement in August 1917, Palestine was likewise earmarked for international administration in a form to be decided. Thus the Foreign Office and the "garden suburb", though more often than not they worked in unison, did not always do so. The Turkish settlement was an especial bone of contention; in the summer of 1917, members of the Foreign Office favoured, and members of the "garden suburb" thwarted, an American plan for inducing the Turks to quit the war on easy terms. Mark Sykes wrote to Clayton in Cairo that he "laid them low" by means of "a few rights and lefts" and "a breakfast with the Prime Minister".

Though Sykes is often held responsible for the worst of the inconsistencies, the War Cabinet discussed many of them and must take the blame for consenting to, even insisting on, courses he recommended. Personalities played a great part in its decisions. Mark Sykes himself was infectiously enthusiastic and optimistic; he was rich, travelled, gay, alert and companionable, and even a detached chief, such as was Balfour, was charmed into ignoring the fact that Sykes had never known the disciplines of consistency at school or university, or of having to carry plans through to their end. A chronology of certain events of 1917 reveals his weak points, but also those of a Cabinet that stampeded after him under a mercurial Prime Minister bent on acquiring a British Palestine.

By February 1917, Zionists in London had heard rumours from Paris about British commitments to France, and on February 7 a group of them met Herbert Samuel and Mark Sykes, and pressed for information. Stein tells that there is no verbatim record of this meeting, but according to notes made by the Jews who were present, Samuel said that he could not reveal Cabinet business, but Sykes, greatly pressed, said that "with great difficulty the British Government had managed to keep the question of Palestine open". His listeners got the impression that he spoke with embarrassment; and no wonder, for in his agreement with Picot Palestine's lot was clear.

In March, Baghdad was captured, and the British cabinet, over-riding the advice of its political officers on the spot, insisted on publication of a flowery piece of Sykes's ebullience. This informed the Arabs of Mesopotamia that the Arabs of the Hejaz had

> expelled the Turks and Germans who oppressed them and have proclaimed Sharif Hussain as the King and His Lordship rules in independence and freedom and is the ally of the Nations who are fighting against the power of Turkey and Germany . . . It is the desire and hope of the British peoples and nations in alliance with them that the Arab race may rise once more to greatness and renown among the peoples of the earth and that it shall bind itself to this end in unity and concord . . . Therefore I invite you to participate in the management of your civil affairs in collaboration with the Political Representatives of Great Britain who accompany the British army so that you may unite with your kinsmen in the North South East and West in realizing the aspirations of your race.[10]

It seems reasonable to read into the Cabinet's insistence on issue of this proclamation a reaction to the Government of India's chilly attitude towards Arab independence in general and the Sharif in particular. But again it was out of key with the Sykes-Picot agreement. It was also over the heads of most Baghdadis, and was deplored by the "politicals" who were handling them—Percy Cox, Arnold Wilson, Gertrude Bell. Wilson, one of the hardest workers ever to serve the British Empire, had put Sykes up during his grand tour in 1915, and had not cared for his restless imagination, or for the zest that captivated men as different as Storrs in Cairo, and Kitchener, Hankey and Lloyd George in London.

A fortnight later, Sykes accepted, as we have seen, instructions from Lloyd George and Curzon to try for a British Palestine, and warned Picot of this intention. In May, he and Picot went to Jidda to demonstrate the indivisibility of the allies to the Sharif; in Cairo later in the month, he and Picot were questioned by some Syrian inquirers, and Sykes admitted to these that a certain part of Syria would be under French occupation, but said that a certain part would be independent and that "for it the British would favour one of the sons of the King of the Hejaz". Here, he was in line with his agreement with the French.

On April 25, Lord Robert Cecil, who was running the Foreign Office while Balfour was in Washington, told a leading Zionist, Chaim Weizmann, who called on him on Zionist business, that it would strengthen the British position if the Zionists would ask for a British Palestine. Yet on April 19 Lloyd George had held with the French and the Italians the discussions at St. Jean-de-Maurienne which the Foreign Office translated into a formal agreement embodying the international administration of Palestine.

Admittedly, the times were full of uncertainty. In the spring of 1917, France was fighting for survival in Champagne and Kerensky's revolution had begun in Russia; the Egyptian Expeditionary Force was stuck at Gaza and the Germans had lent the Turks General von Falkenhayn to run Operation Yilderim (lightning) and retake Baghdad. A conflict of proposals is understandable at a moment of rapid variation in the fortunes of war. Yet muddle is undeniable, and the muddles that did permanent harm to Britain's reputation in the Middle East started in the spring of 1917 and in the dichotomy between the Foreign Office and the "garden suburb". The upshot of the evidence is that the Foreign Office held the professional view that it was imperative to keep in tune with the French and to stick to agreements, however imperfect, as being a better working basis than no agreement. The garden suburb was less orthodox and wider-ranging; to Amery's visions of continuity of territory or control must be added Sykes's of an Arab-Jewish-Armenian band of buffer states between the Turco-German combine and the British interests that stretched from Egypt to India. Sykes pursued this concept to the length of trying to found an Arab-Jewish-Armenian committee in London, but the three peoples had far too few interests in common to fall in with his dream. Sykes simultaneously prepared the ground for Zionism, and sounded the Pope about Christian desiderata in Palestine.

The British promise of a Jewish National Home, when given on November 2, 1917, in the form of a letter from Balfour to Lord Rothschild, created a mere ripple of public interest that contrasts strangely with the flow of ill-consequences that it generated for Britain. To the Jews who went to Palestine, and to many who did not, it signified fulfilment and salvation, but it brought the British much ill-will, and complications that sapped their power. Measured by British interests alone, it was one of the greatest mistakes in our imperial history. Yet at the moment of issue to the public, which was on November 9, 1917, it earned no comment in *The Times*, and when, in the following week, the first questions were asked in Parliament, they merely probed for assurance about French consent to the step—a matter on which Balfour was evasive. British thoughts were elsewhere because the war was in its fourth gloomy year. The headlines of the day were the welcome arrival of an American mission for a war conference, the Italian retreat towards Venice, General Allenby's capture of Gaza and *"Coup d'Etat* in Petrograd".

This last item, though not the most prominently printed, was the main news of the day, and was the crowning reason for issuing the Balfour Declaration, for these reasons were no longer in the same order of importance that had moved Grey in 1916, or Lloyd George in the following spring. General Allenby's advance had altered the picture; the risk of French claims to predominance in the neighbourhood of the Suez Canal was now negligible, and far more menacing was the new bogy of Russian surrender, which would confront the Western allies not merely with military calamity but with a fatal breach in their blockade of Germany. The British hope was that the influence of Russian Jewry would both keep Kerensky in the fighting line and prevent the Russian grain trade, which was largely in Jewish hands, from being diverted to the hungry Germans. The Lloyd George cabinet was also influenced by rumour that the German Government was courting the Zionists;

London was not aware of the limitations imposed on the German Government in this matter by Berlin's worsening relations with the Turks. By November 2, therefore, the British Government

> was thinking of the rapidly deteriorating situation in Russia, of the apathy towards the war of a considerable section of American Jewry, of the propagandist value of a pro-Zionist declaration, and of the urgency of the matter in the light of reports suggesting that, if such a declaration were further delayed, the Germans might blunt its edge and forestall it.[11]

On these grounds, it had obtained President Wilson's consent to the Declaration. But British observers had overestimated the influence of Russian Jewry on Kerensky's government; the Declaration therefore never served its most immediate purpose. Ironically, on the day of its announcement to the general public, Lenin took over power in Russia. Accident thus rid the British Government of one liability—the promise of Constantinople to the Czar—at the very moment, when, by design, it took on another just as damaging to British fortunes in the Middle East.

At least one onlooker at once foresaw the trouble the Balfour Declaration was to bring. William Yale, an American citizen who had represented the Standard Oil Company in Jerusalem from 1915 till March 1917, was sent by the State Department to Cairo as an observer in the following autumn. His most perceptive reports predicted among other things that the arrival of Western standards in Palestine would raise the Arab birth-rate as it had raised that of Egypt, and that argument over respective numbers was bound to arise. He told of jubilant Jewish meetings in Cairo and Alexandria, and consternation among the Syrians in Cairo, who composed a telegram to Balfour saying that Palestine was to Syria "as the heart is to the body". This telegram, he says, was not forwarded to London, and was merely acknowledged by the local British authorities. He retailed how Clayton (back from Palestine where he was serving as Chief Political Officer to Allenby), soothed Arab inquirers with assurances that "only a Home" was promised, and that nothing would be settled till the Peace Conference; Clayton added for good measure that the Jews were in touch with the Turks, and that Arab opposition might lead afresh to Turkish control. Yale also reported that the Syrians were at sixes and sevens; that they have been made to understand by the agent of the King of the Hejaz at Cairo that the Sharif has fully acquiesced in the programme of the British as to the Jews of Palestine and the taking of Syria by the French;[12]

and that British reassurances had brought the Syrians round to the view that, as there was not to be a Jewish government, they would be at some advantage over newcomers. Clearly, the British officials on the spot were handicapped by the vagueness of a policy in which they had had no say; they reported that "nothing hampers so greatly our local relations with the existing non-Jewish inhabitants". As one candid officer told Yale: "Officially I can say not a state, but unofficially I simply don't know."

This avowal was to hold good for a generation. At the time, officials were bound to make the best of their instructions and trust that apprehension was unnecessary. Some Arab experts counted on things shaking down, and advanced the view—put about also by some Zionists—that very few Jews would want to settle in the Levant and that derelict crown lands and reclaimed coastal wastes would meet all their needs. At a large public meeting in London on December 3, 1917, which was the first piece of mass publicity for the Declaration, gentiles of the eminence of Lord Robert Cecil sat on the platform and Sir Mark Sykes made a speech about "bringing the spirituality of Asia to Europe and the vitality of Europe to Asia". The public read of Jews, an Arab and an Armenian sitting beside them, and felt no qualms; Clayton expressed misgiving, but, being by nature both moderate and detached, and by profession an intelligence officer, he couched his reports as information, and not as warnings. No one whose words have yet come to light showed the prescience of William Yale.

With busy politicians and civil servants immediate matters force other affairs into the background, and in the last year of the war with Turkey, Zionism was by war standards a side issue; the two developments that dominated British policy in the Middle East were the collapse of Russia and the problem of occupying and administering sophisticated Arab towns about which promises had been made, or were newly made, as the British army advanced towards Damascus.

Directly Lenin took over power in Russia the Russian armies began to melt. Those in Persia and the Caucasus refused to obey their Czarist officers, and the area to the north of their point of junction with the British force in Mesopotamia became a void through which the Germans or Turks, or both, were expected to thrust in the general direction of India. No one on the allied side realized that neither enemy had by this time any margin of reserves left for use in central Asia. Nor had the British, but there was no one else available to parry the supposed threat, and so three British excursions set off northwards, hoping to hold some kind of a line and to rally Russian waverers. The Kiplingesque adventures that carried all three some way into Russia are not retailed here because they left no permanent mark on British policy. By dint of bluff and resource the columns pressed respectively as far as Baku, Merv and Tashkent. The most westerly group set out from Baghdad under the command of General Dunsterville, the original of Kipling's *Stalky*; consisting of "a few Englishmen of the right type to give our version of the state of affairs" (in the words of Sir William Robertson, Chief of the Imperial General Staff), its strength at the outset was forty-one armoured cars, fourteen officers and a task force of the forty-one drivers. Later, Dunsterville's force served as the line of communication for a British naval flotilla on the Caspian, and there was a period in 1919 during which travellers from Teheran to Constantinople via the Caucasus could sleep in a British mess every night. These expeditions hoodwinked not only enemies but allies into thinking that British power was as inexhaustible and ubiquitous as ever, and one grave result of their piece of conjuring with the Union Jack was to increase French jealousy and suspicion of British designs in the Middle East.

In January 1918, President Wilson launched his Fourteen Points. The twelfth point propounded unmolested and autonomous development for the nationalities under Turkish rule, and word of it soon went the rounds. Arnold Wilson recounts how a Kurdish rebel lying wounded in hospital in Baghdad in 1919 cited it in order to deny the competence of any military court to try him, and wore it, with a subsequent Anglo-French promise, translated into Kurdish on the fly-leaves of a Koran, and "strapped like a talisman to his arm".

The news travelled fastest in the coastal belt that Allenby was conquering, and became a sad worry in the area of complications raised by past promises. Allenby was fighting with French officers on his staff, with Italian officers clamouring to join them, and with the Amir Feisal's Arab army, in company with T. E. Lawrence's guerrillas, on his inland flank. All these had different ideas about liberation, and he needed some rules for the ticklish job of distributing civilian responsibilities between them. Palestine he placed under purely British administration by right of single-handed conquest, and the French, though stirred to anger by both their clericals and their imperialists, were in no position to demur. But as he advanced northwards, he was pursued by diplomatic dispatches from London about the attention he must pay to French and Arab claims. Forced into the realm of diplomacy, and to decide between rival claimants to fly flags, he could find no better basis for his judgements than the maligned and tattered Sykes-Picot agreement. He told all plaintiffs that his arrangements were temporary, and that complaints must await the Peace Conference. Meanwhile, he awarded the coastal zone of Lebanon and Syria to French administrators and the inland one, including Damascus, to Arab ones with—for the time being—British and French liaison officers. (It was when he told T. E. Lawrence that there was to be a French liaison officer as well as a British one in Damascus that Lawrence asked for leave, and went home just before the armistice.)

In Mesopotamia, where the British were fighting on their own (except for the civil war between London and the Government of India about the degree of direct rule to be applied), these international complications did not arise. A less sophisticated Arab population made fewer demands; many of its younger firebrands were serving with Feisal in Syria. Administrators trained in India were therefore able to do the kind of work to which they were accustomed—serenely "bringing in" tribes and keeping order, irrigating parched lands and feeding hungry towns, but— in terms of politics—ruling outright.

Allenby's political problems in Syria were heightened by differences between the various religious communities as to the national future that they wanted. Some of them—the Christians in particular, but also some of the Moslems—had qualms about living under the rule of the Sharif of Mecca. Automatically, the Sharif's control of affairs waned as the fighting receded farther and farther from his seat of power, and, when communications behind the battle-fronts grew easier, visitors from Cairo began to call at the army depots that Feisal had established on his way north, and to report from there that the Sharif was "tyrannical and autocratic". Yale records this news, brought back from Aqaba to Cairo, in one of his reports to the State Department; he also records the fear of the

Syrians in Cairo that the Sharif would consent to distasteful plans for their future as the price of being left to himself in the Hejaz.

These Syrians communicated their fears to sympathetic British officials, and notably to Osmond Walrond, who was working temporarily in the Arab Bureau. Walrond (who had at one time been secretary to Milner in South Africa, and of whom we shall hear again) had in his youth been tutor to an Egyptian prince, and had returned to live in Cairo, where he had many friends among the nationalists. His perceptive reporting about the worries of sophisticated Arabs helps to account for a fresh British promise made to the Arabs in June 1918. This took the form of a reply to a memorial by seven Syrians, and is known as the Declaration to the Seven. It undertook that Arab territories which were free and independent before the war should remain so, and that in territories liberated by the Arabs themselves, the British government would also recognize the "complete and sovereign independence" of the inhabitants. Elsewhere the governments of the future were to be based on the consent of the governed. Two explanations of this document are given by contemporaries and both seem to be right. One is that Turkish propaganda to the Arabs had taken on a new lease of life, and needed countering; the other, which rests on the fact that the Seven had specifically inquired whether the British Government saw all Arab countries in the same light, is that would-be federalists wanted some guarantee of immunity from the vagaries of the Sharif.

But the effect of the declaration was to make confusion worse confounded, for it thrust the Sykes-Picot arrangement farther than ever into the background at a moment when this was proving essential to Allenby as a basis for striking a temporary balance between the contestants for Syria. A crowning piece of insincerity was added when, three days before the armistice, the British and French Governments were goaded into competition with President Wilson's Twelfth Point, and jointly issued a further proclamation to the Arabs. This promised definite emancipation and governments chosen by free choice.

It is these final pledges, given when the burden and heat of the day were over, and when there was no compulsion to compete with enemy verbiage, that were far more flagrantly broken at the peace than the broad but guarded assurances given by McMahon to the Sharif. By the time the 1918 promises were made, there was no excuse for ignorance about Arab opinion; in Palestine, for instance,

Zionist newcomers were causing uneasiness among the Arabs already living there; reports from the spot are full of disquiet. Further, everyone had realized that the Sharif knew little or nothing about Palestine. As Hogarth of the Arab Bureau reported, "his ready assent to Jewish settlement there is not worth very much". As early as January 1918, even Mark Sykes was acknowledging that, where the expectation had been a crop of friendly national units, cross-fertilizing one another, "a whole crop of weeds" was growing up.

As to the French, by November 1918 they had lost a million more dead than Britain in Europe, they were no longer fighting for France's survival, and it was naïve to imagine that they would lie down under a plan that waived the Sykes-Picot agreement in Palestine but maintained it in Syria.

D

TOGETHER AT THE PEACE: 1919–22

ANGLO-FRENCH solidarity was never more heartfelt than on the day in December 1918, when Foch and Clemenceau arrived in London to discuss preliminaries for the Peace Conference. On a dismal Sunday afternoon, crowds lined the pavements ten deep, colours were dipped for Foch as for royalty, and the carriages bowled out of Charing Cross station to shouts of "God Bless you!" and "Good Old Tiger!" Clemenceau and Lloyd George spent several hours closeted together at No. 10 Downing Street. Naturally, the main subject of their *tête-à-tête* was the future of Germany. This topic dominates the whole of Anglo-French relations throughout the years described in this chapter; it is the main bone of contention, and as France and Britain tug at it, morsels of Asia are bandied between them or flung to lesser powers as sops to keep them quiet.

In Europe, Clemenceau was on his own stamping ground; he belonged to the generation of 1870, was an anti-clerical, and was fond of propounding that men live encased in their past: "Auguste Comte said that we live dead men's lives, and it is true." He was less romantic than Lloyd George, and less moved by thoughts of Palestine. But one of them brought up the subject of the Middle East. Neither kept notes, and no one was present, but we know what happened because, eight months later, Balfour reconstructed the scene in a memorandum on the Sykes-Picot agreement written to convince anti-French colleagues that France had some grounds for resentment. Clemenceau's attitude, as Balfour rendered it, was as follows:

In Downing Street last December I tried to arrive at an understanding with England about Syria. I was deeply conscious of the need of friendly relations between the two countries, and was most anxious to prevent any collision of interests in the Middle East. I therefore asked the [British] Prime Minister what modification in the Sykes-Picot agreement England desired. He replied, "Mosul". I said, "You shall have it. Anything else?" He replied, "Palestine". Again I said, "You shall have it". I

left London somewhat doubtful as to the reception this arrangement would have in France, but well assured that to Great
Britain at least it would prove satisfactory.[1]

Naturally Clemenceau did not agree to these two modifications
without corresponding gains. His conditions are nowhere exactly
specified, but can be deduced from later evidence. They were:
British support on the left bank of the Rhine; a share in the supposed oil of Mosul; the province of Turkish Cilicia for France, with
British support against American objections to its acquisition, and
"no dualism in Syria"; by this last phrase, he seems to have meant
no line of distinction drawn between Beirut and Damascus. Of
course nothing could be finally fixed by such a method, but Lloyd
George emerged satisfied from the talks; when the French Foreign
Office was told of their substance, it was horrified.

Yet at the time that the Peace Conference assembled, the British
frame of mind about the Middle East was not wholly complacent.
The stance looked splendid—an empire standing victorious on the
wreck of three others, and in a position to claim the pick of the
spoils from the one romantic campaign of the war.

> Our military power in the occupied regions of Asia [wrote
> Curzon] was sufficient to enable us to enforce not merely the
> agreed terms of the armistice but any supplementary terms that
> were found necessary.[2]

And so they did; Mosul, for instance, was taken over after the
armistice with Turkey, and despite Turkish protests that the
methods used went far beyond the armistice terms. The vanquished
were cowed, awaiting punishment; the fellow-victors expectant,
awaiting rewards. But the scene was marred by the suspicion that
the French were going to want to supervise Syria more closely than
joint promises to the Arabs warranted. Another flaw in British
satisfaction was uncertainty about Russia; in 1919, its "recovery"
from the disease of Bolshevism was still thought to be possible;
not until 1920, when the Red Army lay within ten miles of Warsaw,
was it accepted as a permanent feature of the landscape. Still
another worry was the huge change that had taken place in the
world pattern of naval strength; by 1919, the two-power standard
had gone for ever. In its place was established, at the Washington
Conference of 1921, the ratio between the British, American and
Japanese navies of 5:5:3; further, pressure of American and

Dominion opinion in the Far East had constrained the British to drop their alliance with Japan. The centre of gravity in terms of navies had been transferred from the Atlantic to the Pacific, and for the first time the whole of the British Empire east of Suez was at the mercy of an ambitious and at least potentially hostile naval power. By British standards security of passage through the Suez Canal needed even more guardianship than before the war.

By 1919 the ministries in Whitehall had recovered the ground lost to Lloyd George's "garden suburb", which had ceased to act as a group (Kerr and Sykes were in Paris). The British officials whose job it was to plan for the Middle East with these new uncertainties in mind met in an inter-departmental committee under the chairmanship of Curzon. It worked in spurts rather than regularly because all its important members had other and more pressing duties; its secretary for most of its life was Hubert Young, and his *The Independent Arab* gives a good idea of its handicaps.

The simplest, or seemingly simplest, items on its agenda were plans for the countries in which there was no European competition. The aim for Egypt was unequivocal: "maintenance of the King's Protectorate"—a phrase which recurs throughout all the vicissitudes of 1919 and 1920; for instance, it appears in the abortive Treaty of Sèvres signed with Turkey in August 1920. The British object in retaining a protectorate was not so much to deny Egyptians self-rule as to keep other powers from establishing diplomatic relations on the bank of the Suez Canal.

In Arabia, the British were determined to exert influence, but they did not want protectorates over its inland rulers because of the labours this would entail. War-time experience of handling sheikhs had killed all wish to become involved in settling their quarrels; they could well be left to themselves, since there was no outside competitor for power in the peninsula.

For Persia (which was in its endemic state of chaos, and contained at least three local armed forces none of which took much notice of Teheran) the British aim was the long-standing one of generating some kind of independence run by its elegant, elusive patriots. British interest in a stable régime was greater than ever, because to the old anxiety about the defence of India had been added at least three new ones—security for the oil fields, a good neighbour for Mesopotamia, and a society resistant to Bolshevik ideas.

For Mesopotamia, British intentions were a matter for feud

between the Government of India and London, or, locally, between Arnold Wilson and Gertrude Bell; but this difference of opinion had resolved itself by 1919 into work for an Arab façade with complete British control of administration and finance.

Everywhere else, imposition of British desires was out of the question because of the war-time promises made in the area and the peace aims, imperialist or anti-imperialist, of the major allies. Constantinople—Asia Minor—Armenia—Cilicia—Syria—Palestine: for each a queue of aspirants descended on Versailles, most of them helped by attendant champions from the Foreign Office, or the British delegation in Paris, or the Arab Bureau, or India, not to mention foreigners. A few patterns were open to alteration in that all the inter-allied promises had lost something of their validity through the disappearance of one signatory—Czarist Russia; but most of the contestants were brandishing undertakings that they took to be firm.

There were two main areas about which the Curzon Committee could scarcely plan at all because of these commitments; one was the Arab areas for which the Sykes-Picot agreement prescribed some form of French supervision; the other, the territories inhabited by Turks. Whenever it discussed the Sykes-Picot area, the committee was inhibited by the decision taken at prime-ministerial level to disrupt an agreed pattern by claiming Palestine and Mosul, but to endeavour to preserve that pattern in the rest of Syria; as time went on it received more and more evidence that France would contest this design. For the Turks, Curzon's own recipe was force in Europe: consent in Asia. Always well-informed about the Orient, he rightly judged that reverence for the Caliphate as represented by the Ottoman dynasty was a figment of Europe's imagination rather than a fact of significance in the East. He therefore favoured turning the Turks out of Constantinople but treating them with magnanimity in Asia Minor. The India Office, by contrast, wanted magnanimity in Constantinople also, in order to soothe Khilafat agitation in India. In the end, this issue was referred to the Cabinet, where it was settled by a show of hands that gave a verdict in favour of the India Office, and, as a by-product, of Turkish nationalism.

Settlement in Asia Minor, bedevilled by Greek, Italian and French claims to provinces, led to one of Lloyd George's worst mistakes in the Levant, the decision (supported by some, though not all, members of the Foreign Office) to fight Turkish nationalism by proxy, through the Greeks. In 1919, the Greeks had been encouraged to land at Smyrna by France and America also, but when Greek exuberance and folly had hurried on a Turkish renaissance under Mustafa Kemal, allied support fell away, and only Lloyd George continued to back Greece. By 1922, the Americans had gone home, the French had seen the significance of Turkish nationalism and changed sides, and Britain alone was rebuffed when Kemal, having driven the Greeks into the sea, challenged Europe's power to keep him out. The story of his success at Chanak belongs to Europe rather than the Middle East; its relevance here is that it put heart into many people besides the Turks. His demonstration that a vanquished state could deal with the victors on its own terms, tear up the Treaty of Sèvres, and substitute the very different Treaty of Lausanne, was a tonic to disaffected nationalists in the Arab world, Egypt and Persia; for years to come, the thought of it cheered them whenever it crossed their minds.

Even if the British plans for the Middle East had been executed swiftly and in the flood-tide of victory, not all of them were of good cut for 1919. Done slowly, and with patent quarrelling and fumbling, they came to fruition only at two points—in Arabia and, ultimately, in Mesopotamia. Elsewhere they were twisted to suit other tastes, though not sufficiently so to destroy the paramount position in the Middle East that Britain had won in battle.

Execution lagged because everyone was exhausted. The war had ended very suddenly, and the swift change of mental climate had left men limp. Everyone mentions the strain of the times, even Lord Beaverbrook: "Lloyd George is the only one who never gets tired of power." Inch by inch the Prime Minister grew testier until he was swamping the ministers most immediately concerned with the Middle East by means of a snap poll of the Cabinet, writing them almost intolerable letters, and creating a master-and-servant relationship that alienated his colleagues one by one. The same tired men were simultaneously forcing their way through a jungle of home complications—demobilization, labour unrest, above all, Ireland. Additionally, those handling foreign affairs had constantly to shuttle between London and Paris. Weeks, and on at least one occasion months, passed before the right quorum could attend to business in Curzon's committee, and, when it met, decisions were often postponed because of disagreement between ministers or experts. Sometimes a department pulled this way, sometimes that; for instance, Curzon was at odds with his more liberally-minded India Office colleague, Edwin Montagu, about both Persia and Turkey, whereas over Mesopotamia he had, Lawrence told Yale in 1919,

> recently adopted a more liberal point of view in regard to British control . . . and was inclined to grant the Arabs their wishes;[3]

here, therefore, he contested the conservatism on Government of India lines preached by Arnold Wilson. Men were no less weary, short-tempered and divided after the Second World War, but at least there was in 1945 a sense of impulse and novelty generated by an election that brought a new party to power.

On top of the complications at home, and disagreement with France, the over-ambition of lesser allies had to be dealt with. The Italians, who were just as impulsive as the Greeks, at an early meeting of the Peace Conference suggested for themselves a mandate for the Caucasus (provoking Mark Sykes to a lightning caricature of a Bersagliere grimacing at India over the Pamirs). Yet other expenditure of energy was required to soothe the outraged feelings of countries which felt that they had been made use of without due recognition, such as Egypt and Persia. Finally, overshadowing every debate about the fate of the ex-Ottoman Empire was uncertainty about American willingness to take a permanent hand in the peace settlement; people forgot then, as they often do now, that for a resident of the Middle West the Middle East is, literally, the other side of the world. Procrastination reigned while undecided Europeans hoped that some American Solomon would solve their problems by taking over Constantinople or Armenia or Jerusalem.

Postponements were inevitable when there was half a world to be tidied up but, as they increased in time and number, they exasperated everyone whose place on the agenda was low. The Peace Conference was just sitting down to the main conundrums of the German treaty when the first of the Middle Eastern malcontents demonstrated the effects of inattention. In March 1919 rebellion broke out in Egypt. In this brief affray, the crowd at first confined itself to wrecking property, including the property of anglophile Egyptians, but later it turned on British soldiers, even pulling them out of trains and murdering them in wayside stations. These violent scenes took London by surprise, for it had been misled as to Egyptian opinion by the Egyptian attitude during the war.

Throughout its course the Egyptians, though known to be pro-Turk, had shown singularly little ill-will; they had passively accepted the Protectorate, making no protest at British failure to consult the elected bodies with which those same British had endowed them. They had listened in silence to a British undertaking of 1914 "to bear the sole burden of the war without calling on Egypt for aid". But this promise had not been kept. Requisitioning of animals, collections for the Red Cross, recruitment for the Labour Corps, were all supposed to be voluntary contributions, but once British army headquarters moved northward into Palestine, they were exacted by long-distance means (through Egyptian agents who would usually see to it that they got a commission) and in ways that provoked far more resentment than the actual presence of foreign troops. Peasants as well as townsmen grew angry. Dirges in folk-song have always ranked among the best evidence of public discontent: "Princes have persecuted me without a cause . . ."; "They're after the forbiddin' o' the wearin' o' the green". In the Nile Valley in 1918, the fellahin sang:

> Woe on us Wingate
> Who has carried off corn
> Carried off cotton
> Carried off camels
> Carried off children
> Leaving only our lives
> For love of Allah, now let us alone.[4]

Sir Valentine Chirol of *The Times* records that even where donors were willing they were "never given a chance of gaining credit for conscious and voluntary sacrifice". One reason for such neglect is that military considerations dominated every decision. When the British Royal Air Force sought a base at Aboukir and land was requisitioned for the purpose, the committee appointed to assess compensation did not contain a single Egyptian.

Until 1919, martial law masked reality. Men in London, though warned by the High Commissioner—the Wingate of the song— that tempers were rising, wrote him off as wordy (which he was) and unduly alarmist (which he was not) and said that interviews which he had given to the nationalists who sought representation at the Peace Conference were "unfortunate". They had no notion that slights intended to put nationalists in their place, and preference accorded to Quislings, would infuriate the whole nation. Instead, they listened to the general in command in Egypt, who reported that the arrest of a few ringleaders would deprive the movement of all momentum. The volume of evidence of unrest that piles up in books written after the event is very great, but letters written at the time are also available, and describe the local perturbation; Osmond Walrond, whose personal friendships among nationalists in Cairo have already been mentioned, wrote to Milner at the end of 1918 that Egyptians were borrowing his books on South African union and on the constitutions of the British dominions. Who can say when and whether a volcano will erupt or merely smoulder? Wingate, in the same month as he reported to London that President Wilson's ideas had taken a strong hold, and that the likelihood of an armistice was causing crowds to foregather in the front of the United States consulate in hopes of a sign, wrote home that the nationalist movement might subside if Europe were firm. In assessing the prospects, one of the troubles, wrote Walrond of Wingate to Milner in January 1919, is that "there are so many cooks circling round a very weak and tired man". When on January 21 Wingate left for Paris and London he was bent on conveying a grave warning of unrest. But he accosted other tired men. In Paris, he was listened to by both Lloyd George and Balfour at two meals between Peace Conference meetings, and though cold-shouldered by Curzon when he got to London (no doubt as a reproof for his tendency to respond to nationalists who were by Curzon's standards putting a pistol to his head), he did not go without a hearing. A tragic price was paid by all for his failure to get his message across, for he was superseded, and never got another appointment, while the cost to Britain was a lifetime of Egyptian hostility.

The March rebellion was soon controlled, for Egypt was full of British soldiers—not merely the normal garrison but troops on their way home from the East for demobilization. The appointment of General Allenby to succeed Wingate as High Commissioner helped to damp down demonstration of the unrest; he was chosen with the idea that a man of the Kitchener class, bearing the stamp of a victor in war, would be more effective than an old familiar face. The rebellion had passed its peak by the time he arrived on March 25, and its quick abatement restored British belief in Egyptian volatility. Yet Allenby was tied to maintaining a protectorate with which the Egyptians were determined to have done, and after the first flush of success, his problem became one of handling steady passive resistance, punctuated by strikes, murders and a public boycott of the palliative he produced, which was the Milner Mission.

This mission was attended by more delays. Milner was too busy to undertake the job unless it could wait till the winter. Meanwhile: "Can we honestly say," asked the *Round Table*, "that Egypt's progress towards a life of her own has been rapid?" Its answer was no; Egypt had proved easy to occupy but difficult to ride on a light rein, and impossible to quit for reasons most of which lay far outside its frontiers. No other country affords such clear proof that force of habit kills political sensitivity and imagination.

Allenby's proclamation of November 1919 that the Milner Mission was on its way was the first public intimation of British attention to Egypt's own development that the Egyptians had had for five years. But the proclamation made no concession of principle, so the mission was boycotted in public, though many Egyptians recognized in private that it proffered a hope of progress towards self-government, and were ready to talk to members of its most liberal team, provided they did so behind closed doors. Milner, who was doing the last big job of his life, showed at his best; in the papers which he left at his death is an envelope marked in his writing "Ozzy's letters; well worth keeping"; they are from Walrond, and are a mine of information about public sentiment amongst their writer's Egyptian acquaintances. The fruit of his knowledge and common sense will be described later.

In Persia, as in Egypt, submissiveness while British troops held local strongpoints was mistaken in London for a favourable attitude to Britain, and here too expectations were dashed. Curzon was the accepted authority on Persia, and handled it unfettered, and in his element; since the Persians were not admitted to the Peace Conference, the line of communication ran direct from his desk in the Foreign Office to Teheran. He had India Office agreement that Persia must be reconditioned, be independent and be sovereign, and where his ideas did not dovetail with Edwin Montagu's more liberal attitude, he—the author of the best book on the country and a recognized authority on the whole central Asian question—was in a position to push them through. He reckoned that he must move fast, so as to establish calm on a British model before Russia recovered balance, and he produced, and by August 1919 got Persia's signature to, a forerunner of the unequal treaties of independence that were to be the staple and successful British recipe for most of the Middle East until after the Second World War. But it did not succeed in Persia.

The provision that was unpalatable to Persian nationalists was an undertaking to accept British advisers for military and financial affairs. This was assented to, in a stately way, at a time when the British army had a headquarters at Kasvin in north Persia and the British navy a flotilla on the Caspian Sea. It was negotiated

> on the British side by Sir Percy Cox, and on the Persian side by Vossuq-ed-Dowleh, the Prime Minister. The former had for long been Resident in the Persian Gulf and shared Curzon's affection for, and anxiety regarding, Persian integrity, character, ancient buildings and independence. A silent Apollo, Sir Percy Cox was inclined to take the realities of the Persian temperament more seriously than their aspirations. Vossuq-ed-Dowleh, for his part, was also a realist. Upstanding, handsome and reserved, he combined the traditional distinction of his race with that polish which Vevey and Montreux can add to the culture of Iran. These two distinguished men were born to understand each other. They did.[5]

But by 1920 the military operation that Churchill dubbed "reaching out for Persia" had become expensive; in May, the Red Army began to contest it; commissars appeared and set up soviets in the Caspian provinces, and caused the British Chiefs of Staff to decide that troops in sufficient numbers to hold the necessary lines of communication were not available. Withdrawal began, and though the last units did not leave until May 1921, its start suggested to the Persians that they had better trim their sails. They flourished the article in their constitution that demanded ratification of all treaties by the Majlis before Cox's successor, Herman Norman. Booming telegrams from London instructing him to obtain the necessary ratification were in vain; the feat was impossible in the new conditions that had developed—the rise to power of a determined soldier, Reza Khan, whom the Persians hoped would defy the West as Kemal was doing; support from the Americans for Persian opponents of the treaty with Britain, and, above all, Bolshevik soldiers and their Persian satellites within easy march of Teheran.

Curzon was a ruthless master with a long memory for other people's failure to do as he thought right; he blackballed Norman as he had done Wingate, and neither man ever got another appointment. But in the end his mind took a philosophic turn. When the

Americans, who had opposed his over-positive policy, supplied advisers, he reflected that

> the question by whom Persia is to be regenerated is vastly less important than that her regeneration should take place.[6]

Provided, of course, that the regenerating agent was not the Bolsheviks. These had made an excellent start by repudiating all Czarist privileges, annulling Czarist debts and promising to evacuate all Czarist troops from north-west Persia. Now that a Russian army of different stamp had reappeared, the Persians—given 2,000 miles of undefended frontier with Russia—saw no alternative to signing the Russo-Persian treaty of 1921 that survived until 1959; but they were able to water it down by a subsequent exchange of notes, and to get rid of the Red Army by the expedient of promising to appoint a pro-Russian governor for the northern provinces and then substituting another after it had gone. Curzon was not alone in his chagrin.

Baulked in Persia and resisted in Egypt, he thought that he was sure at least of Mesopotamia, where, he told the House of Lords in February 1919, "more has been done in two years for those places than has been done in the five preceding centuries. . . . There are no shadows in this picture". But in Mesopotamia another round of delays was brought on by the lack of a peace treaty with Turkey, and here too procrastination ended in rebellion. For months on end officials worked in ignorance of what the future held for their districts; as one of them—Leachman, subsequently murdered while on the job—began a report from Mosul: "The limit of masterly inactivity has now been reached." The local peoples, likewise uncertain whether the British meant to go or to stay, were in doubt as to whether to comply with British arrangements, and bided their time lest the Turks should come back. Often in danger from recalcitrant tribes in the remoter areas, the British officials carried on upon conservative Government of India lines. Arnold Wilson (who was holding down far more than one man's job, since he was also responsible for the whole Persian Gulf) slept and ate in his office, and could be relied on by his subordinates personally to answer a telegram at any hour of the night or day. He covered the wilder parts of his parish by air, using R.A.F. machines that sometimes carried the acting High-Commissioner to be dropped at one point, and a few bombs to be dropped at another.

Elsewhere in the Baghdad office Gertrude Bell, immaculately

dressed, catalogued the friendly and unfriendly tribes, welcomed the many whom she knew as old friends, and prayed that Percy Cox would come back and institute some régime more liberal than the pattern favoured by Wilson. Neither of them shared Curzon's illusions about a scene free from shadows, but in 1920 both underrated the effect on Mesopotamia of uncertainty, and of events outside the territory. So did the soldiers, who migrated to a summer camp in Persia. In some ways it was surprising that the "politicals" contrived to hold down the lid of the cauldron for as long as they did; it flew off in June 1920 and not long after it had done so Gertrude Bell wrote home:

> It is true that we are largely suffering from circumstances over which we couldn't have had any control. The wild drive of discontented nationalism from Syria and of discontented Islam from Turkey might have proved too much for us however far-seeing we had been; but that doesn't excuse us for having been blind.[7]

The cost of blindness was fighting which lasted until the spring of 1921 with a loss of some hundreds of British dead and missing and a bill of £50 million in money. People began to wonder, in a way that they never wondered about Egypt, whether Mesopotamia was worth such an outlay.

The Arabs who attended the Peace Conference by right of belligerent status were in a better position to advance their claim than absentees and second-class contributors to victory. Their leader was the Emir Feisal, the son of the Sharif of Mecca whom T. E. Lawrence had chosen and publicized as the best of the four; as to both dress and demeanour, he was the most romantic person called to the conference table. Even a chilly American lawyer like Robert Lansing was moved to flights of romantic prose by it: "His voice seemed to breathe the perfume of frankincense and to suggest the presence of richly coloured divans, green turbans and the glitter of gold and jewels." But romance was of no avail. Feisal's fate at the conference's hands is a byword. Though an often-told story, it needs its European background to be fully understood.

All through 1919, stresses mounted for the peacemakers. During its first six months, the British and French fought a contest over Germany that is, in retrospect, the opening round of the twenty-year battle about appeasement. Ranged on opposite sides were the

French, bent on a reparations policy that stemmed from their suffer-
ings, and the British, guiltily aware that they had got off the more
lightly in the matter of war damage, yet feeling bound to insist
that the only hope for the future of Europe lay in food, coal,
transport and economic revival for Germany. It was the year of
controversy not only over Germany's capacity to pay but over
frontiers; of the march of communism into Hungary and as far
west as Bavaria; of reluctant enlistment of Germany against the
Bolsheviks; and of British pressure to get French agreement to a
pattern for Europe that would hold good only if America helped
to maintain it. Throughout the second half of the year, the British
and French alike were riddled with anxiety first by the likelihood
and then by the virtual certainty that the Americans would refuse
the role—the fear that, says Harold Nicolson, "became the ghost
at all our feasts". And, once suspicion became reality, the French
set off upon the course of reinsurance that they maintained, regardless of British opinion, for the next ten years. Yet throughout this
time of basic disagreement, all major British statesmen, and all
French ones except Poincaré, knew that the two countries must hang
together or Europe would fall apart.

In this clamour, the noise of eastern Europeans fighting for
territory in order to anticipate decisions, or plaintive Middle Eastern
voices describing slights, delays and non-fulfilment of promises,
were heeded only intermittently. Nevertheless, each time the subject of Syria gained the full attention of the Big Four, Lloyd
George made an effort to get for Feisal the self-governing Syria
that had been promised. "Our permitting the occupation of
Damascus by the Shereefians has allayed some of the suspicion of
British intentions", Clayton had written just before the armistice
from his listening-post as chief political officer to Allenby; according to the British undertaking of 1918 to the Seven Syrians, they
had earned it, and so must keep it.

But there were two weak points in the armoury at Lloyd George's
disposal for his battle on behalf of Feisal; one was that he could
not hold the French to the Sykes-Picot agreement (which had specified that the Arabs were to have the inland towns) when he himself
had jettisoned the clause about Palestine; in treaties, as in knitting,
one dropped stitch weakens the whole fabric. The other was that
the British did not wish to lay themselves open to a French *tu
quoque* about the direct rule that they were practising in Mesopotamia.

Lloyd George's retreat before Clemenceau over Syria took place by stages in the course of 1919. In March, at a meeting of the Council of Four, the French brought up the bargain of the previous December. In the course of an acrimonious debate, President Wilson upset both Lloyd George and Clemenceau by bluntly stating that he did not consider the secret understandings binding on the United States; he added that the "only scientific basis possible for a settlement" was to send an international commission to consult the wishes of the inhabitants. This was the last thing that the British wanted either in Palestine or Mesopotamia, or the French in Syria, and in the end a purely American commission—the King-Crane commission—went only to the Levant; and even there its report came to nothing because of Wilson's failure to grasp that consultation is a virtue only if the consulting authority has the will and ability to act on what it learns.

At the March meeting Lloyd George succeeded in getting in word that the British could not let the Arabs down over Damascus. By the autumn, however, a combination of factors had reduced British bargaining power. One was the need to curtail overseas expenditure; another, the attack on the Treaty of Versailles led by Senators Lodge and Borah which, coupled with President Wilson's paralytic stroke, suggested that the United States might fade from the European scene and that Britain had best not quarrel with France. A third was a series of reminders from the General Staff that the army was shrinking fast, and that the peacemakers must not overtax British military capacity. In one of its memoranda, it hoped that

> only such terms will be seriously considered by His Majesty's Government, in the first place, as may be reasonably compatible with the resources which exist or which it may be intended to provide for their execution.[8]

So in September 1919 the British announced agreement with the French to British military evacuation of Syria in favour of the French on the littoral, and of Feisal in the four promised towns and the desert beyond them. By November, the British troops had left Damascus and the French were inching eastwards into the Bekaa valley that is on the way inland; they moved to an accompaniment of Arab protests only, for Allenby had gone, and there was nothing more that the British could do for Feisal. Even so, his cause was not yet hopeless, for while in Paris in the autumn of 1919, he had friendly encounters with French statesmen and officials—notably with Clemenceau and with General Gouraud, newly appointed High Commissioner in Syria and Lebanon. These talks led, in December 1919, to the production by the French Government of a draft, and by Feisal of a counterdraft, of an agreement between them. Apparently Feisal thought the prospects sufficiently promising to take the French draft with him to Damascus, to which he returned at the beginning of January 1920. But tempers had been rising there during his absence, and a draft agreement that had seemed to a sophisticated prince in Paris to merit consideration was scarcely worth showing to the nationalists of Damascus. Even before his return, they had been demonstrating against him, and his ideas of compromise were doomed.

He contrived to hold until the following July the patrimony that he had run for twenty-one months. But his single-handed dealings with France ended in military defeat, followed by a flight that constitutes a black spot in the annals of British support for the Arabs. A shamefaced little band of Englishmen waited on him as he passed through Palestine:

> I went with Sir Herbert [wrote Storrs] to greet Feisal and Zaid when the train of exile passed through Ludd where we mounted him a guard of honour a hundred strong. He carried himself with dignity and the noble resignation of Islam
>
> > Nor called the Gods with angry spite
> > To vindicate his helpless right
>
> though the tears stood in his eyes and he was wounded to the soul. The Egyptian "Sultanate" did not recognize him, and at Qantara station he awaited his train sitting on his luggage.[9]

"He that sweareth unto his neighbour and disappointeth him not, though it were to his own hindrance; Whoso doeth these things shall never fall." But in the short run the fifteenth psalm does not apply to great powers. For thirty years the British, and for twenty the French, withstood the practical consequences of their bad faith; the moral consequences assailed them later. But in Britain, some of the men responsible felt guilty at such treatment of a friend and ally even though, if all the outside circumstances are taken into account, that treatment was unavoidable. The hard core of the British case for letting down Feisal in Syria is contained in two summings-up by responsible men. On July 30, ten days after his collapse at Damascus, Balfour, during a talk with Colonel Meinertzhagen of the Peace Conference staff that the latter recorded in his diary, remarked that

> he was very distressed at the Syrian muddle, all the more so as he perhaps was personally responsible for it. We had not been honest with either French or Arab, but it was now preferable to quarrel with the Arab rather than the French, if there was to be a quarrel at all.[10]

Five months later, the second main reason for defection was communicated in unvarnished form to Feisal in Paris. When he complained to Curzon, by letter, of the French move into the Bekaa, Curzon sent no written reply. Instead a Foreign Office official was instructed verbally to tell Feisal's faithful follower, General Haddad Pasha, that he did

> not see how we can help or intervene in any way. We should very strongly resent any French protest as to our action in Mesopotamia or even in the *vilayet* of Mosul or on its borders and the French position with regard to the Bekaa is somewhat analagous.[11]

Thus did the British indecently bury the Syrian section of the promises given at the end of the war.

One broken British promise directed Arab attention to other samples of British bad faith, and caused the Sharif, who had at first assented to Jewish settlement in Palestine, to add his voice to those of the Syrian and Palestinian Arabs who had from the outset shown their hostility to Zionism. This is the context in which McMahon's careless failure to be specific about Palestine became an issue in general Anglo-Arab relations. Before 1920, not only the Sharif, but at times even members of the Arab Bureau had thought there might be advantage to the Arabs if Jewish settlement were encouraged. Even T. E. Lawrence on one occasion suggested that it might strengthen Feisal because if, coming from the desert as he did, he found the townsmen of Syria slipping from his control, he might find an Anglo-Jewish Palestine a source of support against them. The speculation and confusion of mind into which the indeterminate and multiple promising of Palestine had thrown everyone cannot be overstressed. At some moments the British officials there were wringing their hands at Arab unrest generated by early symptoms of Jewish exclusiveness and chauvinism; at others they were reporting that everything seemed to be settling down. On balance, worry predominated; according to Lloyd George, it helped to kill Mark Sykes, who died in Paris in the influenza epidemic of February 1919.

Even President Wilson had to admit that there was for the moment an irreconcilable conflict between his belief that the Jews must be helped and his belief in self-government and self-determination, and was forced to concur that Palestine must "for the time being" be excluded from the area destined for provisional independence. In retrospect, it is easy to see that both the main problems that were in the end to defeat the British in Palestine were present from the start—the conflict over numbers and the problem of whether or no to use force to settle matters. They are revealed from the moment of the first "disturbance" (the British euphemism for riots) in 1920 and 1921. But for more than a decade the troubles were thought manageable because their dimensions were not great, and because they were directed at one community or the other and not at the umpire, and because the statesman or civil servant who wants to keep his work within bounds expends his energy on day to day issues and keeps his mind off—to use Balfour's phrase—"distressing possibilities".

After scenes that President Wilson once described as "the whole disgusting scramble" for the Middle East, the mandates for former Turkish territories were allotted at the San Remo Conference of April 1920—Syria and Lebanon to France, Palestine and Mesopotamia (Iraq) to Britain. The decisions accorded neither with the wishes of the inhabitants nor with the unqualified end-of-war undertakings about freedom of choice. They were pieces of unabashed self-interest, suggesting to many onlookers that all talk of liberating small nations from oppression was so much cant. Yet extension of the British Empire on these terms was accepted by the British Government and people, though both were on the whole averse to taking on more territory. The explanation of this anomaly lies in the magic of the word "'mandate". It was sufficiently elastic to suggest to the British left that here was a fitting job for the new League of Nations, and to the British right that the essentials of imperial defence would remain safely in British hands.

By contrast, the word struck dismay into all Arab hearts. The adoption of the system of government for which it stood helps to account—together with Feisal's humiliation, fear of the Jews, the exodus of nationalists from Damascus to Baghdad, and the

progressive withdrawal of British military rule from the area—
for the outburst of strikes, murders and rebellions that mark 1920
and that have already been described.

Armed resistance instinctively produces in an imperial power
an unwillingness to capitulate to violence; yet capitulation happened all over the Middle East between the end of 1920 and the
fall of the Lloyd George government at the end of 1922. It was
not surrender to successful resistance, as in Ireland or Turkey;
everywhere, except in rural Iraq, actual violence was quickly
stamped out. It was due rather to pressure from British victims
of Cabinet delays and disagreements—that is, to the British men
on the spot. These, charged with holding down the lid of the
Middle Eastern cauldron with their bare hands, had good grounds
for complaint, for their countrymen in London and Paris would
neither agree that the pot was boiling, nor take steps to move it to
the side of the fire.

The principal servants who spoke up were Percy Cox and
Gertrude Bell in Baghdad, T. E. Lawrence in London and Allenby
in Egypt. Cox, tall, calm and taciturn, was sent back to Iraq in
October 1920 to handle the rebellion. By the time he arrived it
had passed its peak and Wilson, overstrained by delays that had
brought him to the pitch of advocating either governing or going,
went on leave from which he did not return. Gertrude Bell thank-
fully resumed the role of a moon in orbit round her planet, Sir
Percy, and helped him to establish a new policy—the transformation, as quickly as possible, of the whole façade of the administration from a British to an Arab one. Cox, fresh from interviews in
London and possessed of enough Asian experience to outshine
even Curzon, was able to force London to take decisions, however
unpalatable:

> Fortifying myself with the conviction that the project had at
> least an even chance of success and was at any rate the only
> alternative to evacuation, I took heart of grace.[12]

Lawrence, differently placed, used a different technique for the
same purpose; he waged a war of words. From the refuge of All
Souls College, Oxford, to which he had retired after the ordeal
of the Peace Conference, he fought with his pen for the Arab case
and against the evils of administering mandates "from the empty

space which divides the Foreign Office from the India Office".
He poured out letters and articles :

> How long will we permit millions of pounds, thousands of
> imperial troops and tens of thousands of Arabs to be sacrificed
> on behalf of a form of colonial administration which can benefit
> nobody but its administrators?[13]

By the early spring of 1921 his bombardment, added to the force of
circumstances, had shaken the Cabinet and helped to bring about
a change of management for the mandates; responsibility for
them was transferred to the Colonial Office, to which Winston
Churchill was appointed as Colonial Secretary. Churchill had not
known Lawrence for long, but admired his virtues and resolved
to bridle and employ him; to the surprise of most onlookers, he
succeeded in adding him for one important year to a team of "two
or three of the best men it has ever been my fortune to work with".
The outcome of their efforts was mitigation of the sense of guilt
about letting down the Sharif, achieved by placing the Emir Feisal
on the throne of Iraq and entrusting his brother Abdullah with
government of the vacant lot which the British christened the
Amirate of Transjordan. Simultaneously, and to prophecies of
doom from the army, Sir Hugh Trenchard's idea of keeping order
in Iraq by means of the Air Force was put into practice. Photographs of Churchill's Cairo conference of 1921 are good evidence
of the galaxy of talent that evolved and supported these decisions;
Lawrence was not their only begetter, but he used his credit and
renown to set the ball rolling in a way that paid dividends both
to Britain and the Arabs—perhaps the greatest of the several great
services he performed in the Middle East.

Allenby's technique was different again. In Egypt the Milner
Mission, though it had been boycotted, had been able to learn
a good deal about Egyptian nationalism and local British attitudes.
Its report, when it came out in December 1920, came as a shock
to Conservatives in Britain; men like Curzon and Bonar Law were
aghast at its candour about past British shortcomings as well as
the liberalism of its proposals for the future. How were they to
be sure that imperial communications would be safe if Britain
were to agree to abolish the protectorate *before* signing a treaty
with an infant of an independent government and monarchy, and
would not British imperial security be jeopardized if Egypt were
to enjoy diplomatic representation abroad, entailing reciprocity and

the representation of unfriendly powers in Cairo? But these were
not the only hesitations; the Egyptian nationalists also prevaricated;
they refused to say yes or no to novel propositions, and since they,
and not the moderates, had the last word with the Egyptians,
Allenby was faced with further delays and a fresh crop of strikes
and riots. At last, in February 1922, he could stand procrastination
no longer; he decided to take the bull by the horns and left for
London with his resignation in his pocket. Burly, determined, and
a Field-Marshal, he confronted the Cabinet with the presence almost
of a Kitchener. The scene is best told as he retailed it to his
biographer, Wavell:

> Sir Gilbert Clayton and (Sir Maurice) Amos accompanied
> Allenby to the meeting. Mr. Lloyd George was supported by
> Lord Curzon. Allenby was subjected to a sharp cross-fire of
> questions and objections on his proposals; he began to show
> impatience, complaining of the number of occasions on which
> his advice had been rejected. "But," said the Prime Minister,
> "you are now asking me to abandon our entire position in Egypt
> without guarantee." Here Amos broke in: "That, sir, is not a
> fair description of Lord Allenby's proposals." Mr. Lloyd George
> then turned on Amos and again went over the Cabinet's objec-
> tions, to which Amos replied. The argument was proceeding,
> when Allenby broke in with: "Well, it is no good disputing any
> longer. I have told you what I think is necessary. You won't have
> it, and it is none of my business to force you to. I have waited
> five weeks for a decision, and I can't wait any longer. I shall tell
> Lady Allenby to come home." On this the Prime Minister rose
> and put his hand on Allenby's arm. "You have waited five weeks,
> Lord Allenby," he said, "wait five more minutes."[14]

Allenby had won.

The scene is a measure of the debt Britain owes to the men
who brought about the shift to a liberal policy. Though they had
a large sector of public opinion on their side, because people were
sick of Ireland, and sickened—following a notorious massacre at
Amritsar in India—at the prospect of more shooting of Asians,
they also had to contend with the wide range of good imperialists
who thought in terms of a vital British heartland all the way from
the Suez Canal to the Persian Gulf. Ought the cabinet to be given
credit for listening to unfamiliar advice or to be castigated for
failure to read the omens until these were written all over the wall?

All the principal members of Lloyd George's last Cabinet had lived their formative years in the nineteenth century. Balfour was born in 1848, Milner in 1854, Bonar Law in 1858, Curzon was, in Lord d'Abernon's phrase, "born grandiloquent" in 1859. All but Lloyd George were in their forties when the twentieth century began; all had since lived through changes of social outlook just as swift and radical as that which our own generation has known. The surprising aspect of their change of direction in 1921–2 is not that Curzon and Bonar Law were difficult to move, but that Balfour and Milner were so responsive to the thought and climate of a new world. There was only one point at which their new liberalism could make no headway. Balfour admitted to this signal failure. As Colonel Meinertzhagen records in his diary for July 30, 1919:

> He agreed, however, in principle to the creed of self-determination, but it could not be indiscriminately applied to the whole world, and Palestine was a case in point, and a most exceptional one.[15]

Because he and his colleagues had created the co-existence of incompatibles, conditions that they had fought the war to create were out of the question in Palestine, and remained so.

3
THE YEARS OF GOOD MANAGEMENT:
1922–45

THE sequel to this dreadful story of broken promises and friends abandoned should by rights be a tale of retribution. But it is nothing of the sort. The British were powerful, yet their policy was flexible, and serene combination of the two qualities saw them through the ups and downs of the next twenty-five years.

After the men on the spot (backed by Winston Churchill after one of the practical about-turns that distinguish his career) had denounced British force of habit and advised meeting rebels half way, the plans adopted for immediate use were various but the end was the same—to evolve a compromise between the Middle Eastern wish for independence, and the British wish to retain partial control. The British recipe was to give moderate local leaders something to show for their moderation. Such leaders were at hand; men like Adli Pasha Yeghen in Egypt, the Amir Abdullah in Transjordan or the ageing Naqib of Baghdad disliked extremist antics, and wanted an orderly transfer of power. They would, as the Naqib remarked privately to Gertrude Bell in 1920, "a great deal sooner combine with an unbeliever—except always the French—" than with the hotheads at home. Their compliance with British plans blinded British eyes to the fact that they too were nationalists; for instance, Lloyd George saw nothing amiss in taking Adli Pasha, when he was in London in 1921, into the room in which the Imperial Conference had sat, and pointing to a chair which he said was being reserved for Egypt's entry into the British Commonwealth of nations.

The compromises evolved for Egypt and the mandated territories were different in letter but alike in spirit. The mandatory undertakings amounted to a cross between liberalism and adherence to war aims, but were not the same thing as old-style colonialism, primarily because their charter implied a time limit, and also because the mandatory power was responsible to an international body of critics that had the right to review its actions once a year. This

Permanent Mandates Commission of the League of Nations was
the best body of its kind ever so far constituted; it consisted of
men of such experience and impartiality that they were able to
work effectively even though handicapped by the success of the
mandatories in denying them the right to pay visits of inspection.
They sat in their private capacity as experts, and (unlike their
successors on the Trusteeship Council of the United Nations) were
uninhibited by national or ideological prejudice. While serving on
the Commission they were debarred from holding any office which
made them in any way dependent on their own governments, and,
though four out of the nine were nationals of mandatory powers,
Orts the Belgian and Lugard the Englishman were just as likely to
hurl brickbats at a mandatory government as was Rappard the
Swiss.

The solution that the British government preferred in Egypt
was a declaration of so-called independence, which was intended
to lead at once to Egyptian management of home affairs, but turned
into a unilateral British declaration instead of a matter of agreement
because the Egyptian nationalists, led by Zaghlul, were smarting
under past slights and were not ready to commit themselves to a
moderate policy. Most nationalists were prepared to admit that
Britain had local interests that needed preserving, but they refused
to agree that the four reservations on which Great Britain insisted
were compatible with independence. The essence of the disagreement was a question of trust; Britain mistrusted Egyptian ability
to look after the Suez Canal, the Sudan, the rights of minorities and
the defence of Egypt; the Egyptians wanted to be trusted with
these matters, and contended that, short of that trust, independence
was a sham. And they had grounds for saying so, since the independence they were given amounted to independence to do right,
but not independence to do wrong, in situations in which the sole
arbiter of right and wrong was Great Britain.

On paper, the two systems were different, but in practice they
left the British as fully paramount in Egypt as in a mandated territory. Both subordinated the local peoples to British interests outside
the Middle East. Imperialists regarded themselves as entitled to do
this in the name of good management of eastern peoples, and,
though some liberals had tender consciences about the arrangement, most were able to quiet their qualms thanks to the magic
of the word "mandate".

Both systems, however imperfect, worked adequately for years.

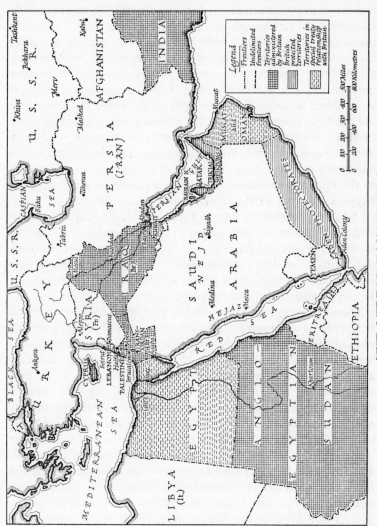

THE MIDDLE EAST IN 1926

Legend

Frontiers
Undelimited frontiers
Territories administered by Britain
British protected Territories
Territories in special treaty relationship with Britain

The main reason why they did so is that the British had the good fortune to impose them in conditions singularly free from outside interference. The Germans were off the map; the French had their hands full in Syria; the Italians were disliked for their doings in Libya; there was no Soviet representative in any Arab country except for a diplomat who, from 1924 to 1938, saw to Russian pilgrims and other business in Saudi Arabia; the Americans dabbled in questions affecting the open door in the mandated territories, but chiefly to ensure that American oilmen were not being worsted. In short, the British were blessed with insulation not only from interference on the spot, but from world affairs. In contrast to the nineteenth century or the nineteen-fifties, when troop movements in the Caucasus or Germany could cause them to alter course in Egypt, all but one of the world crises between the wars left them undisturbed. Mussolini, though he caused them great annoyance, undid his own anti-British propaganda by the methods he used to subdue Cyrenaica and Ethiopia, and the single outside development of the times that deeply affected British Middle Eastern policy was Hitler's anti-semitism, with its repercussions upon the volume of Jewish immigration allowed into Palestine.

Usually, insulation from outside pressure breeds a sense of leisure that slows down political processes; a classic example of this phenomenon occurred in the Sudan, where a devoted British civil service was fortified by legends of previous maladministration in a determination to go slowly and do things properly. India provides another, for progress towards independence could not be called fast until the threat from Japan hurried on the Cripps mission of 1942. In the Middle East, the pace and pattern varied enormously. In Palestine, both were *sui generis* because of the peculiar shape imparted to local politics by the conflicting promises to Arab and Jew, but elsewhere they are worth comparing because of the light thrown on the intentions in British minds. By far the most instructive comparison is that between Egypt and Iraq, where the process was slow in the first country, quick in the second, for reasons to be described.

On paper, Egypt became "an independent sovereign state" in 1922. Yet British Governments of all descriptions, including those run by long-standing critics of imperialism such as Ramsay Mac-Donald, when the Labour Party was in power in 1924 and 1929–31, stuck to reservations that made a travesty of the phrase. The British had intended that the reserved points covering the protection of their imperial communications, of foreign business and other interests, and of the Sudanese should be matters for negotiation, but each amounted to a *Diktat* because of its unpopularity, and because, pending agreement, "British discretion" governed all arrangements. Egypt was therefore anything but independent in the matter of defence, and therefore in foreign policy; even at home Egyptian hands were tied in all questions affecting the rights of foreign residents under the Capitulations. The British High Commissioner had, and used, a right to handle home affairs whenever a member of any foreign minority was concerned; foreign powers were told that the *status quo* of their nationals remained unchanged, and Allenby issued his orders directly to the Egyptian Criminal Investigation Department throughout the run of murders that followed the 1922 Declaration. This Declaration was far more restrictive than the treaty that the Persians had refused to ratify, and galling by comparison with the contemporary arrangements offered to backward areas such as the Hejaz or Afghanistan. But Egypt was by British standards a different matter, and the British stuck to their hold on it through the ingrained habit that caused them to think of rights along the main lines of imperial communication as perfectly natural, and of their large financial interests in Egypt as an addendum that went without saying. Their imperviousness to Egyptian resistance was partly due to possession of the strength to domineer, but partly also to a more praiseworthy impulse. Egyptian antipathy to them was masked by one common interest— the desire to establish parliamentary government. Europe was still at the stage when democracy was regarded as a cure-all, and Egypt's ambition was to make an entry into Western democratic society; thus when its first parliament was opened in 1924, the sense of triumph was shared, even though it was damped for Britain by the overwhelming majority held by Zaghlul's ultra-nationalist party, the Wafd.

The extreme Egyptian nationalists in their frustration kept up the Sinn Fein methods that they had adopted in 1919. In 1924 they carried them to the limit by murdering Sir Lee Stack, the Governor-General of the Sudan and Sirdar of the Egyptian army, in a main street of Cairo. This violent act shocked many of their fellow-countrymen; it was excessive even by Zaghlul's standards and its consequence was a shaking down into a more humdrum, though no less mistrustful, relationship. Each side adjusted its policy. Allenby had on his own responsibility demanded, after the murder, retribution so excessive that it looked like an intention to do Egypt permanent harm; he put his thumb on the country's jugular vein by requiring it to consent to the Sudan drawing without limit on the Nile waters; his terms were thought excessive by London, which dealt with him as if he had always been a reactionary; he departed from his post after less than a year. Zaghlul, for his part, resigned over his inability either to stop extremist outrages or to mitigate British reprisals. His successors, lacking the momentum he had supplied, became immersed in less dramatic matters—party struggles and secessions, differences with the king, new and wider responsibility for the day-to-day running of public administration. Their relationship with Allenby's Tory, imperialist and realistic successor, Lord Lloyd, became one of surly calm.

During the reign of the British Labour Government of 1929, the Egyptians were offered almost everything that they were to accept in 1936, but at the time the Wafd (without the support of which an agreement was not worth the paper it was written on) had been dismissed by the King and would consent to nothing pending elections. A chance therefore slipped by. But all evidence suggested that no politician could afford to take the logical step of easing the British out by stages, and so, unable to adjust conditions that they were powerless to remove at a single stroke, Egypt's party politicians enabled the British to jog along for two decades in possession of Britain's two main requirements—defence of the Suez Canal and preservation of the Sudan from the contagion of Egyptian nationalist agitators.

The contrast with Iraq is striking both as to timing and as to consideration for national susceptibility. Iraq's weak structure was threatened by stronger neighbours and, willy-nilly, a new state needed a protector; King Feisal, inoculated by experience in Syria, probably saw no alternative to working with a great power. In any case, in a far less homogeneous country than Egypt (a fifth of Iraq's population is Kurdish) there was better reason for moderate men to be co-operative. British respect for the Permanent Mandates Commission, and the unimportance of British investment in Iraq at the time, may also have played their part. And undoubtedly an alternative route to India that had not developed into a satisfactory channel of communication mattered less in the British scale of values than did the Suez Canal.

Nor did this accumulation of political and economic factors wholly account for the difference in British conduct in the two countries. British predilection and convention also affected it. The British struck up friendships in plenty with individual members of both nations; but the Englishmen, and still more the Englishwomen, who arrived in Egypt, often from India, in the heyday of a Victorian superiority complex about caste and colour found there a ruling Turkish group that had maintained a deliberate gap between itself and native Egyptians. The British in Egypt never got over these incentives to be clubby, and their exclusiveness was enhanced by differences of upbringing and outlook. Most educated Egyptians of the occupation period were formed on a French rather than a British model, while a large number of the British families on the spot were garrison-born and bred. They felt disdain for a people that had no taste for martial life or field sports, and one of whose proverbs proclaimed that there is no shame in bowing the head if there is no comfortable alternative. In Iraq, by contrast, Anglo-Indian habits never took deep root owing to the forty-year difference in the date of take-over, but also to the different stamp of the Iraqi aristocracy. Sheikhs and notables had lived on terms of equality and fraternity with their Turkish co-citizens of the Ottoman Empire, thought themselves the equal of anyone, and were taken by the British at their own valuation. The Iraqis were not intellectually inclined, took manfully to Harrow and Sandhurst, were good judges of horseflesh or a rifle and—apart from the first white lies due to caution or good manners—less devious than either the Egyptians, the Persians or the Hindus. The Englishman felt at home with Iraqis, and indeed with all Arabs untouched by the Sorbonne, in a way that he seldom did with any of their neighbours except the Turks.

And so it came about that, in Iraq in 1922, local antipathy to the word "mandate" led the British to ban it from circulation, except at Geneva, and to substitute for it a bilateral treaty. What is more, they agreed that this treaty should be subject to ratification by the new Iraqi parliament—the very procedure that had doomed Curzon's plan for Persia. In 1923, by which time the Iraqis had grasped that the change was merely nominal, the British added a protocol shortening the time limit; originally, the mandate or treaty was to run for twenty years; in 1923, the end was to be "the date of admission of Iraq to the League of Nations and in any case not later than four years after the ratification of peace with Turkey"— probably, that was, in 1928. The British motive for thus cutting the tutelary period was not entirely due to causes within Iraq;

home opinion during the general election of 1922 was against
holding the mandate at all, and a cabinet committee of the Bonar
Law Government recommended some concession to this domestic
pressure. But the main consideration was to make sure of Iraqi
ratification of the treaty (which in the end was secured only
narrowly, and with the greatest difficulty) because it was thought
important, for strategic reasons affecting both the defence of India
and the future state of Iraq, to produce a result that would be con-
ducive to the award of Mosul *vilayet* to Iraq by the League of
Nations. In the event of its award to Turkey, a hostile army would
reappear on a frontier devoid of natural obstacles at the north end
of the Mesopotamian plain.

In 1925, as part of an international agreement about the Mosul
award signed in order to satisfy consciences at Geneva, both the
British and the Iraqis agreed to a twenty-five-year term, but it is
obvious that they did so subject to some private bargain about a
loophole, for in 1926 a new treaty between them subjected the
twenty-five-year term to an elastic proviso: "unless before that date
Iraq shall have become a member of the League of Nations".
(This treaty was negotiated very quickly and ratified within five
days, in sharp contrast to the struggle and murders that had accom-
panied the debate about ratification in 1924.) King Feisal was a
man-of-the-world enough to realize that independence in 1928 was
now out of the question, but neither he nor the Iraqi nationalists
were pleased with the next British attempt at settlement, which
proposed admission to the League of Nations in 1932 "provided
the present rate of progress in Iraq is maintained and all goes well
in the interval". They objected so strongly to the proviso that in
1929 the British abrogated it also.

> Feisal of course was delighted (I shall never forget the smile of
> triumph that spread over his face as he listened to the communi-
> cation); but he had to be reminded more than once in the ensuing
> weeks that, whether H.M.G. made the verbal condition or not,
> the League itself was unlikely to admit Iraq unless all did in fact
> go well.[1]

In a word, there is antithesis between British policy in Egypt—
a point of vital importance both to British imperial communications
and to the pattern of the British Empire in Africa—and British
policy in Iraq—a poor and turbulent country, where neither air
communications, nor danger to the head of the Persian Gulf, nor

the probable existence of oil that lay undiscovered until 1927, at the time bulked large in British thinking. Partiality for Iraq cannot be put down entirely to British self-interest. The mandate was terminated partly out of bad conscience about broken promises, and a wish to atone to Feisal for failure to uphold him on the throne in Syria that he had obtained at British hands. Possibly a second reason for liberal behaviour was a wish to offset the dismal failure to progress towards self-government in Palestine that was by now all too apparent at Geneva whenever the Permanent Mandates Commission examined the situation there.

For in Palestine no such progress was possible. The original hopes that the Jews would prove to be "promising mediators" between Europe and Asia were soon dashed; even before the final award of the mandate at San Remo in 1920, pro-Zionist Ministers of the Crown, if they were also practical politicians, were expressing the opinion that it was "no great catch" and that "if only our own convenience is to be consulted I should prefer someone else" as mandatory; the authors of those two remarks were Robert Cecil and Balfour respectively. But Palestine was part of the hallowed area round the Suez Canal, and their misgivings were overridden by a succession of British Governments. Late in 1922—that is, some time after the first Arab revolts of Easter 1920 and Labour Day 1921 had outlined the shape of trouble to come—*The Times* was of the opinion that

> if we do not solve the problem that Egypt presents it is, to put it no higher, wise strategy to have in Palestine a state that owes us thanks for its birth and early development.[2]

This optimism lasted until 1930 in spite of slow evaporation of the reasons for it. It survived because Arab refusal to consider anything short of Arab dominion over a Jewish minority was written off as local non-co-operation, and never seen as a manifestation of the wider kind of Arab nationalism that was at work also in Syria. It was further strengthened because, until the United States Government imposed the quota system for immigrants in 1924, most Jews emigrating from Europe preferred America to Palestine, and, after 1926, economic depression in Palestine reduced Jewish immigration to a trickle. In 1927, more Jews left than entered the country. The British therefore hoped to live down their incompatible promises, and, up till the very eve of the grave disturbances of 1929, were able to get representative Jews and Arabs to meet and discuss their differences. Sir Harry Luke, then acting High Commissioner, records such a meeting at his house (at which the arch-nationalist Mufti of Jerusalem led the Arabs, and Ben-Zvi, later to be president of Israel, led the Jews) on the evening before the 1929 explosion. But this was the last scene of its kind.

Looking back at the 1920s, it is possible to discern other reasons than the sheer weight of British power why, in spite of local resistance, and in spite of failure in Egypt and Palestine to secure the compromises that were the goal of British policy, the British remained supreme in the Middle East without a vestige of military effort between 1922 and 1929. Ask a foreigner why, and he will answer that they succeeded because they divided and ruled. Admittedly they divided the Arab world with France, though less in order to rule it than to satisfy France's historic claim and to meet a situation in Europe. Admittedly, also, they divided their own share of Arab territories into portions, but, Palestine apart, the British secured these portions to a single family, the Hashimites. They had no objection to Arab unity because their primary interest was in through traffic, and good inter-Arab relations improved the thoroughfare. In Arabia, they paid subsidies to the two major rulers, Ibn Saud and the Sharif, but did not create the division between these two princes, which dated from Ottoman times; further, when, directly they stopped the subsidies, Ibn Saud set out to overthrow Hussein and in 1924 succeeded in doing so, they accepted his victory and the unification of Arabia. There is no evidence that the British tried to profit by Arab disunity until the 1950s, when their singling out of Iraq for special treatment did not work out as they had hoped. Far more difficult to assess is for how long they envisaged the establishment of two communities in Palestine as a means of retaining a base so conveniently placed for watching over the routes to India, and from the oilfields.

Certainly the idea of dividing and ruling in Palestine weighed with Great Britain in the beginning. But when, instead of settling down under British sway, Jew and Arab began violently to disagree over the question of numbers and fair shares, British prospects of fulfilling the idea began to fade. For dividing and ruling is a purposeful process whereby a third and ruling party obtains a hold over two others each of which depends on it for security, whereas, after 1929, the British were confronted with unruliness that impaired their purpose. From 1930, they lost control of the situation in Palestine, because they started to vacillate, and the two communities took advantage of the vacillation to become so obstreperous that the British were reduced merely to holding the ring.

At the time, they themselves scarcely noticed the change of role because they attributed the 1929 rebellion simply to imprudent reduction of the garrison, and not to deeper causes. The garrison had been reduced, during the quiet years in which the question of Jewish numbers did not press, to two companies of armoured cars supported by a squadron of the Royal Air Force, responsible between them for the whole of Palestine and Transjordan; the armoured cars were all in Transjordan when the rebellion broke out, and too much reliance had been placed on the Trenchard scheme of policing by means of the R.A.F.: this had worked in Iraq but was of no use in Palestine's built-up areas. In Palestine in 1929, therefore, the British sent for reinforcements from Egypt and Malta and hoped that their luck would hold. But in retrospect it is obvious that, from the fatal date in 1931 when they substituted for a White Paper that favoured the Arabs a "Black Letter" that favoured the Jews, they revealed a flaw in their policy, and began simply to register trouble, instead of controlling it. In 1930, they admitted to the Permanent Mandates Commission that self-government was impossible; in 1931, they reversed a policy rather than enforce it; they did the same in 1937-8, when they accepted the Peel Commission's recommendation that they partition Palestine, and a year later rescinded their approval because execution of the plan entailed carrying it out in the teeth of both Arab and Jew. Because of their reluctance to enforce a solution, the British seemed incapable of any decision except a postponement. All they could do was to jog on in unwillingness to admit that the Palestine problem was beginning to exceed the range of their experience and their persuasive powers.

And yet, in spite of these vicissitudes, Britain remained paramount in the Middle East, unchallenged by any power of equal magnitude, and able to maintain order thanks to its serenity, and aura of empire, and its ability to summon reinforcements from Malta or India in case of need. British paramountcy endured until the end of the Second World War, and for longer in Middle Eastern imaginations; the shadow of power is long, and remains after the substance has gone.

There are several reasons why Britain weathered the years between the wars in such excellent fettle. For one thing, the British personnel in the area were still full of hope and confidence

F

and the habit of authority, which had its effect not only on their demeanour but on Middle Eastern acceptance of their orders. For another, they rendered the area some very great services, and brought it the kind of economic gain which, while breeding no gratitude, produces a grumbling tranquillity. The British itch to administer maladministered peoples found scope as great as any in Britain's imperial career in places neglected during the Ottoman decline, and later victimized by wartime campaigns and shortages. A pattern of service existed already, in the Sudan; the civil service there was famous for its devotion and single-mindedness, and on its model, even more than on that in India, were formed the teams of men in the mandated areas many of whom gave a lifetime of service to the Arabs, and still refer to Iraq and Transjordan as "we" and the British Government as "they". The relationship was different wherever there was no scope for a dash of paternalism —for instance, with the Egyptians after 1922, or the Persians, or the self-contained, competent Palestinian Jews. But elsewhere the devotion of hundreds of individuals left its mark. The effect was widespread so long as the worse conditions of a previous era remained in mind; just as Arabi Pasha, on return to Egypt from exile in 1901, told friends that he appreciated changes made by Cromer that he himself had proposed to make, so senior Iraqis or Palestinians in the public service valued some of the British innovations and actively enjoyed working with the men who introduced them. This brand of respect, while it lasts, forges a human bond far more deeply felt than the impression created by the roads, schools, hospitals, public security, mounting trade balances or impartial courts of law that all formed part of the endowment at British hands.

But the sentiment is impermanent; indeed, it died out in less than a generation because the main appreciators of British predilection for a quiet life were the older men with vested interests, who feared the birth of left-wing ideas that might lead to encroachment on privilege, and who counted on British conservatism to retard the pace of change. Reciprocally, Britain relied on these kings and pashas and rich merchants, and there were times when members of the ruling class in the Middle East were closer to Baldwin and his pipe of peace, or Churchill and his fingers opened in a V for victory, than to mutinous hotheads belonging to their own kith and kin. This was certainly true of the Hashimite royalties, and perhaps also of Chaim Weizmann at moments such as the twentieth

Zionist Congress's rejection of partition in 1937, or the murder of Lord Moyne by Stern Gang extremists in 1944.

Another Arab contribution to British power sprang from the despondency, uncertainty and division of opinion into which the Arab nationalists were plunged by the fruitlessness of their effort between 1916 and 1918. Instead of enjoying the lustre, dignity and independence that they had been led to expect, they had merely undergone a change of master that by no means all of them thought was for the better. No Kemal sprang up and rallied them. In the presence of so many foreign troops, they judged their lot hopeless, for outside backers who might have been worth turning to, such as the Americans, had packed up and gone home. People bereft of plans and backing are apt to fall out among themselves, and the Arabs of the 1920's proved this dictum. They could not afford to quarrel with both Britain and France at once and, judging the odds to be hopeless, spent themselves in argument, and in negative criticism of conditions they were powerless to alter. A display that is typical of their despairing state of mind in the middle 'twenties is to be found in the records of the conferences they held about restoring the Caliphate. They could never agree what to do and the last meeting in 1926 adjourned on the plaintive note that though the Caliphate was "the soul and the manifestation of Islam" it was

> incapable of realization at the present time, in view of the situation in which Moslems find themselves.[3]

In 1925–6, the failure of the Arab rebellion in Syria depressed their spirits still further. No leaders of magnitude were produced in such doldrums, and lesser lights such as the Mufti of Jerusalem were therefore able to shine. The idea of unity between the Arabs of the former Ottoman Empire never died out. It was pursued by Syrians who struggled against France's decentralization schemes in Syria, and cherished by the Hashimite Kings and their supporters; it found expression, years later, in the Blue Book on the unity of the Fertile Crescent that Nuri Pasha was to publish in 1943. But the British, contrary to French and Jewish suspicions, never actively promoted it between the wars, partly out of recognition that it would embroil them with France and the Jews, and partly because they could not afford to antagonize either King Farouk or King Ibn Saud, each of whom was violently opposed to Hashimite aggrandisement in any form. For years, therefore, the Arabs in their impotence merely thought about unity. And for more than a decade, the British were able to take advantage of Arab inability to combine. They had little difficulty in keeping afloat in a sea of doubts and unresolved arguments; in 1930, they enjoyed enough such assets to see them through the twenty years of vicissitude to follow.

After 1930, the British halo of power and glory grew less bright on account of two developments—the challenge of rivals and the mounting evidence that Britain's Palestine problem was insoluble.

The challenge offered by Fascist Italy was disquieting, but never seriously weakened them in the Middle East because Italy was not popular in the Levant. The Turks disliked Mussolini and his ideas of "historic objectives" because they had not forgotten Italy's seizure of Libya in 1911 and its wartime ambitions in Anatolia, and many Arabs despised and laughed at Fascism for the way in which it had caused Italians long resident on the North African shore, particularly in Tunis and Alexandria, to drop their quiet habits and strut about in black shirts, shouting slogans. Mussolini won adherents only in Syria and Palestine—that is, in places at some distance from his own colony in Libya and where (in the words of a Syrian nationalist exile, Shakib Arslan) Arabs were "confident that Italy will not treat us as England and France have done".

In one respect, however, Mussolini's expansionist policy had an adverse effect on British power; it revealed British vulnerability. His successful conquest of Ethiopia in 1936 is often rated as of benefit to Britain because it frightened the Egyptians into dropping their internecine party politics, and combining in the all-party delegation that signed an Anglo-Egyptian treaty of alliance—the mutual agreement for which the British had been angling off and on since 1922. (This was the occasion on which Anthony Eden appeared on an Egyptian postage stamp—the only European ever to do so.) But the spectacular gain of a treaty that provided, indefinitely, for British garrisoning of the Suez Canal was offset by an equally impressive revelation—that the British Navy, though able to make a dash for Alexandria as soon as Mussolini attacked, was not able to stop him, and that British fatherliness towards small states did not necessarily extend to crusading against an aggressor at Geneva. Yet this discovery did not gain wide currency, for by the time it was apparent, all eyes in the Middle East had become focused on Arab rebellion in Palestine.

The challenge of Hitler in the Middle East was more insidious, and much more damaging. It began to sap British strength there very soon after his accession to power in 1933, but, unlike Mussolini's assault, it was involuntary. The Wilhelmstrasse documents of the Hitler period show that neither he nor the German Foreign Office ever calculated that to push German Jews into Palestine was to embarrass and weaken Britain. They got rid of the Jews in order to purify their Reich, and all they thought of when they discussed Palestine was the effect of possible British policies upon themselves. For instance, when partition was discussed in 1937, they speculated whether, if a Jewish state were to materialize, Germany would benefit by concentrating all the worst Nazi-haters in one place, or would lose by the endowment of Jewry with international standing. They fêted Arabs; they received disgruntled nationalists in Berlin, including the Mufti; they learned from their tireless envoy to Iraq and Arabia, Herr Grobba, that

> Yussuf Yassin replied that not only Ibn Saud but all Arabs are sympathetic to Britain, the one exception to this attitude being in matters relating to Palestine.[4]

But they never exploited this exception by using their Jewish policy in order to do so, because right up to the end of Ribbentrop's ambassadorship in London their aim was to appease, not to embarrass, the Chamberlain Government. Their most open exception to this line of policy was the anti-British propaganda that they began broadcasting to the Middle East when Italy dropped the practice after Neville Chamberlain reached agreement with Mussolini early in 1938.

But though Hitler's anti-Jewish policy struck at the British in the Middle East only by accident, it struck home because it found out their weakest point. It dispelled for good their hope of muddling through in Palestine. It caused them to double the authorized rate of Jewish immigration between 1932 and 1933; immediately, the Arabs rebelled, and struck for the first time at Britain as well as at the Jewish community. In 1933, out of compassion, the British trebled the 1932 figure, and went on raising the quota until 1935, when they admitted over 60,000 Jews—a number small by comparison with Jewish needs but large in relation to the population of Palestine. Again the Arabs rebelled, and from 1936 onwards they sustained until 1939 a rebellion that proved most difficult to quell, and that reduced the Jewish rate of entry in the years of greatest Jewish need just before the Second World War.

The question of numbers was, throughout, the core of the Palestine problem. Until 1939 no British promise or statement ever defined the relative size, or the limits, of the two communities, so that each was free to scheme for numerical superiority. Arab numbers greatly increased during the mandate, chiefly naturally though to some extent by immigration, but the Jewish increase was proportionately greater. The percentage of Jews in relation to the total population rose from 11 per cent in 1922 to 29 per cent in 1939. A cause of all the Arab rebellions, and the chief cause of the last, biggest and most successful of them, was fear that this progression would never stop. Minor causes there also were—hints dropped by Mussolini's broadcasts from Bari, deductions drawn from Ethiopia and the Rhineland that the British were not invincible, despair at mounting evidence of the strings that Zionists were able to pull in London and New York; but the chief and simplest cause was a matter of arithmetic. Given the known natural increase, plus a Jewish immigration rate of 30,000—that is, half the 1935 figure—the Jewish population would overtake the Arab in 1962.

The Arab rebellion of 1936 started with a strike. This form of resistance frightened the conservative Arabs in the neighbouring states, and their kings hurried forward to mediate. This act of class solidarity was welcomed by the British as a manifestation of Anglo-Arab unity—an impression that was not altogether false at the start, but which became so long before kings and pashas faithful to alliance with Britain were stabbed to death by Arab republicans many years later. In 1937, the British parried criticism by proposing yet another Royal Commission. This was the Peel Commission which recommended partition as the only way out of the British dilemma.

Maybe it was right to recommend a surgical operation, but where was the surgeon? By now, all Europe was at grips with the Nazi struggle for *Lebensraum*, the Japanese were conducting another in north China, ideological war had broken out in miniature in Spain and the shadow of general war was visible. Also by now, Britain's whole problem of keeping a hold on its lifeline through the Middle East in the event of that war was concentrated in Palestine, for elsewhere people were less concerned with grievances against Britain than with their own affairs: Egypt with getting rid of the Capitulations and grooming itself for a role at Geneva, Iraq with political turbulence including Bakr Sidqi's moment of military dictatorship, Syria with its chances of a treaty with France. Most Arab rulers did their best to induce the Palestinian Arabs to co-operate with the Peel Commission.

But all its fact-finding came to nothing. Its report is the best account of Britain's Palestine dilemma in existence, and is likely to remain so, because it was written with the rare double advantage of access to all the documents as well as personal encounter with the human beings involved, and so with the extra evidence supplied by the inflexion of a voice, or by a gesture. Although the British Government approved the partition it recommended, the approval was rescinded in 1938 because opposition to partition came from both communities, and because a second Royal Commission reported that it was not feasible. In fact, partition was impossible of execution without armed enforcement which, given the state of world affairs, the British were in no position to undertake.

The Arab rebellion therefore continued, and became more difficult to control because it became a matter of interest to Arab nationalists outside Palestine. Leaders slipped across the frontier and directed operations from outside, recruiting bands of supporters in Syria. The British increased their garrison, but numbers are seldom the answer when a resistance movement has the support of a whole population. A volley would be fired from a hillside at a passing convoy, but by the time a breathless guard had climbed to the level of the olive-grove from which it must have come, the guns were hidden in one of a thousand trees and peasants were innocently plying their mattocks, having "heard nothing". Life was rendered so insecure that Orde Wingate and other British officers were detailed to train Jewish settlements in methods of self-defence.

We have come to 1938—the year of Munich and the seizure of Austria, of Italian demands for Tunisia, Corsica and Nice, of Japan's "new order in East Asia", of the slow collapse of the Spanish Republicans under fire from shells made in Germany. In Palestine, there were only two ways open to the British of stopping a bad situation from worsening: one was to impose partition by force which, as we have seen, was impossible in the context of world affairs; the other was to define British intentions as to numbers, and stick to the definition. The British postponed a decision on the second step until they had held one more conference—the Round Table conference of 1939. Once again they summoned the other

Arab Governments to help them with the Palestine Arabs; but kings and pashas, confronted with the Jews, moved closer to their own people than they had been in the year of the strike. "I against my brother; I and my brother against the world."

Between the dissolution of this fruitless conference and the outbreak of world war, Hitler occupied Prague and Mussolini Albania, Neville Chamberlain realized that he had been duped, and the British fastened their safety-belts. As part of this operation they issued the Palestine White Paper of May 17, 1939. This tackled the problem of numbers: it fixed an annual total for Jewish immigration for five years, after which further increase was to be dependent upon Arab acquiescence; thus far, it was a capitulation to Arab resistance. But it did not give the Arabs a free hand; there was to be no independence without Jewish consent.

Many people in Britain disliked the measure. It was repellent to them because it caused a humane people to look monstrously inhumane; it obscured the fact that in their own islands they were doing as much as any country for Jewish refugees coming from Germany; as members of a nation that worships fair play, they disliked such behaviour towards people in distress. But there were now two such peoples, for conscience about the Arabs on the part of a mandatory that had never promised the Jews a majority had been nagging for some time. It had slumbered during the years in which Jewish immigrants had only trickled into Palestine, but had reawakened once Hitler set going a never-ending stream of them. The 1939 White Paper is seldom dispassionately analysed because of the emotions that it aroused in all three of the peoples concerned. According to Jewish sources, the British in effect said: "It is in your interest to accept this until better times, for without it, we may both succumb to Hitler." But it was also the first official British attempt to come to an honest and definitive decision about reconciling the two halves of the Balfour Declaration—the half which gave British blessing to a Jewish National home, and the half that said "it being clearly understood that nothing shall be done which may prejudice the civil and religious rights of existing non-Jewish communities in Palestine." Caught between these two undertakings, the British sought a way out by attempting to force the Jews to behave less exclusively, and to lubricate their own entry into a mixed community instead of expecting a mandatory power to provide the lubricant for them. But these aspects of that pre-war statement of British policy are long since forgotten; they were burnt up in the Nazi holocaust. The point that is usually remembered about the White Paper is that it saved few Jews from the gas-chambers. But it served one major purpose. It was the first of a second British series of "convulsive gestures of self-preservation", and the only one in the Middle East that preceded the actual fight for survival. From the purely British point of view, the point that counts for most is that it helped to secure enough Arab compliance to tide Great Britain over the war years.

But not unscathed. As in 1914-18, a great number of the war measures that Britain was forced to take in the Middle East in order to save its skin had long-term repercussions that reduced both British repute and British power.

The broad outline of British strategy in the Middle East in the Second World War is true to type. India, for itself and as a base for the Indian army, was the prime asset to be defended; oil supplies for a potential theatre of war came second. So necessary to salvation was the holding of a line from the Caucasus to the Sahara that the famous decision was taken in August 1940 to denude the British Isles of tanks, in spite of the threat of invasion, in order to reinforce Egypt. So important was maintenance of that line against both Germany and Italy that distant members of the Commonwealth—Australia, New Zealand and South Africa—all sent contingents to help. Twice during the war this British stockade was gravely threatened, once in May 1941 when the Germans had captured Crete and their aircraft began to hop onwards into Vichy Syria, once in the summer of 1942 when they reached a point only sixty miles from Alexandria. But the line held, and one of the reasons why it did so is that no unmanageable trouble developed behind it. Twenty years of British policy, however faulty, made this negative but substantial contribution to Britain's survival.

For purposes of a study of British fortunes, the war in the Middle East falls into two halves—before and after the tide turned at Alamein in November 1942. During the first half, impressive propaganda to the inhabitants of the Middle East was usually impossible for lack of any good news to provide raw material for it. Nearly all of them reckoned that the British might lose; Egyptian peasants in the delta held meetings to decide how to parcel out the land when Hitler came, and Palestinian Jews desperately discussed whether the flower of their young people should die in a

last-ditch battle or withdraw with the British towards India in order
that a nucleus might survive for another Return.

Doubters took out reinsurance policies. The Jews were of course
in no position to do so, but the rest had plenty of scope. Some, including the Mufti of Jerusalem, took the full plunge and went to
Berlin, and others, including King Farouk of Egypt, entered into
correspondence with Germany or Italy. The Hashimite house and
Ibn Saud, by contrast, stuck to the belief in Britain, subject to
reservations about Palestine, that Grobba had accurately reported to
Berlin.

Reza Shah of Persia had a predilection for Germans; they had
never put pressure on Persia, as the British and still more the
Russians had done; they were obliging trading partners and supplied many of his country's technical services; they also ran, under
the supervision of a competent and vigorous Nazi minister, a much
admired *deutsches Haus* in Teheran. Arab admiration for the Nazis
was less manifest. Nevertheless, it gathered strength when the
Germans reached Crete in 1941, and were preparing to support a
putsch in Iraq. Opponents in Iraq of the alliance with Britain
reckoned that the time had come to show how great was the
nationalist desire to get rid of this tie. The immediate impulse
for the Iraq army's rebellion of May 1941 was belief in the immin-
ence of German help (which never came because it had been noise-
lessly diverted to eastern Europe for the attack on Russia). But
the underlying causes were old sores—Iraqi nationalist resentment at the degree of British control that had survived the mandate,
and burning animosity about Palestine. Though one squadron of
King Abdullah's forces in Transjordan mutinied in sympathy with
Iraq, most of his troops were ready to serve their king, obey their
British officers, and help to stamp out the Iraqi rebellion.

In Egypt, the depths of the local brand of resentment were
plumbed when Rommel was pounding Auchinleck and the news
from the Far East was at its worst, in February 1942. Already,
politicians with pro-Italian leanings were under arrest; now came
King Farouk's turn. He too had been flirting with the Italians; in
the Abdin Palace, surrounded for the event with British tanks, a
towering British ambassador—Sir Miles Lampson—demanded that
the King install a government with which the British could co-
operate. Lord Chandos' *Memoirs* tell how, during the encounter, an
instrument of abdication was produced, but in the end Farouk did
not have to sign it. All these arbitrary British acts may have been

necessities of war, but they were by local standards never-to-be forgotten indignities, and all were entered on a bill of reckoning for presentation after the war.

A particularly large store of this resentment accumulated in neutral Persia, where, once Germany had attacked in Russia and was advancing towards the Caucasus, it became important to offset Reza Shah's partiality for Germans. In 1941, in co-operation with Soviet forces, British troops invaded the country, in order to ward against the classic thrust towards India, and to open a supply line to Russia. (The Shah, fearing the Russian troops that were within a few hours' march of Teheran, abdicated and slipped into exile.) This arbitrary act of invasion made sense, in the emergency of 1941, even to an anti-imperialist Secretary of State in Washington, for when Reza Shah complained to the American President,

> our response (says Cordell Hull) placed the dispute in its true light as one small element in the vast effort to stop Hitler's ambition of world conquest.[5]

But Persians saw the proportions differently. They were powerless to retaliate; as in Egypt and Iraq, criticism was held in check not only by the strength of the British military forces on the spot, but by censorship. Nevertheless, though rulers had to give in and though, in Persia, the Government saw no alternative to signing a treaty of non-military alliance with Britain and Russia, a growing block of younger men in each of the occupied countries, including Syria under the Free French, shared the sentiments of La Fontaine's ass when urged by the old man to flee the invader:

> *Et que m'importe donc, dit l'Ane, à qui je sois.*
> *Sauvez vous et me laissez paître;*
> *Notre ennemi c'est notre maître*
> *Je vous le dis en bon françois.*[6]

Set against the prospect of a victorious Hitler in Cairo or on the Persian Gulf, the contemporary cost of arbitrary acts was a small price to pay; compared with the magnitude of the decision taken after Dunkirk to reinforce Egypt at the expense of the British Isles, they were as nothing. Yet they were difficult to explain away even at the time, and BBC broadcasters in Arabic, speaking indiscriminately to listeners in all countries, were hard put to it to compose reassuring bulletins about British policy. In November 1941, however, Anthony Eden—then Foreign Secretary—had a flash of inspiration and decided to swim with the stream of Arab thought and desire by giving a boost to the cause of Arab unity. These were his words:

> This country has a long tradition of friendship with the Arabs, a friendship that has been proved by deeds, not words alone . . . The Arab world at the end of the last war, and many Arab thinkers desire for the Arab peoples a greater degree of unity than they now enjoy. In reaching out towards this unity they hope for our support. No such appeal from our friends should go unanswered. It seems to me both natural and right that the cultural and economic ties between the Arab countries, and the political ties too, should be strengthened. His Majesty's government for their part will give their full support to any scheme that commands general approval.[7]

This bid for Arab favour at a depressing moment was shrewd enough as an immediate sweetener; as usual, it was calculated more with reference to Iraq, where Nuri Pasha and others had long cherished a scheme for union with immediate neighbours, than to Egypt, where there was as yet no popular feeling of belonging to the Arab world. It pleased the Hashimites, who had never given up the Sharif's conception that Arab Asia ought to be one, and to have one head. But the statement had its drawbacks; it had been devised in London, and some at least of the men on the spot at once inquired what relation it bore to declared policy towards the Jews and the Free French. Both these last it horrified. Both saw it first and foremost as a threat to themselves, but also as fresh evidence of the extent to which British partiality for the Arabs led to delusions about Arab feelings for Britain; in their eyes it amounted to the digging of a pit into which the British too would ultimately fall. And so it might have been, had not the Arab League to which it gave impulse allowed itself to become a chatter of shifting and quarrelsome cliques.

The esteem in which Britain was held by most Middle Eastern states improved after Alamein. In the flush of Montgomery's victories even Egyptian cartoons showed glad faces beneath the tarbooshes. But whereas by Arab, Jewish and Egyptian standards war dangers were past, and changes were due, by British ones there was still far to go before Germany and Japan were beaten. After 1943, the continued enforcement of war measures in the Middle East irked its inhabitants almost as much as the drastic treatment meted out to them before victory in Africa.

Restrictions of all sorts had to continue, and one of their symbols was a body called the Middle East Supply Centre. This well-managed organization—at first British, later Anglo-American—was responsible from 1941 to the British Minister of State whom the Churchill Cabinet had installed in Cairo, and ran shipping and supplies, besides dictating the pattern of local production, for the whole area. It worked with the local governments and, if Arab protagonists of unity had been less suspicious of British imperialism, could have been taken over and converted into a piece of machinery of value to the Arab League. Instead, it merely earned a bad name for Western bossiness, and became another grudge against the British, fit only to be discarded when they gave it up in 1945.

A restriction for which the British were later to pay a heavy price was that on Jewish immigration into Palestine. In 1939, the Jewish slogan had been "to fight the White Paper as if there were no war, and the war as if there were no White Paper". But as soon as the danger of extermination by Rommel's army was past, the Jewish community, driven to grief and despair by the news of mass murder of their kin that began in 1943 to seep out of Hitler's Europe, turned on the British, and blamed them, and them alone, for callous unwillingness somehow to organize a rescue. Jewish acts of resistance multiplied. The Palestinian Jewish war record is therefore a mixed one, compounded half of sturdy service in fighting units, great industrial effort and deeds of bravery performed by volunteers parachuted into the Balkans, and half of subterfuge to promote illegal immigration, gun-running, thefts of British arms for future use, and murder. During 1944, the extremist group called the Stern Gang killed many members of the police, ambushed the British High Commissioner though without success, and murdered the British Minister of State in Cairo, Lord Moyne. By no means the whole Jewish community approved of terrorism, but under stress of tragedy more and more of its members determined to wrest control of immigration from British hands. They were helped to this conclusion by the support of American Zionism. In the blackest days of the war, in May 1942, the Zionists had run a conference at the Biltmore Hotel in New York which had resolved

> that Palestine be established as a Jewish Commonwealth integrated in the structure of the new democratic world.[8]

How this end was to be brought about was left open, except that most of those present envisaged that an assault on British policy would be entailed. Thereafter, much Palestinian Jewish energy was devoted to furthering the Biltmore programme, causing inconvenience and embarrassment to the British war effort.

Everywhere, the two years after victory in Africa were therefore years of mounting Middle Eastern impatience and nationalist kicking against British authority. There were plenty of displays of both moods—speeches from the throne in Egypt proclaiming the certainty of rewards to come, a sharpened struggle against French wishes to retain bases in Syria and Lebanon, whispers from Zionists that a Jewish state was bound to materialize in Palestine because Churchill favoured partition, a law passed by the Persian parliament (introduced by a deputy named Musaddiq) making it punishable for a Cabinet Minister to grant oil concessions to foreigners without prior parliamentary approval. All told, the bills that everyone was preparing to submit when peace came promised to be as long as those presented at Paris in 1919, or longer.

4

THE ROLE OF OIL IN BRITISH
GOVERNMENT POLICY

THE modern image of the Middle East is one of lands swimming in oil, and people forget how lately this asset began to dominate the region's economy and disturb its politics. In 1938, its oil production amounted to less than one twentieth of the world's output. In 1948—at the birth of the Marshall Plan for rehabilitating Europe by means of American aid, European self-help, and fuel from the Middle East—the figure was one-eighth. By 1960, the Middle East was producing one quarter of the world's total. The great leap forward took place at the beginning of the nineteen-fifties and was the outcome of more than one post-war development. The chief of them was purely commercial, and was the desire of the American companies that had discovered vast quantities of low-cost Arabian oil just before the war to exploit that discovery in an oil-hungry world. Another was the stimulus of Europe's dollar shortage, and of the Marshall Plan.

Between 1939 and 1948, expansion had been slow because of shortage of shipping and of steel; wells had been sealed, awaiting development, in several places where oil in commercial quantities had been discovered just before war broke out. Once war began in earnest, short haul was a first consideration; Britain was supplied from the Caribbean, and pipelines from the United States to Alaska had priority over pipelines to the Mediterranean. The main Middle Eastern producer to increase wartime output was Persia, which became an important supplier for the war with Japan thanks to its oil-fields close to a seaboard, and its sufficiency of pre-war apparatus. To make the point in terms of British imports, today 50 per cent of the total comes from Kuwait, but large-scale Kuwaiti production began only in 1949, and people have forgotten that, in 1938, 57 per cent of British oil imports came from the Americas and only 22 per cent from the Middle East—18 per cent of it from Persia.

To glance through company records for the years between the wars is to be struck by the uncertainty in which they worked in the Middle East—unaware both of the rosy future of world consumption, and of the exact location of the hypothetical oil. On the Arabian shore of the Persian Gulf, for instance, at key points in Kuwait and Saudi Arabia where rich finds were made later, rights secured by a New Zealander named Holmes were for sale in the nineteen-twenties, but Holmes found no takers. A good example of the oil outlook of the period appears in the report of a British Minister for Air, Lord Thomson, who visited Iraq in 1924 and reported that "wheat production for years at least has greater possibilities". Although Iraq, given proper irrigation and drainage, could be a great granary, he was wrong; three years later there followed the major oil discovery at Kirkuk.

There are no rules for taking government action in support of the private overseas investor. Foreign ministers of all nationalities are deterred by the bogey of discriminating in favour of one company as against another, and by the invidious task of distinguishing between the bona-fide promoter of his country's trade, who ought to be helped, and the speculator who goes in at his own risk and must take the consequences. The power to give official help is wholly discretionary, and as often as not depends on the temperature of current politics. The Victorian habit of sending a cruiser to collect a debt diminished with diminishing power; once the ships of all nations had been shelled with impunity by a miscellany of Chinese armies on the Yangtse in 1926, faith in gunboats began to dwindle and economic sanctions became more popular. They were used by both the British and the American Governments when Mexico nationalized its oil in 1938.

In general, it can be said that a government applies pressure, or seeks to keep up appearances on behalf of investors, in two or three sets of conditions that can be defined. The most obvious is when other governments are competing on behalf of their nationals, as they did in the Ottoman Empire, in China, and in Egypt. Another is in regions where there are traditional strategic interests, such as Britain's along the route to India or those of the United States in the Monroe Doctrine area. The wronged Egyptian bondholders got unusually vigorous protection in 1882. Sometimes, on the other hand, strong government action is taken where there is no strategic stimulus; in Mexico in 1938, the British Government gave wronged oil companies as much assistance as economic sanctions can provide; here its display of temper and energy was undoubtedly due to the peculiar significance of oil.

Strategically all-important, oil is also a cardinal commodity from the standpoint of society. Shortage leads to more fuss, bad temper, exaggeration and publicity than shortage of any other industrial raw material because it so quickly produces discomfort as well as fear—no warmth for American homes in the cold winter of 1947–8; serious threat to industry in Luxemburg during the Suez crisis. For the modern citizen, one effect soon felt is curtailment of transport. Another reason for edginess of temper is that oil, unlike hard fuel, cannot easily be stockpiled for eventualities. For a known date, a special effort can be made; in 1944 the United Kingdom was able to tuck away 23 million tons for D-Day. But large quantities cannot be put by in artificial containers for some time or never, both because containers of the necessary size are so expensive that the capital investment is almost prohibitive, and because the oil deteriorates. The only proven way of hoarding oil is to discover it and close it in till wanted—that is, to conserve it in its natural subsoil.

A further complication is the variety of products in use; stock-piling, even when practicable, entails keeping the right kind of refined product—jet fuel, kerosene, naval fuel oil—in the right place. A final cause of strain is that the world oil trade has long been in the hands of a very few major companies. These companies compete fiercely for markets—witness the array of their rival pumps on any main road; this commercial rivalry over marketing has sometimes given them an appearance of political rivalry in the field of production. But this impression is largely false. In the Middle East, they often combine to organize production, regardless of their nationality of origin; all over the area, mixed Anglo-American or Anglo-Franco-Dutch-American companies are commoner than companies of a single nationality. But between them "the majors" control the bulk of the trade all the way from the well to the pump and into the private carburettor. The oil industry is "vertically integrated" (which means that the same major companies control the process throughout—discovery, production, transport, refining, marketing) and participants who do not share in the venture all the way down the vertical line are often suspicious of it. They suspected it even when its practices were beneficial to them, as, for instance, was its practice of relating Middle Eastern selling prices to the American "posted prices", so providing Middle Eastern states with a share of a bigger income than they

would have had if price had been related to the local cost of production, which was relatively low.

Governments—the American and French as well as the British—
have interfered with a plain commercial operation whenever seized
with fear of shortage in wartime. By a famous Churchillian operation of 1913–14, the British Government actually bought its way
into the trade. Its interest in the future of oil dated from the findings
of an Admiralty committee of 1903; by 1912, the drive of Admiral
"Jacky" Fisher had led to a widespread naval change to liquid fuel,
and a Royal Commission of that year visited the Persian fields in
order to report on the maintenance of a reliable supply for the
navy. At the time, world production and distribution were almost
wholly in American and Dutch hands, and the Commission recommended that the Anglo-Persian Oil Company* should be "financially supported" by the British Government. There followed in
1914, and under the wing of the then First Lord, Winston
Churchill, the famous transaction whereby the British Government
put up £2.2 million of new capital, and so became the majority
shareholder in the company. Because of its date (the Royal Assent
was given to the relevant bill six days before the outbreak of the
First World War) the purchase is often attributed to the fear of
war that hung over Europe when it was made, and to the risk that
the British Navy might be held to ransom in the matter of price.
In fact, peace-time immunity from such pressure also counted with
the government of the day. As Winston Churchill told the House
of Commons:

> Nobody cares in wartime how much they pay for a vital com-
> modity, but in peace—that is the period to which I wish to direct
> the attention of the committee—price is rather an important
> matter. . . . I cannot feel that we are not justified . . . in consider-
> ing how in years of peace, and in a long period of peace, we may
> acquire proper bargaining power and facilities with regard to
> the purchase of oil. The price of oil does not depend wholly,
> or even mainly, on the ordinary workings of supply and demand.[1]

In a word, there was a desire to protect Britain both in war and
peace against what was then called "the oil combine" of companies.
The purchase accounts for a world-wide impression of British

---

* In deference to a Persian wish, this company became "Anglo-Iranian"
  in 1935; it is referred to as A.P.O.C. till that date, and as A.I.O.C.
  after it. In 1954 it became the British Petroleum Company.

Government interference in the trade. But in practice it produced no such thing. By the terms of the 1914 agreement, the Government was to appoint two directors to the board of management, one or other of them was to sit on all its committees and they were to have a right of veto on decisions. This veto has never been used. It was in any case limited by a Treasury letter of May 20, 1914. In the letter, several safeguards against undue interference with the trade were offered; the commercial directors were provided with a right of appeal, and the Government said that it did not propose to play its trump except in cases that it defined. These were: matters affecting foreign naval and military policy; or if a sale of the company's undertaking were contemplated; or if new exploitation plans seemed to it unsuitable, or if contemplated sales of oil to foreigners or on long-term contracts seemed likely to endanger naval supply.

> Their interference (if any) in the ordinary administration of the company as a commercial concern will be strictly limited to the minimum necessary to secure these objects.[2]

These undertakings, which lapsed from disuse and now read like a message from another world, are listed only because they were not made public until 1929 and are seldom quoted; they were published in the context of a Government refusal to use its special position as the majority shareholder in A.P.O.C. in order to influence the price of oil in the United Kingdom. The chief outcome of the whole arrangement was not a government venture in trade, but a highly profitable investment of public funds. But it was speculative; thanks to the Admiralty fuel oil contract, the company, which had run short of funds, was able to carry on; but it did not pay a dividend until 1917.

Against the financial advantages must be set a diplomatic drawback. The Government shareholding was a liability whenever the British Government wanted to act *as a government*; third parties in general, and Middle Eastern governments in particular, seldom credited it with acting in any role but that of a self-interested shareholder. This handicap was foreseen by at least one intelligent onlooker. Arnold Wilson, then a young man in his thirties in the Indian Political Service, and serving in South Persia, wrote home on July 28, 1914, rejoicing that the company had found the money for carrying on, but added that:

> the government may in practice find it harder to exercise diplomatic pressure on behalf of a company it controls than in the

interest of a company in which it has no shareholding. Moreover, its control . . . might in certain circumstances lead to difficulties with foreign governments. It is a strange reversal of the established order that such a step should be taken by a liberal government.[3]

His forecast was right, but did not become patently so for years. Few people noticed that when, in 1923, Ibn Saud was granting a concession for oil prospection in Nejd, he discarded the suggestion of his old friend Percy Cox that it should go to the Anglo-Persian Oil Company because he was shy of employing a semi-governmental concern. After the Second World War fresh light was thrown on Asian shyness of foreign government participation in concessions. On the one hand the Persians, though they had been so mistrustful of the British Government's stake in A.I.O.C., in 1957 granted a concession to the wholly state-owned Italian Ente Nazionale Italiano (E.N.I.); on the other the Kuwaitis on one occasion turned down E.N.I. in favour of Shell because the former was "a foreign-government owned company". No Middle East state has yet leased a concession to the greatest of government-owned oil concerns—the Soviet oil industry. The inference is that government ownership is more likely to be feared if the owner is a great power.

For years, the drawbacks of government participation were so little envisaged that the American Government, through fear of shortage in the Second World War, favoured the same process as the British Government had done before the first war, though with a different result. In 1943 President Roosevelt signed his consent to a proposal that the United States Government should buy a part interest in the American companies then functioning in Saudi Arabia and Bahrain. A little later the American Office of War Mobilization put up a proposal for acquiring a one-third interest in A.I.O.C. as part-repayment for oil supplied under Lend-Lease. In 1944 it contemplated laying a government pipeline from wells on the Persian Gulf to the Mediterranean. All these proposals fell through because of the objections either of American domestic oil producers, or of isolationists who thought that government expansion into the Middle East would embroil the United States in the perennial Anglo-Russian quarrel there. The American Government therefore merely prodded American companies to extend their Middle East operations.

. . . . .

In the early days of search for Middle Eastern oil, governments often exercised pressure on behalf of their nationals. The occasions on which they did so prior to the granting of concessions can be fairly easily enumerated because they fall into four clear categories. These were: in order to secure equality of opportunity; when frontiers were being fixed or were in dispute; when the laying of pipelines was contemplated, and—more rarely because of the risk of drawing invidious distinctions between their citizens—in order to help a national to get a concession.

In Ottoman days the struggle for equality of opportunity was brisk, particularly at the point where oil had been known to exist since ancient times—in Mesopotamia. There, the Germans were the first to secure rights; they did so as part of the bargain for building the Baghdad Railway, made in 1903. But there were competitors over the ensuing years, and by 1914 the most forceful was the British d'Arcy Group (a participant in A.P.O.C.) which had strong support from the British ambassador. When in March 1914 three of the competing groups, one British, one Anglo-Dutch and one German—agreed jointly to participate in a reorganized Turkish Petroleum Company (T.P.C.), the d'Arcy Group secured a 50 per cent interest, the agreement was signed in the British Foreign Office, and government representatives as well as company officials signed the document.

By the end of the First World War, the role of the British Government had somewhat changed. The Ottoman and German Empires had disappeared, and the British, as the victor in Mesopotamia, had first say in the disposal of former rights. France headed the list of claimants, and its title to a share was obvious if only because—as will be remembered—the Sykes-Picot agreement had accorded it a sphere of influence that included Mosul. Neither Lloyd George nor Clemenceau had forgotten about oil during their private exchange of pawns in December 1918, in the course of which Mosul province had changed hands; the nature of France's share in Mosul's hypothetical oil was debated in several diplomatic conversations in the course of 1919, and was finally fixed when the mandates were distributed at San Remo in April 1920; France was to be heir to the former German quarter share in T.P.C.

The American campaign for fair shares was bitterer, and more public. From the corridors of the Peace Conference, William Yale reported home that the petroleum wealth of Mesopotamia was causing much political excitement, but within the British delegation

Balfour, with his customary common sense, circulated a memorandum that was meant to curb "all the ordinary talk I hear" about Mesopotamian oil "belonging" to Britain if it were found. Such speculation, he reminded his colleagues in September 1919

> is quite inconsistent with the assumption underlying the whole Covenant and expressly embodied in its clauses. For in all mandated territory the "open door" is to be completely maintained and all nations are to enjoy equal opportunities.[4]

At the time when the mandates were being distributed, the United States (though it did not itself want a mandate) was in the throes of an oil scare, and was being led to believe that its domestic reserves would run out because it had sold oil unstintingly during Europe's war. One current estimate was that American reserves amounted to no more than six years' supply, and fear, as usual, produced stridency and loss of proportion. Except in Persia, no oil in commercial quantities had yet been discovered in the Middle East, but "England", boomed Senator Lodge, "is taking possession of the oilfields of the world". The treaty arrangement with Iraq that did away with the word "mandate" was regarded in America not as a gloss on an unpalatable name but as a device to plunder Mesopotamia, and to strike a blow at American chances of getting in there on the strength of the Open Door clause. Foreign Secretary in London and Secretary of State in Washington exchanged a cross-fire of incommensurable statistics—Curzon setting the Middle East share of world production against that of the United States (at the time 4·5 per cent to 82 per cent) and Lodge replying with comparisons of American consumption and American reserves. The quarrel ended only in 1929, when two American oil companies joined with the French *Compagnie des Pétroles*, A.P.O.C., and Shell to form the Iraq Petroleum Company, with its well-known five-per-cent share for Calouste Gulbenkian, the Armenian who had helped to found T.P.C., and who had first reported to the Ottoman Government on the possibility of oil development nearly forty years earlier. From 1929, the United States Government agreed that the companies' restrictive agreement of that year, known as the Red Line Agreement, did not infringe the Open Door. A door that is ajar always feels more open to those inside than to those outside it.

In matters of frontier limitation in the Middle East, oil has played less part in government calculations than is often supposed.

In the classic case of a frontier dispute that is reputedly connected with oil, which is the Anglo-Turkish quarrel in 1923–4 over Mosul, the evidence as to how far oil influenced British support for Iraq's claim, and against Turkey's, is conflicting. According to Curzon, who was still Foreign Secretary when the dispute began:

> Oil had not the remotest connexion with my attitude, or with that of His Majesty's Government over Mosul;[5]

and he is borne out not only by the then Colonial Secretary, Leo Amery, but by more than one surviving member of the Mosul Boundary Commission. But the Labour Government Colonial Secretary of 1924, who was J. H. Thomas and a renowned chatterbox, told Parliament that: "It is true to say that oil had some bearing on the frontier." He also mentioned that the British Government had discouraged exploration pending a frontier settlement.

The explanation of this flat contradiction is that oil, though suspected in Mosul province, had not been discovered, and the likelihood that it would be found was not the prime concern with the British at the time, because their chances of securing the concession were good even if the verdict went in favour of Turkey. The brief for the British negotiators dealt not with potential discoveries but with present problems: what was to happen to the Nestorian Christians who had risen against the Turks in 1916 and, after reprisals and other hardships, were now stranded near Mosul and without a home? And how was Iraq to acquire a defensible northern frontier unless it included Mosul? Anyone who knows the terrain will appreciate that, here, all the old north-west frontier instincts of servants of India came into play. Iraq without Mosul province would possess a northern frontier on a plain, and on the other side of it would lie an army of irredentist Turks—at the time, outcasts on good terms with the fellow-outcasts in Bolshevik Russia. In British eyes a frontier in the mountains to the north of Mosul was infinitely preferable. There was substance, therefore, in Curzon's lusty denial about oil, which is repeated in the best subsequent book on the Mosul Commission—C. J. Edmonds's *Kurds, Turks and Arabs*:

> Although the world Press was wont to represent the battle as part of a gigantic struggle for the control of oil, it is interesting to recall how very little oil figured in our calculations, at my level

at any rate; I do not remember a single document in which oil
was mentioned as a factor of outstanding importance.[6]

Yet the world Press, though wrong about the prime British reason
for securing Mosul to Iraq, had some grounds for its tall stories;
though the presence of oil in commercial quantities was still only
suspected, it had certainly been a secondary thought in the minds
of some of the British statesmen who had struggled for the
province, notably in that of Lloyd George. In the end, the Turks
got a few crumbs from the British table; by the Anglo-Turco-Iraqi
treaty of 1926, the British Government secured them a 10 per cent
interest in the hypothetical oil royalties for twenty-five years—a
period that lapsed just as really big earnings began to come in.

A second point at which disputed frontiers and oil interests are
often linked in the public mind is eastern Arabia. Here the inland
boundaries between the Saudi kingdom and the British-protected
sheikhdoms and principalities along the coast are undelimited over
long distances, petering out all round the great central desert that
the Arabs call the Empty Quarter. But here, even less than at Mosul,
is the connexion apposite. When, in 1935, the British failed to
agree with King Ibn Saud about his eastern frontier, the stumbling
block was not undiscovered oil but his wish for an outlet to the sea
in territory which Britain recognized as belonging to the coastal
Ruler of Abu Dhabi—a sheikhdom under British protection since
the nineteenth century. Frontier delimitation was abandoned
through lack of agreement. Nearly twenty years later, during King
Ibn Saud's last illness, some of his subjects exploited this failure
to agree, as well as the king's weakened authority, in order to make
one of a series of claims by large states against small in Arabia.
In 1952, these Saudi expansionists attempted to push the boundary
to a point a hundred miles beyond the maximum line that the king
had suggested in 1935, and seized the oasis of Buraimi. They may
have been prompted partly by the smell of oil, but British resistance
to their advance was determined not by oil interests but by the same
reasoning as in 1935—fulfilment of the old obligation to look
after the defence and foreign affairs of the coastal rulers.

From the earliest moment at which the layout of trans-desert
pipelines became a consideration, British Government action was
taken, principally because the site of pipeline terminals was a
matter of concern to the Committee of Imperial Defence. For
instance, when, by an Anglo-French convention of December 1920,

the line of the frontier between the British mandate in Palestine-Transjordan and the French mandate for Syria and Lebanon was adjusted, the new line was specifically stated to be drawn with a potential railway and pipeline in mind. Again when, in 1931, the wayleaves for the line from northern Iraq to the Mediterranean were being negotiated, commercial interests, if left to themselves, would of course have chosen the shortest and flattest way to the sea, which was to Tripoli in Lebanon. But with politics in mind, the British Government intervened to promote a forked lined to an alternative terminal at Haifa. The reason for doing so, which seemed sound in 1940, but became ironic in the light of later events, was uncertainty about French prospects in Syria by comparison with its own in Palestine.

Apart from the efforts that the British Government made before 1914 in the Ottoman Empire, and the few words that it spoke to the Persian Grand Vizir in 1901 in support of d'Arcy, it seldom used its influence on behalf of concession-hunters. Even in places where it was entitled by pledge or treaty to approve the nationality of the concessionaire (as it was in Kuwait or Bahrain), it preferred to leave British aspirants to fend for themselves. The list of occasions on which it gave no help is very long. It gave none, for instance, to the British negotiator in Jidda in 1933 when he sought from Ibn Saud the prize (now the Arabian American Oil Company fields in Eastern Arabia) that he saw pass to an American rival because the Iraq Petroleum Company had authorized him to

speak only of rupees, where gold was demanded.[7]

It gave none when the western Arabia concession, later fruitless, was negotiated in 1936; none when the Turkish (later Iraq) Petroleum Company negotiated and re-negotiated agreements with the Iraq government in 1924–5 and 1931; none in Syria in 1937–8; while in Bahrain in 1929–30 it was amenable about waiving exclusive British rights, and agreed to operations by American firms which took Canadian nationality for the purpose.

Developments in Kuwait were less straightforward, but the end-product was the same; the British Government never tipped the scales with the Ruler in the two years (1932–3) during which the American Gulf Oil Company and A.P.O.C. waited on his decision between them. The story is interesting because it illustrates two former characterstics of British Middle Eastern policy—the suspicion evoked by government participation in A.P.O.C., and the delays that tended to arise when agreement with the Government of India was necessary. Kuwait had been excluded from the area bounded by the Red Line, and so was a territory open to all-comers, subject to the Ruler's pledge of 1913 that the British Government was to determine the nationality of any concessionaire. In the winter of 1931–2, the American suitor became convinced that its British rival was being favoured, and the American Government pressed officially for equality of opportunity and relaxation of the nationality clause. But Kuwait also lay on the join between the parishes of several British Government departments and the Government of India. Months passed because, as one British official in London confessed to his American colleague,

> the views of various government departments have been so divergent.[8]

The Americans were sure that the British Government was procrastinating in order to influence the Ruler in favour of its own godchild, A.P.O.C.; their suspicions grew when they were told of further delays because the British were comparing the offers made by the two companies in order to advise their protégé which would best suit his interests. Naturally, outsiders deduced that a piece of special pleading was being concocted, though in the end, the Ruler was impartially advised to reject both offers. But the question gave rise to a double embarrassment. In London, the British Government was averse to opposing the American Government on such a matter at a time when Anglo-American harmony was important; the incident coincided not only with the Hoover Moratorium on war debts, but also with American support for collective protest against Japan's aggression in Manchuria. In Kuwait, the Ruler too was embarrassed because, though free to make the choice, he seems to have been loth to turn down a company of the same nationality as his protecting power. Neither company would withdraw, but in the end neither the Ruler nor the British Government had to take an awkward decision; the matter was settled when the two companies decided to apply jointly for the concession. Farther down the Persian Gulf, the British Government was ready to say a word in favour of the I.P.C. when, in 1938, it signed agreements with the Rulers of the smaller sheikhdoms, but no such inducement was necessary.

A government becomes embroiled after, rather than before commercial enterprises of its nationality are installed on foreign soil. For one thing, it must help them with day-to-day matters such as passports and residence permits; if security is poor, as in south Persia or Saudi Arabia or Kurdistan in the early days, it may have to help them to obtain protection of property. These services it does for any national, and the notoriety of certain occasions on which the British Government has given legal aid to British oil companies is due chiefly to the element of sensation that always surrounds oil, owing to its strategic and social significance, and to the glamour that attaches to a commodity in which some of the world's great fortunes have been made—Rockefeller's, Gulbenkian's, those of the Saudi royal house and the Ruler of Kuwait.

Persia was the country in which Asian nationalism made its début in Middle East oil affairs. By the late nineteen-twenties Reza Shah, who had been impressed by Mustafa Kemal's success in dealing with foreigners, had shown the way his mind was working by denouncing the Capitulations. He had visited the oilfields in 1925, and soon afterwards began to show his interest in getting his country greater advantages from its oil. He is much revered, since his death, for the way in which he upheld national rights, and, though he was in the nineteen-thirties unpopular with Persian liberals for his autocratic ways, all Persians agreed with him in disliking foreigners. They were with him in thinking that the original oil concession, even as revised in 1920, was inadequate to the scale that A.P.O.C.'s operations had reached. He wanted more control of a great natural resource, and bigger receipts from it, but discussion of new terms led to no result because the company thought his demands excessive.

The agreed method of calculating Persian receipts from the oil industry was based on profits, and fluctuated with world market conditions. In 1932, the royalty payment fell off sharply owing both to Britain's departure from the gold standard and to the slump in oil sales caused by the world economic crisis, and the Shah unilaterally cancelled the A.P.O.C. concession. Loss of revenue was the immediate cause of his act, but there were deeper causes as well. The Persians mistrusted the company's contract with the British Navy at an undisclosed price and for undisclosed quantities of oil; they mistrusted, more generally, a technical operation that no Persian then had sufficient training to understand, and they wanted a share in running a concern that, because it determined the relation of Persian output to world demand, dictated the size of the biggest single item of their national revenue from a board-room in London.

The situation seemed to them incompatible with Persia's great past.

The British Government was all-powerful in the Persian Gulf area; it could have sent cruisers and a landing force, as it had done, in company with other wronged powers, to Shanghai in 1927. But times were changing; British public hopes were centred on the Disarmament Conference, and a League of Nations Commission—the Lytton Commission—was struggling to stop Japan from using force in Manchuria; in any case the British Cabinet was deterred by the perennial reason that such a move might provoke a counter-move by Russia. So it chose another course. All local oil concession agreements contain an arbitration clause, and nearly all Middle Eastern nationals dislike recourse to it because they would rather argue behind closed doors than in front of third parties. In 1933, however, the British Government succeeded in taking Reza Shah to law by appealing to the League of Nations under Article 15 of its Covenant, and the dispute was thrashed out in front of Eduard Benes of Czechoslovakia—a rapporteur of renown. Though the Persians were later to argue that the settlement over which he presided was an unfair deal, it was at the time thought so favourable to them that Anglo-Persian shares dropped several shillings on the London stock-market immediately his award was announced. In fact, Reza Shah won his round with the company—first tearing up the agreement and later emerging from litigation with a new one much more advantageous than the old.

But the role into which the British Government was pushed at his hands pales by comparison with that forced upon it by Dr. Musaddiq in 1951. Here again it felt itself compelled, after diplomatic representations had failed, to bring Dr. Musaddiq's nationalization law before an international tribunal on the grounds that a British national had been treated in violation of international law. The violation was not the act of nationalization (which, as Persians pointed out, was a legally permissible act that had been practised by the British Labour Government); it was Musaddiq's unilateral annulment of the agreement freely concluded between Reza Shah and the company in 1933, and his refusal to submit the dispute to arbitration in accordance with that agreement. The issue was never decided, for the International Court of Justice decided that it lacked jurisdiction, basing its view on the date at which Persia had signed the so-called Optional Clause accepting its compulsory jurisdiction. It was of opinion that a natural and reasonable way of reading the text [of Persia's very restrictive Declaration of adherence to the Optional Clause] leads to the conclusion that only treaties subsequent to the ratification come into consideration.[9]

The decision hung on grammatical interpretation, but the British Government failed to establish its point, or to make good a subsidiary contention that the 1933 agreement, having been arrived at through the mediation of the League of Nations, had the status of a treaty between the United Kingdom and Persia.

The Persians, naturally, were delighted with the Court's ruling, and Dr. Musaddiq was able to turn the occasion into a personal triumph. But at this stage he missed a golden moment. Perhaps he was over-excited at the success with which he had stirred up nationalism and Anglophobia; perhaps he was nervous of responsibility for taking decisions in a matter of great difficulty; in any case he was ignorant of conditions in the world oil trade, and showed no will to learn about them; for instance, he seemed to have no idea how easily Persian oil could be replaced, and how eager neighbouring states would be to see their exports rise. He had every opportunity to negotiate suitable terms of nationalization and compensation. These chances were afforded not only by the British company and Government, but by the World Bank, which tried and failed to get him to resume oil operations under its temporary management, and by the American Government. But it was becoming difficult for him to agree to compromises that were bound to be insufficiently nationalist for his more fanatical supporters, and he turned down a succession of opportunities; by mid-1953, the American President, thoroughly alarmed about the effect of business stagnation in Persia on the spread of communism, told him that there would be no more aid while he continued to be unreasonable about earning revenue and negotiating compensation.

He failed through a mixture of his own obstinate adherence to conditions that no one would entertain, and to an extraneous cause that was decisive—his virtual inability to deliver oil to overseas buyers. These were soon available, notably in Italy and Japan, but delivery was difficult because (quite apart from A.I.O.C., which went to law over "stolen oil" in Aden and Japan) the other major oil companies refused to handle Persian oil pending a settlement and, owing to their virtual monopoly of the world's marketing network, no one else was immediately in a position to do so.

Mexico, somewhat similarly placed in 1938, had been saved from ruin by the seller's market of World War II. No such extraneous boon came to save Musaddiq; quite the other way, the rival exporting territories on the opposite shore of the Persian Gulf profited by Persia's discomfiture to take its place in the world's markets. Never since has Persian output caught up with that of either Saudi Arabia or Kuwait.

The British Government suffered considerable public discomfiture through the Musaddiq affair. At the outset, he had the sympathy of more than half the world—of anti-imperialists, pronationalists and everyone who enjoys seeing a small nation stand up to a great power; he was the man-of-the-week on the cover of *Time*; when he went to New York, huge crowds waited to hear his low-voiced, repetitious speeches to the Security Council. Yet the damage done to Britain's name and power by its surrender of rights and loss of face was grievous to it outside rather than inside Persia. Within Persia, British power suffered little reduction; it had been diminishing for years, had dropped to zero after the grant of independence to India, and no longer existed except in Persian imagination. The possibility of using such power had for a generation been limited by fear of Russian counteraction, and in fact it had been exercised in the twentieth century only in two conditions; either in agreement with Russia, as in 1907 and 1941, or when Russia was dormant, as in 1918. As a shareholder, the British Government got adequate compensation for all material loss when, under the settlement of 1954, the A.I.O.C. came to share its assets with a consortium of foreign oil companies. At times of political bargaining, the British position is no weaker because of combination with a group of nationalities; on the contrary, the arrangement deprives the Persians of some latitude for flirtation of a kind at which they excel.

Over the years, the British Government might have acted more astutely than it did about meeting Persian grievances, which were freely aired and generally known. There would have been advantage in waiving habit in order to mitigate the two sorest points: the Persian belief that the Admiralty contract for oil was cheating a poor country of revenue, and the knowledge that the British Government got far more in tax from A.P.O.C.'s worldwide operations than Persia got in revenue from the oil that had been that company's start in life. For instance, was it really necessary to conceal from the Persians the amount of Persian oil sold to the

British Navy, and the price paid for it? Churchill had said in 1914 that

> it has never been the practice of the Admiralty to publish the terms of its contracts or even the names of its contractors for important munitions of war such as oil must be regarded.[10]

But it is surely better to change a practice than to lose a source of supply; unless the amount sold represented the whole of British naval requirements, security need not have been undermined by disclosure. Or when, in the financial crisis of 1948, the British Treasury request for dividend limitation automatically reduced Persia's income from A.I.O.C., would not adjustment by the British Government have been politic? Anthony Eden records in his memoirs that, on return from a visit to Persia in that year, he thought the matter so serious as to ask the Labour Chancellor of the Exchequer, Stafford Cripps, to make an exception for a company "whose dividends influenced the receipts of a foreign government". But Cripps said no, and left the oil company to offer compensation, which the Persians refused unless paid as part of a wider settlement. Throughout the three-year period during which that settlement was abortively sought, the British Government told inquirers that it had best not interfere with the minutiae of the negotiations whereby the company was trying to arrive at a new basis of payment; it left the Americans in Saudi Arabia to display the virtues of shock treatment when at the beginning of January 1951 they bounced out like a jack-in-the-box with the simple "fifty-fifty" formula that caught local imaginations and held good for a decade. In the course of A.I.O.C.'s long haggle with the Persians, an equal sharing of profits had been considered, but was abandoned because the Persian Government had insisted that its share apply to the company's earnings outside as well as inside Persia.

Perhaps no scheme short of total foreign capitulation to Persian demands would by 1951 have been acceptable, for the tide of anti-foreign feeling in Persia had been running so high since the Second World War that a succession of Persian Governments felt bound to swim with it. Unnoticed in the clamour of vituperation against the oil company was the short shrift that they gave to other foreign enterprises. A government of 1949 passed legislation restricting foreign banks that in fact hit only a British bank of sixty years' standing, and in 1952 Musaddiq further restricted foreign banking privileges to a degree that caused that bank to abandon its operations in Persia. Again, an American firm of planning consultants to whom Persia had paid a large fee to produce a co-ordinated plan for economic development was—despite its excellent work—given one month's notice to quit in December 1950. The more paternally the oil company dispensed housing and hospitals, the more praise it got from I.L.O. for its labour relations, the more effortless its bland superiority, the more often the British Government protested at discrimination against it, the angrier the Persians became. Perhaps there was no way of averting a British humiliation the main blast of which was felt in countries outside Persia—the first of them Egypt.

Since 1882, troop movements on behalf of wronged investors have not been common in the Middle East; oilmen have placed their faith in the local police, and in barbed wire. In 1946, during serious strikes about post-war shortage of amenities at Abadan, the Government of India made its last contribution to British Middle Eastern policy by sending troops to Basra "for the protection, should circumstances demand it, of Indian, British and Arab lives, and in order to safeguard Indian and British interests in south Persia". But circumstances did not so demand and, having done nothing beyond causing affront to Iraqi nationalists, the troops re-embarked. Again in 1951, H.M.S. *Mauritius* stood by off Abadan; it was revealed during the general election campaign of 1951 that she had orders to land marines for the protection of British lives, though not of British property. But again force was not used. Happily, the Royal Air Force has never yet been given the unenviable task of scooping British citizens off inland oilfields, though at the time of the Suez crisis rumour had it that aircraft were available for a rescue operation in northern Iraq.

The use of troops to defend oil supplies has therefore only taken place in time of war. In 1914, the force dispatched by the Government of India to look after British interests at the head of the Persian Gulf landed a few troops at Abadan, though its main task, which was to push the Turks back in Mesopotamia, was conducted from Basra. In 1940, a major reason for reinforcing the Middle East at the expense of the British Isles was denial of its oil to Hitler, whose need of fuel was proved in 1941 by his drive for the Caucasus rather than for Moscow. Also in 1941, British reinforcement of Iraq during the pro-German rebellion of that year included the dispatch of a Government of India expedition to Basra both in order to make sure of an assembly base there, and to shield Abadan. Lastly, during the cold-war a perennial reason given for clinging to British military bases was a desire to "protect the oil". Naturally, plans for doing so changed with changing weapons, but whether or no the feat is practicable in the nuclear age (except in terms of some puny local quarrel) the intention survived all hazards. As Eden said to Khrushchev in London in April, 1956

> I thought we must be absolutely blunt about the oil, because we would fight for it.[11]

Six months later, he did so; for, as some of his messages to Eisenhower indicate, one of his reasons for wanting to topple Nasser was the risk that Egypt would mount Arab revolutions that would produce governments which would have to

> place their united oil resources under the control of a united Arabia led by Egypt and under Russian influence.[12]

The Suez adventure of November 1956 was to prove, however, that armed attack is no longer the best way of ensuring an oil supply. For, quite apart from Egyptian blockage of the Suez Canal route, it caused the Arabs to cut other supply lines: to blow up two pumping stations in Syria on the trans-desert pipelines from Iraq; to refuse to pump from Saudi Arabia to the Mediterranean any oil that was to be loaded into French or British tankers, and to stop all pumping from the Saudi fields to the refinery at Bahrain; even in relatively friendly Kuwait, some not very effective explosives were laid under the oil installations.

Successive British Governments of the nineteen-fifties and sixties were confronted with a number of new developments that altered their standing, and their capacity to make sure of Middle Eastern oil supplies by the exercise of might. The first in date order was the disappearance of the Indian army as an instrument of policy, and of protection against Russia; the only imaginable Great-Power adversary thereafter had the advantage—for what it is worth in nuclear war—of living closer to the Middle East oilfields than does any Western power. Next, shortage of dollars in western Europe and the adoption of the Marshall Plan, which depended on a lavish and continuous supply of Middle Eastern oil, for a while placed the oil-owning states of the Middle East in a position of strength

H

such as the peoples of the area had not enjoyed since the seven-teenth-century heyday of Suleiman the Magnificent. The sellers' market for their oil that lasted from Pearl Harbour until 1960 placed them at an advantage that would have been enormous had they hung together. But they never did so until a buyers' market was on its way. None of them, except Iraq, applied an oil sanction in order to exercise pressure in favour of the Arab cause in Palestine; far from closing ranks round Musaddiq, the Arabs were delighted with the extra earnings that they gained from his plight. Not until the Suez crisis did they club together and use their asset as a weapon of retaliation.

The third and much the most profound of the developments that altered relations between British buyer and Middle Eastern producer was the growth of antipathy to foreign control over any Middle Eastern asset. This phenomenon will be described in the next chapter, but oil spreads its sticky stain over the whole topic for more reasons than one. In the early years, lack of local engineering and mining skill led to nervousness of being cheated of treasure; subse-quently, resentment swelled at the uncommon degree of control exercised by companies that managed not only production but the marketing end of the operation as well. Lastly, there was under-standable confusion in local minds between company and govern-ment. To most Arabs and Persians these are Gog and Magog—twin giants equally avaricious. (A good illustration of local feeling in the matter is a clause that the Kuwaitis inserted into a contract of 1958 with Japanese oil interests, which stipulated that no re-course might be had by their company to its own government for protection; in international law the proviso is flimsy because no national can sign away his government's right to intervene, but to psychologists it is revealing.) Against governments and com-panies alike, therefore, are directed a whole gamut of local grievances, including some that have nothing to do with oil—chagrin about social inequality, resentment at Western power, anger at the indignity of watching the one great national resource used for the profit of foreigners. The emotions that were first discernible when Reza Shah struck his blow for nationalism in 1932 suffused the whole scene by the 1950's, and forced all com-panies into the field of diplomacy or all parent governments into the field of oil policy. Middle Eastern nationalism narrowed to vanishing point the gap between the commercial and the diplomatic handling of oil affairs.

From a moment in the nineteen-fifties that differed from country to country, the British Government, inextricably confused with the company in all local minds, was confronted with new choices. Either it could accept that it was implicated, and make common cause with British companies by giving joint displays of strength; or else it could read the writing on the wall, recognize that local ill-will could deny oil to the West, encourage a search for politically and strategically safer sources of supply, and, till they were found, adjust itself to the new mood in the Middle East.

The oil concessions are not everlasting. The reason for making them long-lived was the size of the investment needed for oil prospection. Most of them end at the end of the century. Between now and then, the responsibility for working out a form of take-over that meets the needs both of the Middle Eastern governments for steady revenue, and of the companies for continuing efficiency, lies between the two of them, and not with any Western government.

Hazard has played its usual large part in the oil era. It was a fluke that almost all the great oilfields in the area matured under the very sod that the British had chosen to protect all along the line of their alternative route to India—Kirkuk, Basra, Kuwait, Qatar, Abu Dhabi. It was a fluke that the discovery made in Persia in 1908, happening within a year of the Anglo-Russian share-out of 1907, adjoined the British sphere of influence, and could easily be added to it. It was a fluke that in 1948—just one year after the Indian Independence Act had reduced the importance of protecting the passage to India—the adoption of the Marshall Plan rapidly increased western Europe's need for Middle Eastern oil, and so rendered the safe passage of oil a Western and a British interest of magnitude. A sequence of British Governments has made what it could of these bonuses, and engineered what it could of other advantages, but all told, British Government action in pursuit of Middle Eastern oil has been taken less often, and over much shorter periods, than is popularly imagined.

THE SPECTRUM OF MIDDLE EAST
RESISTANCE

THE annals of resistance to domination are romantic and the annals of policing it are not. Before 1914, British liberals had often been on the side of romance in Europe, particularly in Greece, and they had occasionally been so in Asia—for instance, when E. G. Browne took up the cudgels for the Persian Constitutionalists in 1905-6. During the First World War, the British Government had a spell on the side of romance when it sponsored the Arab revolt—the opposite of the role it played in relation to the Egyptians. This association with the Arabs seemed the more romantic because the fight that the British fought in company with the Sharif's forces was the only dashing land campaign of an otherwise drab war. The two peoples shared a great experience, though as far as the Arabs were concerned this was quickly overlaid by bitter disappointment.

The attraction that Arabs held for Englishmen long pre-dated the First World War. It started towards the middle of the nineteenth century when travellers (till then chiefly traders, or pilgrims with their eyes glued to the ground for Bible evidence) began to take an interest in the contemporary inhabitants. Kinglake and Robert Curzon in popular books, David Roberts and Lear in paintings, were forerunners of a new mood of observation. Interest blossomed into excitement over literary discoveries (sixteen volumes of the Arabian Nights were printed in Richard Burton's translation between 1885 and 1888) and on account of the daring of explorers. The chief creators of a vogue for Arabs were Burton, whose journey to Mecca in disguise is commemorated by a symbolic tent-tomb in the Catholic cemetery at Mortlake, near London, and Doughty, who took the risk of travelling as a Christian and an Englishman in order to record the way of life that he described in *Arabia Deserta*. Englishmen who had long ceased to live and work in Indian clothes put on Arab robes and headdress without embarrassment. The Arab counterpart of these British sentiments was respect for British institutions. Before 1914, Arab nationalists saw in Britain the first champion of liberalism, and Syrian Christians even envied the Egyptians the freedom of their lot under good British management.

In Britain the Lawrence legend therefore fell on fertile ground when first propagated by the American publicist, Lowell Thomas, in 1919. Thomas's illustrated lecture, *With Allenby in Palestine and Lawrence in Arabia*, drew audiences so large that they overflowed Covent Garden and had to be transferred to the Albert Hall. Lawrence's *Seven Pillars of Wisdom* (sub-titled *A Triumph* and first printed in a limited edition in 1926) needed no Lawrence mystery in order to be sensational. Like the Thomas lecture, it satisfied two British cravings—for Arab lore, and for a war epic of a kind never evoked by the trenches.

But resistance is romantic only in other people's territories; a struggle to be free that was rightful when directed at domination by others became subversion in India or Ireland. When the British, by conquering Baghdad, Jerusalem and Damascus, took over the role of military ruler from the Turks, their relationship to the Arabs changed automatically. This change was much more obvious to Arabs than to most Englishmen. The Arabs would of course far rather have beaten the Turks by themselves, but had been obliged to accept a helpmeet. Now they saw that helpmeet turn policeman in Iraq and Palestine, and assist the French to do the same in the Levant States. So that, from the Arab point of view, the whole area, instead of being liberated, remained in bondage. Nevertheless the intention of many Englishmen towards Arabs remained liberal, and, as we have seen, their liberalism found part-fulfilment in Iraq and Transjordan owing to Lawrence's influence on Churchill. Honour part-satisfied, there grew up in these territories a band of British public servants whose predilection for Arabs, or whose sense of guilt about Palestine, caused them to view Arab resistance with indulgence.

British policy-makers seem to have visualized Middle Eastern nationalism as of three brands, and when the distinction that they drew is scrutinized, it turns out to be based chiefly on the scale of British interests in three different areas. The distinction was of course also affected by the relationship that Britain bore to the various areas—here to independent states, there to dependencies— and it was coloured by the old love for Arabs.

Seen through British eyes, the first brand of nationalism was that of independent peoples—the Turks and Persians. It was represented

in Turkey by the Kemalist movement that threw out all Western
nations (first ejecting the Greeks and then tearing up the Capitulations and the peace treaty signed at Sèvres by the last of the
Ottomans) and in Persia by adroit politicians who—after experience
of interference by four belligerents—in 1921 cunningly evaded
the attentions of both Curzon and the Bolsheviks. In Turkey and
Persia the British, soon perceiving both countries to lie beyond the
range of their immediate interests, reconciled themselves to making
concessions to opponents—Mustafa Kemal in Turkey and Reza
Khan (later Reza Shah) in Persia. Britain was obliged to trust to
luck that these two unknown soldiers would build some kind of
buffer between its Middle Eastern dependencies and Bolshevik
Russia.

Egypt the British placed in a category by itself. Here, where
their interests were vital to their empire, they saw nationalism as
subversive, stamped quickly upon it, and when agreement with
moderate Egyptians did not follow, firmly maintained the *status quo*
until such time as the Egyptians should come round to the British
view of Suez Canal defence and of the Sudan. Between the two
world wars, British cruisers steamed into Alexandria if riots broke
out, part of the British army was in any case on the spot, and
Britain played makeweight in the endemic struggle between the
Palace and the main nationalist party, the Wafd, whenever its
interests prompted it to do so. The arch-champion of British firmness whenever the reserved points were touched upon was Allenby's
successor as High Commissioner, Lord Lloyd; during his reign
(1925–9) he had some major differences of opinion, even with a
Conservative government, on the degree of firmness to be applied
and he was invited to resign as soon as Labour came to power.
But he was unrepentant and carried many of his countrymen with
him when, in the following December, he brushed aside Liberal
and Labour criticism and told the House of Lords that

> the only place from which the Suez Canal can be economically
> and adequately defended is from Cairo.[1]

In the Arab areas for which Britain was responsible, the British
attitude was different owing to the feelings of affection tinged with
remorse that have been described. Resistance to Britain was seen
only as a temporary demonstration made by people who were
friends at heart—a mood soon curable by working shoulder to
shoulder with the sons of the Sharif whom Britain had installed

as rulers of Iraq and Transjordan, and by reassuring the Arabs of Palestine. The British believed themselves able to make up for a bad start, and to restore a former affinity.

And up to a point this belief was well founded. For years, Great Britain achieved a tolerable, even a satisfactory, relationship with the Arab class that mattered most for British purposes—the ruling class. In this were grouped older men who appreciated some of their qualities, and from whom they won respect. The group included kings and sheikhs who liked the public order that Britain introduced; merchants who were glad to have stable conditions in which to trade, and men with enough experience of Ottoman public service to appreciate British standards of administration and justice. Among these, Britons who, in the course of their work, made their homes in the Middle East found congenial neighbours or colleagues, and made good friends. The links they forged included that with the Sharif's family, the Hashimites. Though the Sharif himself had even by Lawrence's standards turned into an obstinate and difficult old man, and had finally lost his throne to Ibn Saud in 1924–5, the Anglo-Arab connexion survived through his sons, Feisal and Abdullah. But virtually all the friends of Britain belonged to a single generation, and generations die out.

British qualities and methods had not the same attraction for younger men. Here was a generation bred in the turmoil of the Young Turk revolution, and a succession of Ottoman wars. Some young people were adrift because their families had lost the bearings provided by tradition and dogma and an established pattern of behaviour; new religious movements such as the Moslem Brotherhood (founded in Egypt in 1928) inadequately answered their need because the Brotherhood wanted to restore the past, whereas most young men wanted to look forward. The great mass of the younger generation was ready to leave religion aside and proceed with public life on the admired Western model. But these young men, instead of enjoying freedom to experiment with democracy in their own way, found themselves obliged to try it in leading strings held by foreign mentors; the people in the worst case were the Palestinians, who were scarcely able to try self-government at all. Hostility to Britain grew, and the British often misjudged the reason for it. They encouraged schooling that taught liberty and equality, and forgot that most Arab and Egyptian schoolmasters belonged to a generation that did not feel free. When students shouted for freedom, British observers drew little distinction between youths who were parading at a piastre a head on behalf of some politician, and serious young nationalists whose main grievance was the British presence in countries that were independent only in name, because a pro-British foreign policy was in fact imposed upon them. A shrewd French analyst of Middle Eastern sentiments has written of France's failure to appreciate the nature of Arab nationalism in Syria in terms that apply equally to the British attitude:

> As it (nationalism) was often expressed by young lawyers and publicists, the product of our schools, we tended to regard it purely as a verbal exercise. . . . The powerful echo that nationalism was to find in the masses thanks in particular to the inter-penetration of Arab and Muslim sentiment was not sufficiently heeded, or at least was not appreciated at its proper value, in French administrative circles.[2]

An example of British complacency of the kind described is the reduction of the Palestine garrison in 1926 that has been mentioned, and that was made in spite of warnings, subsequently justified, from the Permanent Mandates Commission that so small a force was inadequate. Another example is British ascription of the rebellion in Syria in the same year entirely to French shortcomings, instead of seeing that it was part of an Arab nationalist movement that would sooner or later turn against Britain also.

Nationalism was not peculiar to the Middle East. It was sweeping the whole of Asia. The slow, steady growth of self-confidence in the Far East and India, with its gain of momentum when Japan scored a victory over Russia in 1905, and its further spurt in 1914–18 as a result of the spectacle of "European civil war" is well described in K. M. Pannikar's *Asia and Western Dominance*:

> The Indian soldier who fought on the Marne came back to India with other ideas of the Sahib than those he was taught to believe by decades of propaganda . . . Among the Chinese who went to France at the time was a young man named Chou En-lai.[3]

Suddenly, Asian doubts that had been maturing for years found expression in a whole series of anti-western acts, starting with demonstrations by Chinese revolutionaries that they could with impunity shell the gunboats of great powers on the Yangtse-kiang.

Early in 1927, the Chinese turned the British out of their concession at Hankow; later in the same year, Reza Shah, trading on the victory won by Mustafa Kemal over the West at Lausanne, denounced the capitulatory privileges of foreigners in Persia. In 1929, there were troubles in Palestine. In 1930, Gandhi gave notice that he was defying the government salt monopoly and led his march to the sea for a symbolic "making of salt". In 1931 he launched his civil disobedience movement, Japan defied the League of Nations in Manchuria, the Mufti of Jerusalem summoned an Islamic Congress to rally support against British policy in Palestine, and in 1932 Reza Shah unilaterally denounced the Anglo-Persian Oil Company's concession. As the Sadhu said to Alden in Edward Thompson's *A Farewell to India*, published in 1931:

> Haven't you realized that nothing is ever going to be normal again, as you islanders count normality. The unchanging East has become Vesuvius.[4]

A boost to Asian resistance in general was given in 1928 by the Sixth Congress of the Communist International; held in Moscow, this produced a long document on the *Revolutionary Movement in the Colonies and Semi-Colonies*, which gave the Communists some marching orders about circumventing the "semi-colonial *bourgeoisie*" that was collaborating with the imperialists in countries such as India and Egypt, and instructed them to

> learn how to utilize each and every conflict, to develop such conflicts and to broaden their significance.[5]

Fortunately for Britain, the Soviets were so busy in China, Anglo-French dominance in the mandates was so complete, and the buffer provided by Mustafa Kemal and Reza Shah was at the time so adequate, that these instructions had no immediate effect in the Middle East. Nevertheless a storm was rising. The contemporary world economic crisis swelled it. The Palestine troubles of 1928–9 that gave the first of a long series of shocks to British serenity had local causes, but they were also part of the wider movement whereby Asia had begun to demonstrate that it was sick of Europe.

By the nineteen-thirties, the difference between regional brands of Middle Eastern nationalism had disappeared, if indeed it had ever existed anywhere but in British imagination. Young Egyptians, young Persians and young Arabs all thought alike. The immediate butt of their abuse might be some local British activity—in Egypt, the British troops; in Persia, the British oil company; in Arab Asia, British policy in Palestine; but their main aim transcended frontiers, and was to get rid of the British presence, British influence on their elders, and British restriction of their right to choose their friends for themselves. Yet still the British sense of affinity with the Arabs survived, and still it had some foundation. It even survived dealings with a young and anti-British Hashimite king of Iraq—King Feisal I's son Ghazi—who from 1933 to 1939 did many of the things that most young nationalists only dreamed of doing; intermittently, he ran a private broadcasting station from his palace which attacked British policy in Palestine, flirted with Hitler and laid claim to Kuwait. The British ambassador of the day wrote him off as a person of "total irresponsibility", and the label was apposite in that he killed himself by driving a racing car into a lamp standard. But his views were those of his generation to a degree that was masked from British eyes by the array of elder statesmen who continued to hold office, and by the traditional Arab respect for age and custom that still caused sons in middle age to take their place behind the chairs on which their fathers sat with guests.

Until the Palestine Arabs broke into serious and prolonged rebellion in 1936, the Arab and Egyptian dissatisfaction with Britain that had followed the various settlements of the early nine-teen-twenties had vented itself chiefly in talk, but from 1936, desperation about the mounting Jewish immigration that would produce a Jewish majority in a matter of years, caused Arab resistance to become general and substantial. It gained substance through concentration on the single cause of Palestine, and because this cause drew together first the generations, and secondly, all Islamic states. Some fellow Arabs, Syrians in particular, enrolled in guerrilla bands actually to fight in Palestine; others lent moral support by organizing two congresses that were held in 1937 and 1938—the first at Bludan in Syria, the second in Cairo. There was a significant difference in the range and composition of these two meetings. The first, which was summoned by a Palestine Assistance Committee, largely composed of Syrians, consisted of Arab delegates representing themselves alone, or else unofficial organizations; the second was a World Inter-Parliamentary Congress of Arab and Moslem Countries for the Defence of Palestine. It was summoned by Egyptian senators and deputies; it enjoyed the considerable machinery of publicity that is always available in Cairo, and it included delegates from India, China and Yugoslavia and the Arab diaspora in the Americas. King Ibn Saud and King Abdullah both used their absolute powers to prevent their subjects from attending it. Its weakness was that its members could not agree upon what to do; its strength, that it was attended by elder statesmen as well as young demagogues, and that it committed some prominent Egyptians to an Arab cause about which they had till then been lukewarm. It produced neither the pertinacity whereby the Zionists were later to gain American support, nor the weight of that support, but it revealed a unity of Moslem sentiment that an empire containing 70 million Moslems could not afford to ignore.

But the kind of unity shown was far from sufficient to shake Great Britain's hold on the Middle East. Though the British authorities in Palestine were much disconcerted by the ability of the rebels to paralyse civilian life (the paralysis was at its worst at the time of Munich) they were able to meet the crisis by falling back on their network of Arab cronies. And these responded to an appeal to help stabilize matters. Each for reasons of his own, the kings accepted a British invitation to send representatives to London early in 1939 in order to try and work out a compromise acceptable to the Palestinians. One hated the Mufti; another feared Mussolini; some wished to show the decorum incumbent on newly independent states; no one wanted to be left out of a display of Arab unity. Lastly, all preferred to play for safety at a time of great risk of world war. When the White Paper was promulgated by the British in May 1939, the kings reckoned with justification that their solidarity had furthered the Arab cause. But their peoples, who felt no responsibility for government and no interest in wider world affairs, were not of the same mind, and applauded the Palestine Arabs when these rejected the White Paper because it was only half a loaf.

Among the huge majority of Arabs, the grievance about Palestine destroyed every shred of regard for Britain. But to argue that, had it not been for Palestine, a special Anglo-Arab relationship would have lasted—as the Anglo-Greek relationship forged by Canning and Byron lasted—for several generations is to underrate the other ingredients of anti-imperialism. Nationalism just as virulent as that of the Arabs consumed the Persians, who were unmoved by the Palestine cause, and the Egyptians, most of whom adopted it only after the Second World War. Among Arabs, anger at the unfairness of the British in imposing Jews on the Palestinian

Arabs exacerbated stock nationalist emotions and turned many old friends into enemies, but in Egypt and Iraq hostility to the British for other reasons—their insistence on sticking to military bases, and their "treaties of independence" that did not give independence —was mounting in any case.

By no means all the Middle Eastern grudges against the British were political. Some were social, and were generated by the assured British manners and the obliviousness to foreign civilizations that moved E. M. Forster to chastise his fellow-countrymen and country-women in *A Passage to India*. Ascendancy of social over political grievances can best be sampled in Persia, to which many of the comments just made about political hostility to British tutelage did not apply, since Persia was an independent state.

Nevertheless, the Persians contrived to be politically affronted. They cast back to the Anglo-Russian agreement of 1907, and to the summary treatment they had had at the hands of several belligerents during the First World War; no Persian appreciated that owing to events in Europe, Britain's alternative to the 1907 compromise had been to wash its hands of Persia and leave the Russians to do as they pleased, or that, during the First World War, the British intruder had been kindly and munificent by comparison with requisitioning Russians and Turks. Once Reza Khan was in the saddle and was ruling either without foreign advice, or with foreign advisers of nationalities other than British, the Persians had far less grounds for political grievance against Britain than had the Arabs. Yet they were the more disgruntled of the two peoples; for them, Britain remained the villain and the reason why was that there were still British citizens in exalted positions on Persian soil.

There were in Persia a British oil company and a British bank, and on to the oil company in particular a people with a permanent inclination to carp and criticize projected all its grievances, relevant and irrelevant. Persians have a great sense of their past. They never forget that their forbears led the world in many branches of civil-ization, and they disliked seeing evidence of the long start that the modern Western world had gained over the Orient in material and technical matters. This dislike they directed at the Western power within easiest range—Great Britain. Their mental processes were most in evidence during the oil dispute with Britain in 1951 and will be described in that context. But for years before the final outburst they found fault even with the good deeds the British firms did—for instance, with the high level of labour and social conditions for workers which the oil company maintained. The British were hated, not admired, for their efficiency by all Persians outside their employment because the standards they set were reached by no Persian employer. Now and then, Arabs felt a similar annoyance at the sight of Europeans managing their industries or running their public transport, but they were always much more jaunty about their discontents than the Persians, much more aware of the amount of ground they still had to cover in order to catch up with the West, and much more content with what they were doing for themselves. The Iraqis, for instance, in the 1950's employed two foreign technical experts as full members of their Development Board, and were well served by these outsiders; the Persians thought it beneath Persian dignity to hire foreigners except in subordinate roles.

On one account, but one only, the Iraqis grew almost as disgruntled as the Persians, and this exception was due to the accident that the Middle East's one great commercial asset—oil production—called for investment risks and scientific skills that were far beyond local compass. This thought irritated young Iraqis, though it never ate into their souls as it did into those of Persians. Most inhabitants of both countries had never seen an oilfield, but those who had found their way to the spot were misled by the apparent simplicity of the apparatus that meets the eye—a few derricks, some stopcocks and a neat array of pipes snaking away to the horizon. They forgot that forbears of theirs had known of the existence of the fuel for millennia, but had made little use of it, and that not until Western money and skills had been applied had production become profitable. They ignored the whole debit side of the oil operation—the fruitless searches, investment without recompense, years of drudgery and narrow shaves experienced prior to commercial discovery, and considered only how easily they could run the flow once it was turned on. The oil companies helped them to facile conclusions by telling a glossy and continuous success story, and never mentioning either effort or failure. The Syrians, for instance, were astounded and unbelieving when the oil company prospecting in Syria (a collateral of the successful I.P.C. in Iraq) told them in 1951 that it was abandoning its concession; they had taken in none of the implications of seventeen years of search without result.

Faults were not all on the Middle Eastern side. Though local talent overestimated the possibility of skipping the stepping-stones to technical skill, there were fields in which Europeans miscalculated the balance between efficiency and expediency, and hung on for too long to levers that local hands were competent to pull. After the Second World War, a handover began in earnest, but by the time it took place, local blood was on the boil. Even in Egypt, where firms under joint Anglo-Egyptian management began to be set up before the war, transfer of managerial responsibility to Egyptians within British firms was not general. The unforgettable example of too long a Western wait occurred when, in July 1956, an Egyptian organizer of genius, Mahmoud Yunes, proved on Nasser's behalf that European theories about the technical difficulties of pilotage were moonshine by taking over and running the Suez Canal.

The Persians, cherishing anti-British grievances that were social in origin, formed one end of the spectrum of resistance; at the other were the Palestinian Jews, whose grievances were purely political. Socially, the Jewish community in Palestine was by its own wish self-sufficient and self-contained. But politically, it began at an early date to regard Great Britain not as a benefactor but as an adversary; the turning-point was the moment at which the British first set a limit to Jewish plans, and was when Churchill's White Paper of 1922 stated that the Balfour Declaration did not apply to Transjordan. Once broader lands were out of the question, the Jewish target became more people on the land available; the hard core of Jewish resistance to Britain was thenceforth the question of numbers. Between the wars, the Zionists fought their case not in Palestine, but in London. More than once, they won it by causing British cabinets to abandon some new project for improving execution of the mandatory's dual obligation to Arab and Jew and to carry on as before—that is, with the Jewish population steadily overhauling the Arab one. By 1939, all eyes were on Arab resistance because it was armed and violent, but Jewish resistance to British policy had acquired a potency far greater than the British realized. This potency the Jews could not turn to account until someone had destroyed Hitler.

By the time that the Second World War broke out, Middle Eastern society as a whole was simmering beneath a crust consisting of British military power and royal conservatism (or, in Persia, of the conservatism alone). The war pierced the crust at many points, and up bubbled emotions that were in the end to cause kings and the British to collapse.

The new political resentment that British war measures induced when they included arbitrary interference in local politics was described in Chapter 3. In addition, the Second World War, by greatly increasing local mobility and by spreading the habit of listening to broadcasts, presented Middle Eastern nationalists with even more new ideas than the First World War had done. For instance, it offered them the spectacle not only of Europeans fighting one another in Europe, but of European allies stooping to quarrels under Arab eyes. The Syrians and Lebanese are, for a number of age-old reasons, more attuned to European ways of thought than are other Arabs; they therefore watched with relish and amazement first the bitter quarrel between Vichy France and Free France, and then the bickering between the Free French and the British about what was to happen to the Levant States. Anglo-French differences that sprang from a conflict of personalities as well as of policies was personified for them on the British side by Sir Edward Spears and on the French side by General Georges Catroux. The policy for which Spears stood aimed both to redress the British breach of faith to the Syrians over Damascus in 1920, and to avoid a Syrian repetition of the 1941 rebellion in Iraq. In 1941, the Free French had proclaimed the Syrians and Lebanese "free and independent", and the British objective was to get General de Gaulle to live up to this proclamation and to meet Syrian nationalist wishes. General Catroux interpreted this British policy as an *"arrière-pensée d'éviction"*—an understandable piece of reasoning if he compared this sector of British policy with Britain's determination to keep a base in Egypt; where he wholly misjudged the British was in believing that they wanted the French to go in order that Britain might take France's place in Syria; such "places" were out of date. In the course of his arguments with Spears, the Syrian and Lebanese politicians who ran from one man to the other, and served both as confidantes, drew the conclusion that if the Arabs played their cards well they could get rid not only of France but of Britain as well.

New political impressions were far outstripped by new social ones. The passage of British troops through the Middle Eastern countryside, and British purchasing of supplies all over the region, between them produced a revolution. People moved about as they had never done before, found new jobs, and saw spectacles that they had never dreamed of. They saw poor men earning regular money; peoples of whom they had long thought as equals, such as Greeks, fighting in "Free" contingents that wore good boots and red tabs, and neighbouring countries with living standards different from their own. Egyptian drivers gaped at the land of promise in Palestine, and Persians at the unimagined quantities of useful goods such as sugar and textiles that crawled up their passes on lorries bound for Russia. Workers ate regular meals in canteens; some were issued free with protective clothing; many learnt new skills; all acquired new tastes, some of which turned out to be expensive in terms of post-war earnings. A new idea of social justice was born.

Socialists helped the new notions along, directing them against pashas and merchants who were turning British war expenditure to account, and making fortunes out of all proportion to the profits gleaned by the artisan or labourer who had found war work. But the animosity was directed against Britain also. As the belligerent most in evidence it was blamed exclusively for the inflation that was making food so dear. Though wages had risen for those with new jobs, no one else could afford even the low level of nutrition on which he had subsisted before the war. Peasant families began a migration towards cities, and into shanty towns where anti-foreign sentiment breeds much faster than in villages.

The belligerents, far from checking social resentment, in-advertently increased it. For one thing, Russia was their ally, and Soviet propaganda was therefore respectable. For another, Britain's own propaganda services had Germany's to compete with, and each of these vied with the other to preach the more attractive social programme. In 1943, British puffs of new social services in Britain temporarily projected the word "Beveridge" into Arabic.

Not that the British were loth to open Middle Eastern eyes to the fact of social inequality; on the contrary, during the war, and still more after it, British officials were instructed to give all possible help to Middle Eastern states that were organizing new social legislation and promoting trade unions. But the drawback of spreading such thoughts in wartime was the difficulty of dissociating them from reflections about British responsibility for hardships and in-equalities—particularly for inflation.

One by-product of the war was identification of the British with the rich and ruling class to an even greater degree than before. Another was disillusionment with parliamentary democracy which that class had contrived to convert to its own ends. For though all grown men had a vote, they had not a voice because the parliaments so joyfully installed in the nineteen-twenties turned out to be clubs to which the old landed gentry got itself elected, and in which it dissipated all its energies in party and personal quarrels. Democratic systems were later to be discarded in country after country with a readiness that was tacit acknowledgement of their unsuitability for the less developed countries of the world. But while they lasted, they were a target for critics not only of the aristocracy but of the West.

A crowning wartime grievance advanced by sophisticated Egyptian, Arab and Persian nationalists was that the British had no business to be fighting their war across Middle Eastern territory; all Middle Eastern literates were daily reminded of this irksome fact by British censorship of their newspapers and mail, carried out in the interests of British security. Were their countries for ever to be a passage or a thoroughfare, never dealt with for their own sakes? Even their one commercial asset—their oil—was extracted for use outside the Middle East, and at a pace dictated by other people's requirements. These contentions were difficult to answer during a war in which the peoples of the Middle East felt no concern, followed by a cold war in which most of its inhabitants had no interest either.

At all stages short of open revolt, measurement of the volume of a resistance movement is difficult. It is especially so in countries where the régime is intolerant of criticism, and where foreign embassies create a furore if they consort with anyone who is out of favour. (In Egypt in 1953, a British embassy official was severely taken to task by the Egyptian Government for meeting the head of one of the biggest organizations in the country, the Moslem Brotherhood.) In accusing the British of dealing only with "the old gang", nationalists forget that a diplomatic mission is bound both by diplomatic convention and common prudence to deal with the government to which it is accredited, and that any other course lays it open to charges of interference in internal politics.

But this handicap need not lead to foreign ignorance or complacency. Though an ambassador cannot himself hobnob with resistance movements, he has ample access to information about them. Members of his staff—for instance, his press, commercial and labour attachés—all meet every shade of opinion in the ordinary

I

course of their duties, and in addition newspaper correspondents, technical advisers, instructors on loan, business men and private residents are all eager to air their view of the local state of mind. But their estimates vary widely, and at some point in the process of policy making, their information has to pass through the filter of one man's mind. For exactly one generation, a succession of such British representatives weighed the evidence, but against it they naturally set the British interests at stake, and so usually saw the Middle East through the spectacles of convention, of British authority, and—in the case of the Arabs—of friendships with loyal but ageing men. In all the states of the Middle East, British embassies hoped that social reform would bear fruit in time to stave off revolution. In a situation about which diplomats could do little without being accused of unwarrantable interference, they followed the course of human nature, and hoped for the best. Plenty of onlookers thought that an eruption was inevitable and could "see it coming"; but not until after the event can anyone put his finger with certainty on all the signs that a revolution is about to take place.

6

THE DECLINE OF BRITISH NERVE

MOST nations that have concentrated on resistance to tutelage believe, and go on believing in spite of modern evidence to the contrary, that the imperialist always wants to cling to empire. But they are wrong. The desire for empire is subject to fashion, and, like the changing cut of coats, is partly dictated by economics, though not wholly so. Before 1870, the British ideal, made in Manchester, was trade with the world at large for a people that had won an industrial start over all others. Successive governments sought security for that trade by means of the exercise of influence without the expense of a take-over—influence with the Khedive, or the Sublime Porte, or the King of Ashanti. In 1865, a House of Commons committee resolved that "all further extensions of territory or assumption of government or new treaty offering protection to native tribes would be inexpedient".

There are books in plenty on the reason why this attitude changed, and why for the rest of the century Great Britain galloped after just these ends. The motives were by no means all economic; they were often strategic and sometimes emotional and always dog-in-the-manger. A key to the puzzle is the growth of foreign commercial competition, so that the British, instead of enjoying what Tim Healey called a gift from the Almighty of a lease of the universe for ever, had to struggle to keep their feet; but it is not the only key. Reference was made, in the introduction, to the British attitude to this contest and the extent to which all British actions in Africa, including the Boer War, were conducted in order to preserve the long and the short routes to India against European challengers; by and large, British policy extended into Africa the system it used when parrying Czarist Russia in Asia.

The Diamond Jubilee of 1897 was the product and final sunburst of an unalloyed belief in British fitness to rule, subject to the support of the Lord God of Hosts; this last was seldom forgotten. The Jubilee celebrated dominion over palm and pine, over nearly a quarter of the earth's land surface and more than a quarter of its estimated population. It is a monument to the fascination of size, and to the satisfaction of belonging to a big community. When

Rhodes took his honorary degree at Oxford in 1899, to shouts from undergraduates in the gallery of "Cape to Cairo" and "Through Trains", no one paused to think how odd it was that the British Isles should be exporting white paupers to the United States while taking on coloured ones in Asia and Africa.

With the exception of the British Isles and India, the Colonial Office looked after this whole range of races and conditions of men. In the talk and writing of the time, therefore, the word "colonies" meant, primarily, places of white settlement with which there was a blood tie to be kept up. If and when thought was given to the second colonial task—that of remodelling alien races on the British pattern—most people anticipated that, given British fitness to rule, the founding of loyal brown and black dominions would be straight-forward. A suspicion that this was not so lurked in some minds from the time of the Indian Mutiny, but few cared to put it into words. Doubts were allayed by applying all possible energy to building up a superb administration and judicial system. (This tradition, founded in India, was bequeathed to the Middle East via the Sudan, whence it passed into the mandated territories of Palestine, Transjordan and Iraq.) Yet time was to prove that administration, however impeccable, would never wipe out some fundamental differences that exist between colonies that share the home country's language, spiritual and literary heritage, and tradi-tions and colonies different in history, principles and outlook. The first, if promoted to independence, can almost always be counted on, the second cannot, and it is with the spread of this piece of know-ledge that this chapter is concerned.

The experience that dispelled the Jubilee spirit was the Boer War. South Africa was a hybrid, being neither one kind of colony nor the other, in that it contained both black and white subjects with the added complication that more than half the whites were non-British, and did not share British standards or desires. This complication led to war, and the war (which to its British pro-tagonists was the only way in which to deal with a self-righteous Boer dictator and muddler) was seen by the rest of Europe and by British liberals as a piece of bullying of the weak by the strong. The very act of waging a war in this climate of opinion denuded imperialism of some of its moral content.

Complacency was further reduced when attention was diverted from the cause of the war to the way in which it was being fought. Its course revealed an unimagined degree of military muddle and inefficiency; the war cost Britain three years of effort, £222,000,000 of money and 450,000 troops for the purpose of quelling a population of only 87,000 combatant Boers. Next, the stage called pacification led to more moral self-questioning about burnt farms and concentration camps for women and children; finally the Peace of Vereeniging was secured only by abandoning a moral principle—that now known as the equality of human rights—and agreeing that the natives should be enfranchised only after the whites became self-governing, thereby surrendering their fate into other hands. The shock of these discoveries was great for a nation that, according to an analyst in the *National Review*,

> did not question itself, did not set its house in order, accepted its own prowess as beyond dispute and only awoke to indignation when its arms were dishonoured.[1]

Traditional power is resilient. Reaction to the shock produced new policies including an alliance with Japan, an African bargain struck with France, and a naval and military reorganization in the course of which the Committee of Imperial Defence was inaugurated in 1904. On the imperial front, it set going two new and vigorous but contrary streams of thought—one imperialist, for which Milner's celebrated kindergarten was a source, and one anti-imperialist, inaugurated by J. A. Hobson.

At the beginning of the century, the school of thought that Milner fathered was still thinking chiefly of the colonies of British stock. The British people, wrote his follower, John Buchan, was "hungering and thirsting for a living faith". The imperial spirit could be given new life if the public in general could be fired with enthusiasm for a concept that had long been the province of the few—of aristocratic pro-consuls and younger sons eager for a taste of danger. It was a mistake to think of imperialism simply as painting more territory red; enough of the map was red already. The point of importance was Britain's place in the world—best preserved by improving the spirit of the peoples already flying the Union Jack, and turning their feeling of kinship into an imperial patriotism.

A popular version of these ideas can be studied in a Buchan symposium of 1906 called *A Lodge in the Wilderness*—a period piece now forgotten, though it was reprinted in 1916 in the flush of imperial solidarity created by the war. It describes a group of imaginary people born within the political and social pale (some of the prototypes are obvious), who are hand-picked by a hero modelled on Rhodes for a house-party on an escarpment in East Africa. They represent the whole range of empire builders— politicians, pro-consuls, traders, men who can pass as natives or stay *impis* with a word. They spend the day shooting lions and visiting chieftains, but as soon as night falls settle to the real business of their meeting, which is to decide how to fire the empire with their spirit:

> The average man [says one of them], may be described as a confused imperialist. He wants to make the most of the heritage bequeathed to him; his imagination fires at its possibilities; but he is still very ignorant and shy, and he has no idea how to set about the work. The first of imperial duties is to instruct him.[2]

Thought along these lines led in 1909 to the foundation of *The Round Table*—a periodical and a study-group which have played a role in British imperial affairs that has never yet been properly analysed or described.

The opposite line of thought was set in train by J. A. Hobson's book of 1902 called *Imperialism*, the theme of which was grimmer and less easily adapted to romance than the Buchan theories, but which suited the puzzled mood of many intellectuals of his day. Hobson thought that empire was the product of surplus savings for which capitalists could find no profitable use at home. He argued that since these tycoons saw no reason to redistribute the national income, they must find outlets for their money abroad, thereby inducing governments to hurry after them and protect them, and to enter into rivalry with other imperialists. Hobson despaired of stopping this process; he thought it so profitable to a minority of capitalists that they would be sure to come to some mutual arrangement to live off Asia and Africa, and would strike bargains rather than go to war; he predicted that their next meal would be China.

Hobson was wrong not only about China, but about imperial motives, and so were some other anti-imperialist prophets in the years immediately before the First World War, notably H. N. Brailsford in *The War of Steel and Gold*. Their mistake (which was repeated when people thought that Hitler could be appeased by a sop of colonies) was their belief that men go to war for money, and not for power. But Hobson was right on many points; he foresaw, for instance, that market forces in the under-developed world would, unless someone controlled them, render the rich richer and the poor poorer than before. Many of his thoughts seem commonplace in the light of subsequent experience, but they were original and ahead of their time, and his theories as a whole made an impression in rarified intellectual atmospheres such as that of the Fabian Society. Here they dovetailed with the reflections of political scientists such as Graham Wallas about the stirrings of Asian nationalism, and provoked week-end discussion in the studies of the Webbs and the J. L. Hammonds, Bertrand Russell and Bernard Shaw. On a less intellectual but no less thoughtful level, they stimulated the beginnings of socialist debate on lines that led, thirty years later, to inauguration by a Labour Government of the Colonial Development Fund of 1929.

Hobson was an economist and a dry writer. In the *Encyclopaedia Britannica* of 1911, he is singled out, among authors cited in the bibliography on the British Empire, as the lone "anti-imperialist". His theme got no help from romance and little from satire, for the anti-imperialist rhymes of Hilaire Belloc about bravery against blacks ("Whatever happens we have got The maxim gun and they have not") and about the derring-do of the Randlords ("When Beit came striding through the flood And fair young Albu died") were read, like his *Cautionary Tales*, for their comic rather than their moral value. Reinforcement from popular writers did not materialize until the Agadir incident of 1911, when the Kaiser's behaviour over Morocco suggested to the general public that land-grabbing was about to start again, conducted by more empires than before, competing for less of Africa. Until then, the other pillar of support for anti-imperialism had been the oriental traveller who had fallen in love with some Eastern people, and therefore constituted himself its champion against oppression by founding a protection society, and jogging Parliament about it. Professor E. G. Browne of Cambridge did so for the Persians, Wilfrid Scawen Blunt for the Egyptians, Aubrey Herbert for the Albanians; some people took up cudgels for the Turks who, although composing an empire of their own, were being eaten alive by bigger empires out of greed for railway concessions.

The Morocco crisis of 1911 mixed the strains of imperialism and foreign policy. It proved beyond doubt that rivalries in Africa were inseparable from the European struggle for power and alignments; it also brought to light the secret clauses about Egypt and Morocco in the Anglo-French agreement of 1904. It therefore drew into the anti-imperialist fray a number of readable writers on foreign affairs who commanded more of a public than Hobson had ever been able to do. Several of them belonged to the breed that A. J. P. Taylor has christened *The Troublemakers*—that is, effective fighters against the Establishment whose novel thoughts become the commonplaces of a generation later. Between the Agadir crisis and the war, these men campaigned in *The Nation*, the *Manchester Guardian*, *The Economist* and other public places against secret bargains, imperial gambles on Moroccan iron ore or Persian railways, and barter of the Portuguese colonies—a fight that carried most of them, soon after war broke out, into the Union of Democratic Control under the leadership of a tireless campaigner, E. D. Morel.

It is not easy to measure the amount of attention commanded either by the idealistic imperialism of *A Lodge in the Wilderness*, or by the anti-imperialists, before 1914. In terms of numbers, neither had a great following, for among the people who gave any thought at all to empire, the Jubilee sensation of imperial glory and good fortune survived. *Punch*, in December 1901, was still arguing against European entanglements, and showed Britannia dancing with her colonies at an international ball ("After all, my dear, we can always dance together, you and I"); and the Conservatives who founded Empire Day in 1904 fixed it on May 24 to commemorate the birthday of the good old Queen. Parents gave their children imperialist best-sellers by G. A. Henty to read—*With Buller in Natal* and *With Roberts to Kandahar*—and at the coronation in 1911, the hero pointed out to strangers was Kitchener, of the South African blockhouses and of Khartoum. But on the whole Edwardian England was busy with other topics—new social legislation, naval rivalry, the problem of alliances and with whom to make them, and always and above all, Ireland. "Ulster will fight and Ulster will be right"; because a civil war that would have split the British army was averted owing to the outbreak of world war, people have forgotten how nearly Ireland became the Algeria of 1914, rebel generals and all.

The great mass of the nation missed both the neo-imperialist and the anti-imperialist message. So did many of the writers. Georgian anthologies, including those of the war poets, never mention empire as an ideal. Most young men of the time seem to have been unimpressed by the controversies that raged in learned journals for years after the Boer War. Their attitude is well summed up by Rickie in E. M. Forster's novel of 1907, *The Longest Journey*.

Spellbound by a view where "the fibres of England meet in Wilt-
shire", he remembers that:

> People at that time were trying to think imperially. Rickie
> wondered how they did it, for he could not imagine a place
> larger than England.[3]

Between the Boer War and the First World War, the two bodies
that did most consciously to develop the empire were the civil
service and the missionary societies. Most of their representatives
were fully absorbed by day-to-day tasks of management; they got on,
simultaneously, with the tasks of earning their living and improving
the lot of their charges without much leisure for worry about the
future effect of the changes they were bringing about. But some
of them, and some of the statesmen they advised, were peering
ahead—for instance, John Morley at the India Office with Edwin
Montagu as his under-secretary; 1909 is the year of the first short
step, which the British took voluntarily, towards self-rule in India.
Among such workers, the doubts generated by the Boer War were
transient because of the number of colonial tasks to be carried out
for people too ignorant to set up good or healthy living for themselves. These tasks were executed by men in search of a livelihood,
by no means all of whom thought of themselves as performing an
imperial service, but who, for lack of money and good communications with home, discovered more about local civilizations, and
forged closer links with them, than Europeans are wont to do
today. At the top of this pyramid of service stood George V, who
hated "abroad"—in the sense of the continent—and loved the years
in the Navy that had carried him round the English-speaking
world, and who told Lord Esher just after his accession that he
meant "to do for the Empire what King Edward did for the peace
of Europe".

The First World War forced every intelligent person to take an
interest in politics. It also altered most people's scale of values. It
brought anti-imperialists to acquiesce in additions to territory and
to bargain for spheres of influence; even they now found the idea
of empire precious and heart-warming.

The imperial idealists gathered strength for a new leap forward,
propelled by a mass of evidence that the white empire was one
and that, over and above the Indian army fighting under British
officers, Indian princes were ready to supply troops to fight in a

European cause. The preface to the 1916 reprint of Buchan's *A Lodge in the Wilderness* proclaims that:

> We understand now as we have never understood before that our empire is a mystic whole . . . and our wisest minds are now given to the task of devising a mechanism of union adequate to this spiritual unity.[4]

Temporarily, they did so; an Imperial War Cabinet was founded in 1917. But it led to no imperial peace cabinet; it was followed by Imperial Conferences that pointed no royal road to unity, and that produced—in a vain effort to keep Ireland and South Africa within the fold—the watery compromise of the Statute of Westminster. The obituary notice of the work in this context of men like Philip Kerr (later Lord Lothian) and Lionel Curtis is written by Professor A. P. Thornton in his *The Imperial Idea and its Enemies*. They were men who

> were to spend many of [their] days trying to add cubits to the stature of their political contemporaries; if never quite failing to influence, never quite succeeding in guiding, and themselves remaining (though often in high positions) on the fringes of the country's political life, eccentrics and seers whose prestige was never commensurate with their powers.[5]

In the short run of the First World War, they were uppermost, but in the long one the anti-imperialists outdistanced them, sometimes in most unexpected ways. Anti-imperialism was in eclipse while war fever lasted, but emerged in good heart as soon as there was talk of peace. For it had meanwhile applied its now formidable store of brainpower to the problem of forestalling another such war by eliminating war's known and suspected causes, among which it included secret diplomacy, arms deals, colonial barter and annexations.

Its power-house was the Union of Democratic Control ("We refuse to recognize the right of the Executive to put the intellect of the citizen in chains") with E. D. Morel as its main generator and thinkers such as Hobson, Brailsford, Normal Angell, Bertrand Russell and the mayor of Stepney, Clement Attlee, in his train. Its attitude to the conduct of war is beside the present point; its attitude to organizing peace is important for it helped to produce the League of Nations and so, inadvertently, sabotaged the ambition of the Round Table group to found new imperial machinery. For the League called for loyalty to the world as a whole; when the British dominions (and, by an anomaly India, though it was not yet independent) became individual and separate members of the League, family unity was unavoidably and irrevocably impaired.

Before the end of the war, the U.D.C. was one of an army of people and institutions, all for their different reasons wanting the same prophylactics for removing the causes of war—a League of Nations, self-determination, arms control, supervision of colonial rule. Marching alongside were Liberals such as Grey and Gilbert Murray, Conservative internationalists such as Robert Cecil, the Labour Party and the Trades Union Congress. On the narrow front of anti-imperialism, the biggest acquisition to their strength came from an odd assortment of powerful foreigners—from socialist congresses conducting the first nervous meeting with Germans; from President Wilson, preaching self-determination and no annexations, and from Lenin. Hobson's highbrow argument, which had for years passed over the heads of the broad masses, had at last found its hot gospeller. Lenin, drawing on Hobson and adding an injection of Marx's prediction of the course of capitalism, published in 1917 his book also called *Imperialism*. Writing as a successful revolutionary against the most oppressive of empires, he commanded an audience all over the world. To Hobson's original theory about capitalism as a cause of empire-building, he added his prophecy that the colonial people would rebel. The development that he did not foresee was the extent to which some democratic empires would trim their sails to forestall the rebellion that he foretold.

Two major changes brought about by the 1914–18 war eliminate the white dominions from the anti-imperialist agenda. One, already referred to, was their promotion to individual membership of the League of Nations, with a consequent reduction of former ties. The other was Britain's loss of naval supremacy in the Pacific, which rendered Australasia and the west coast of Canada dependent for speedy defence, in the event of general war, upon the goodwill of a foreign navy—that of the United States. From 1919 onwards, men who worried about the management of empire from a base in Britain begin to dwell almost exclusively upon Asia and Africa; dominion is over palm only, and it is in this field that zest for empire ebbs and flows on the way to its decline. The conception that Asians and Africans have an identity that is worth preserving, and must be helped to preserve it, has gained ground; the matter in debate is how to do this while retaining their affection and confidence and—more important in many eyes—their reliability for imperial purposes that may be as much to their advantage as to Britain's own.

The anti-imperialists had hoped for a universal League of Nations. To their dismay, the organization that materialized turned out to be a League of Victors, and a League that lacked not merely the vanquished powers and Russia, but the United States; the hopes they had placed in the tempering influence of President Wilson were dashed. But they had some grounds for satisfaction. The League was different from the old Concert of Europe, and by its very nature began to weaken the fabric of colonial power. As we have seen, the blessing it gave to self-determination made Asians tingle; it also—to do Europe justice—made British imperialists think out new theories. So did the Russian revolution, with its transformation of the northern half of Asia from a dumb and dominated area into a pulpit for Lenin. For instance, *The Round Table*, turning from the dominions to the colonies, printed in September 1919 and September 1920 two noteworthy articles on the law of minimum goodwill. In the first, called "The Harvest of Victory" an anonymous author (believed to be Philip Kerr) argued that it was the duty of a democratic empire to export self-government to all its component races, or else it must admit to democratic failure. The second (known to be by T. E. Lawrence) was called "The Outlook in the Middle East" and specified ways of catching the attention of, and imposing responsibility upon, its peoples, both in their own interests and Britain's. With percipience, Lawrence put his finger on the local milieu that was and is the key factor of successful dis-imperialism:

> In pursuing such courses we will find our best helpers not in our former most obedient subjects, but among those now most active in agitating against us, for it will be the intellectual leaders of the people who will serve the purpose, and these are not the philosophers nor the rich, but the demagogues and the politicians.
>
> The alternative is to hold on to them with ever-lessening force, till the anarchy is too expensive, and we let go.[6]

Even as he wrote, a live sample of the alternative was maturing on Britain's doorstep. The success of Sinn Fein, and British inability to quell a movement for self-determination within the British Isles, led to a loss of imperial nerve greater than most people cared to admit. The setback was the greater because the nature of the Irish treaty of January 1922, was not lost on "abroad"; it excited much comment in India. Later in the same year, an incident in Turkey further stirred Asian thought, and disturbed British peace of mind. When Mustafa Kemal and his nationalists, advancing westward out of Anatolia, challenged Allied arrangements for Constantinople and the Straits, the British found themselves facing him single-handed because his thrust happened at the height of the Anglo-French quarrel over whom to back—Greek or Nationalist Turk—in Anatolia and Thrace. Lloyd George and Churchill checked Kemal at Chanak in September 1922 by a piece of bluff, but bluff that ran the empire too close for the public taste to the risk of war. A symbol of public doubt as to how far overseas responsibilities were always British responsibilities was soon available. At the general election of October 1922, Lloyd George fell, amongst other counts over Chanak, and Winston Churchill was defeated at Dundee by E. D. Morel, the U.D.C. leader.

As we have seen, the mandates system of the League of Nations was converted by the victorious empires into a cloak for a good measure of imperialism, or, as Salvador de Madariaga once admitted that he had thought it at the outset, "the worst fig-leaf in the whole show". Nevertheless, it passed muster with most anti-imperialists for the first ten years after the peacemaking, largely because the world was living in illusory security which few people attributed to its two real causes—the voluntary withdrawal of the United States and Russia from the League fray, and the consequent con-centration of power in the hands of empires that wanted no change in the *status quo*. The mandates system was acceptable because it seemed to temper the old colonialism by offering dependent peoples someone to turn to; and up to a point it did so. For one thing, it assumed that the tutelage was temporary; for another, it restricted exploitation by establishing the Open Door; it also set up a public forum before which a mandatory power had to appear when sum-moned, and face an examination that was on the whole conducted without bias, and that could be a gruelling experience for the representative of the mandatory power. As time went on, an accumulation of these innovations dealt glancing blows at the colonial system proper because they implied the existence and worth of indigenous institutions and qualities; it suggested that the relationship of the European to the Asian or African was not always and in all respects that of the polished to the rough diamond, but rather an adjustment between two civilizations at different stages of development. Hitherto, only territories containing at least some white settlers had progressed from colonial to independent status; now, Asians and Africans were being marshalled into a queue at the barrier.

Yet a worldwide Empire with a range of 500 million subjects to consider cannot change direction overnight. Each successive British Government as it comes to power finds that more has gone before than it imagined—too much to alter quickly. So that, in mandated areas as well as in colonies, the spread of Sinn Fein tactics was nipped in the bud by classic methods, and curbed by them for a generation. Even a one-time pacifist like Ramsay MacDonald discovered, on assuming office, that a strong line must often be taken, and found himself thundering to Allenby, and in opposition to Zaghlul, that

> no British Government can divest itself wholly, even in favour of an ally, of its interest in guarding such a vital link in British communications [as the Suez Canal].[7]

Cabinets might move with the times, and yield concessions, but not capitulate to Asian or African demagogues, either because this would unsettle India, or wake the Sudan, or because moderates must not be let down, or because to hesitate or quit might produce unpalatable results such as Turks in Basra, or Frenchmen in Gaza. Modern imperialism, whether by sea or land, is a game of spillikins in which the moving of one piece is difficult without disturbing the others.

After the First World War, there were, however, some advocates of discarding territory. On grounds of cost, a campaign against holding the mandates for Iraq and Palestine was opened in 1922. In the first place, it was sponsored by the Beaverbrook and Rothermere newspapers; out of anxiety to get rid of Lloyd George they were ready to exploit any topic that would serve. Some of their contentions were ridiculous ("Why do we stay in Mesopotamia"— "*Cherchez la femme*" . . . Miss Gertrude Bell . . . "the Diana of the desert") but, in years when the two British mandates in the Middle East were costing the taxpayer some tens of millions, they gained a hearing and their campaign spread to other quarters. In March

1923, the *Morning Post* reasoned that it was "impossible to jettison Mesopotamia because of Turkey", but urged getting rid of "the *damnosa heritas* of Palestine before we become too embroiled"; in 1924, speakers from the Labour benches described Iraqi refusal to ratify the proposed Anglo-Iraqi treaty as "a heaven-sent opportunity to get out", and in the *Empire Review* of July 1923 Churchill argued that it was better to spend on "what we've got" than on "fumbling with Mesopotamia and reaching out for Persia". But this triggering off of doubts and fears stopped as soon as running Iraq and Palestine became less expensive; the cost had fallen to £5·7 million by the financial year 1924–5.

A second line of attack concentrated on the undemocratic way in which the victors had disregarded the wishes of the inhabitants. In June 1922, a motion against the Palestine mandate was carried in the Lords on the ground that it broke the McMahon promise, and in 1924 both Liberal and Labour writers contended that it was wrong to invite the British Parliament

> to ratify a treaty the acceptance of which has been secured by improper methods. This should be rejected, [said *The Westminster Gazette*], as it does not represent the views of the people of Iraq.[8]

In the final decade of belief in world progress, two conflicting strains of imperial thought—one confident, one doubtful—can be picked up in any year. On the one hand are brave attempts to rally zest, such as the Wembley Exhibition, and votes in the House of Lords that the right place from which to run Egypt is Cairo; on the other, League of Nations Union meetings in distress about continued bullying by great powers in China, and agog for the march-past promised by Professor Alfred Zimmern in his book *The Third British Empire*, which was to consist of a single great community on the road to self-government, whites in front, browns in the middle and blacks behind.

The first major onslaught of British public opinion upon the imperial idea happened in the nineteen-thirties, and was brought about by two outside agencies—the one, Gandhi; the other, the Axis powers.

As a stimulant to doubt and uncertainty, nothing succeeds like non-success. Inability to quell Gandhi's civil disobedience movement, with its implication that here was an Indian who could keep his temper, and make it unbecoming and fruitless for the British to lose theirs, both baffled them and caused them to question their competence. Might he be right when he told them with decorum that they lacked the knowledge and philosophy to handle India's religious and social problems? Was imprisonment an effective answer to his creed? Lord Cromer had once said that

> the British . . . possess in a very high degree the power of acquiring the sympathy and confidence of any primitive races with which they are brought in contact;[9]

but had admitted that they "succeed less well when once the full tide of education has set in". Could he be right also? In 1936, the British Government answered the problem with an India Act that instituted almost complete self-government in the provinces, and would have given a measure of it at the centre had Congress accepted it.

Their perplexity about recalcitrance in India was crowned by a second blow in Asia—Japan's aggression against a chaotic China. At the time, very few people interpreted this act as likely to impair the fabric of the British Empire; the whole of public attention was concentrated upon the effect upon the League of Nations of failure to deal with defiance by a great power. The minds of League supporters were in bad training for coherent thinking; they had just spent three years in a dream inaugurated by the Briand-Kellogg Pact of 1928 for the total renunciation of war, and they were getting ready for the "immediate and supreme objective" of disarmament. British thinking was further confused by the world economic crisis, with its attendant domestic crises—departure from the gold standard, the naval near-mutiny at Invergordon, the formation of a National Government. In any case it was difficult to act effectively, or collectively, in an area in which the United States and the Soviet Union—two non-members of the League— were the paramount powers. So Japan snatched a win in Manchuria in 1931, and with it a piece of the touchstone of empire.

The confusion into which this failure threw British thinking about overseas commitments is well illustrated by the course of the acrimonious "peace or war" debate that followed it. For instance, at a by-election at East Fulham in 1933, a Conservative campaigning for rearmament (and by implication also for imperial self-reliance) dropped a majority of 14,000 and lost the seat to Labour by a further 5,000 votes—votes cast "against" armaments and "for"

collective security as if the two were alternatives, instead of comple-
mentary. Again, when a poll called the "Peace Ballot" was held in
1935, the questions posed failed to make this relationship plain,
and enabled 11 million people to vote for British membership of
the League of Nations, whereas only 6·7 million were in favour
of using military sanctions. Everyone, Conservative as well as
Labour, is to blame for three years of argument at cross purposes;
even politicians who saw plain held their tongues because to tell
the truth was to be disbelieved and would be, as Baldwin once
admitted, to lose votes. The awakening to the connexion between
sanctions and rearmament did not come until a second dissatisfied
power—Italy— had made a strike at the *status quo*. Distance had
blunted the impact of Japan; Mussolini, in seizing Ethiopia, struck
nearer home and closer to sensitive parts of the British Empire.

Before Mussolini used force in 1935, the prospect of Italian
expansion in Africa did not seem too daunting to British imperialists. The phrase "peaceful change" was in fashion, and Ethiopia's
lack of control over its borderlands was a nuisance in Kenya and
the Horn of Africa. In 1935, a confidential British inter-departmental report on interests in East Africa (the Maffey Report, which
can be consulted because it was somehow acquired and published
by a Fascist newspaper) concluded that

> there was no important British interest in Abyssinia with the
> exception of Lake Tsana, the waters of the Blue Nile and certain
> tribal grazing rights.[10]

Pathetically narrow though this view may look in the light of after-
events, it seems to have been general at the time, for the report
added (according to the Italian summary) that imperial defence
interests would be affected only in the remote and improbable
context of a war with Italy.

This complacent thinking continued after the start of the
Ethiopian war; three days after Mussolini attacked, Amery told
his Birmingham constituents that "I am not prepared to send a
single Birmingham lad to his death for the sake of Abyssinia". The
British Government's speech of sturdy support for the League in
September, made to the Assembly by its Foreign Secretary, Sir
Samuel Hoare, seems to have been partly an attempt to bluff
Mussolini, and partly a wish to capitalize public devotion to the
League before an imminent general election. It was not, as

foreigners believed, an attempt to preserve the British Empire on the cheap and at collective expense, for in official eyes the Empire was not even threatened. The notion that a threat to it might develop does not seem to have worried the Baldwin Government until it was awakened by a cold douche—the public furore created by the notorious Hoare-Laval plan of December 1935.

This plan partitioned Ethiopia with nineteenth-century aplomb. Italy was to have part outright, and another part as a "zone of economic expansion and settlement". The Baldwin Government, which had won the election on a ticket of support for the League, blanched when it learned what its Foreign Secretary had done. But as he was ill and had gone on from Paris to Switzerland, it decided to uphold an absent colleague. Public opinion thought the opposite. Its famous rejection of the plan was the outcome of two emotions—one, disgust at the winning of an election by false pretences, the other, dismay at a bland return to the secret negotiations and sharings of Africa that it had thought were done with for ever.

But this sudden, immense exhalation of public anti-imperialism had no sequel. Exhausted either by the effort of making it, or by disappointment that it did not put things right, the British failed to follow it through by demanding collective measures to stop the war. Mussolini therefore demolished Ethiopia. Yet the gesture, though so negative, was not entirely without effect; it helped to divert attention from Europe and Hitler on to Africa and empire, and to bring to light one awkward aspect of British weakness:

> The small nations [wrote Sir Abe Bailey from South Africa]— and the Dominions, relatively speaking, are small nations—are once again uneasy, and some of them are in despair.[11]

The sobering thought occurred to many people that those in despair were bound to include the Empire's coloured peoples. Finally, the defeat of Ethiopia by European force brought at least half of a baffled and angry Britain up against the reality that collective intention was not enough, and that in the last resort the security of the weak depended upon the armaments of the strong. The people who reached this conclusion were helped to it by Hitler's reoccupation of the Rhineland on March 7, 1936; they included groups ranging from confirmed imperialists on the one hand— Churchill, Amery, Lloyd and Grigg—to the trade unions on the other; both of these began to support rearmament without the

ambiguity and backward looks at the Geneva spirit that character-
ized many members of both their political parties.

At the time of the Hoare-Laval fiasco, anti-imperialist critics
of Britain—Americans as well as Nazis and Fascists—were wont to
remind English friends that much of the British Empire had been
conquered by Mussolini's means. To this home-truth, the short
answer was that times had changed. But those who uttered it were
brought to wonder whether the date of an imperial acquisition
entirely altered its moral and material significance, and this thought
acquired currency because it was quickened by nagging reminders
from Hitler about the unfairness and unwisdom of the Treaty of
Versailles. Ever since J. M. Keynes had retired from the British
delegation in Paris in 1919 to publish *The Economic Consequences
of the Peace*, there had been qualms about the wisdom of that
treaty. Now, people remembered that it had deprived Germany of
colonies, and Hitler's claim that this act had robbed them also of
"bread and honour" fell on half-cocked ears. This is the explanation
of the mushroom growth of two new notions that debased the
imperial idea—the one, that the hunger of the dissatisfied powers
might be assuaged if arrangements were made to give them freer
access to raw materials, the other, that "peaceful change" might
suitably include the placing of more colonies under mandate, or
even a redistribution of colonies. A strange assortment of thinkers
put forward these ideas in their hope of avoiding the trying task
of deciding where to draw the line about fighting for rights; its
very variety reveals the extent to which imperial fervour had
dwindled by 1936.

The short answer to powers claiming a right to colonies was
that these filled no economic gaps; that apart from rubber and
tin (largely concentrated in Malaya and the Netherlands Indies)
all the world's main supplies of strategic raw materials were located
in sovereign states. But since honour as well as bread was Hitler's
target, this argument sounded thin, and peace-lovers pressed forward with other propositions. Lord Lothian "would not rule out
the possibility" of transfer of territory; a number of League of
Nations supporters—Arthur Salter, Arnold Toynbee, Norman
Bentwich, Leonard Barnes—suggested some form of extension to
colonies of the kind of mandates system that guaranteed equality
of economic opportunity and the prohibition of military bases; one
confirmed imperialist, Amery, suggested that the European nations
west of Russia should, with their colonies, co-operate in a mutual

preference system, and abandon most-favoured-nation rights for the purpose. Barnes was for forming an Empire low tariff group open to other countries to join on the same terms. But this short burst of pamphlets and articles subsided because Hitler soon made it plain that his "Reich Colonial League" was a sideshow, and that his real ambitions lay in Europe. If the suggestions had any permanent result, it was still further to reduce the emotional content of colonialism.

Imperial fervour had slumped, but once it had cause to rally, there was life in it yet; it burst into flame in 1939, and flared again while Britain debated joining the European Common Market in the nineteen-sixties. Hitler's war was, like the Kaiser's, a tonic to it, not merely in terms of mutual defence, but of exhilaration. At the Teheran Conference in 1943, it was a cause of discussion and head-shaking between two anti-imperialists, Roosevelt and Stalin. We know now that they paid it more attention than it merited, in view of the degree to which British inclination was declining, and British strength was being impaired by the war, but at the time they had some justification for thinking Britain forceful and un-regenerate. Roosevelt, at least, had seen many splendidly full-blooded memoranda ("If we have to quit Gibraltar we must immediately take the Canaries"), and, as we know, Marx and Lenin had failed to warn Stalin that the imperial technique of the democracies might change.

In 1939–40, the initial emotion that suffused the whole British Empire was the obvious one created by common danger. But others were at once added to it—in Britain, a pang of conscience about failure to share social progress with peoples who were now offering to shed their blood, and the passing of the Colonial Development and Welfare Act in the black days of 1940 as an earnest of better intentions for the future; in India, the impatience to be done with Europe that led to open rebellion (in contrast to passive resistance) in 1942.

But the strongest impulses to rally to the imperial cause sprang from the need to meet attack—not merely the physical attack from Japan which precipitated the Cripps Mission to India, but the verbal attack from the enemy and—much more galling—from the United States. American criticism of empire forced the United Kingdom and the Dominions not only to formulate, but to utter, thoughts previously held to be embarrassing about the nature of the connexion with one another, and with Asian and African fellow-combatants. For years, British critics had dwelt on the failings of empire, often enough in order to get them remedied, and had said little about its successes. Now they found themselves being confounded out of their own mouths, and were forced to shed their diffidence, and to retort. "Look at the contribution that we are making to the cause of freedom," in effect they said. "See how much the greater because we stand together. Should England fall, we shall fight on from the New World and Africa. We are looking ahead to the time when the whole world will have to try and improve itself, and at that stage our community will, on account of combining unity with diversity, have a great contribution to make to the pattern. Mistakes in the pace of growth we may have made, but at least we are all marching along the same road." The best current statement of the case was made by the Australian Professor W. K. Hancock, in a short Penguin book called *Argument of Empire*, long since out of print, but worth reading at any time.

This renewal of pride and resilience was mitigated by disaster. For the first time since the eighteenth century, British defenders surrendered colonies—Hongkong, Malaya, Burma, Somaliland. Rebellions broke out in Iraq, India, and, briefly, in Transjordan. Apprehension might well have been increased by worry about future Asian and African demands, or about future British penury. When the Beveridge Report came out in 1943, British propaganda services hastened to make the most of it as evidence of confidence, social conscience and vitality. The corollary that the home country would be expected to contribute to improvements of the same kind in teeming and penniless colonies was brushed aside; at the time, most people in Britain had other things to think about, and awareness of the new contents of the white man's burden did not dawn until after victory.

The decline of confidence about empire is not an isolated phenomenon. It is part of a contemporary decline of certainty about a whole range of human practices, such as prayer, or judgement of art forms, or Communism, or civilization as represented by the American way of life.

To the men of my youth [said Gilbert Murray when he gave the Romanes Lecture of 1935 and called it *Then and Now*], Western, especially British civilization was simply the right road of human progress; other civilizations, if one could call them civilizations at all, were just false roads or mistakes . . . (Now) there is a loss of confidence, a loss of faith, an omnipresent haunting fear.[12]

Where our fathers went to the priest for exhortation, our children go to the psychiatrist. The gulf between Kitchener's "consciousness of the inherent superiority of the European that has won for us India" and Attlee's assessment of Gandhi—"a combination of saint and astute politician—Gladstone must have been a bit like him" is as great as the difference between G. F. Watts and Graham Sutherland or Newbolt's *Vitaï Lampada* and the Auden-Isherwood *Ascent of F6*.

In a Middle Eastern context, this break-up of confidence can be seen to coincide with the years between the British zenith in Egypt —which was when the Anglo-Egyptian Sudan was added to the British safety-zone in 1899—and the British exodus from Palestine in 1948.

7

THE YEARS OF IMPOTENCE: 1945-54

AT the end of the war with Germany in May 1945, the British were astride the Middle East, where their position looked as strong as ever. British strategic motives for holding on to the area had been vindicated—so much so as to stand in a class by themselves:

> There are other interests: oil in particular, commerce, air routes and a large number of British subjects [reported a contemporary study group of experts]; but except perhaps for the first, they are of relatively minor importance.[1]

British strength seemed all the greater because Britain had manned the Middle Eastern fronts almost single-handed, and because the Middle Eastern peoples had bowed to the inevitable and been co-operative; only now and then had they disturbed British security behind the lines. British troops were everywhere and to all appearances could keep within bounds the local restiveness that had been increasing since the end of the war in Africa. Great Britain appeared to be unchallenged and to enjoy the advantages that enable a great power to behave generously.

The Labour victory in the British election of July 1945 seemed to increase the chances that the Middle East would achieve satisfaction of its main ambitions. Except for the Palestine Arabs, who were alarmed at known Labour leanings towards Zionism, everyone in Asia and Africa thought that a new spirit was bound to prevail in London, bringing new social policies and an end to coercion of the weak by the strong. These hopes were justified; Labour ministers were soon making statements about having "no desire to retain unwilling peoples", as Attlee said of Burma, and wishing "to leave behind for ever the idea of one country dominating another". The author of this remark, Ernest Bevin, was the new Foreign Secretary and possessed attributes which suggested that he would pay attention to under-privileged peoples; he had begun life in great poverty, knew the kind of effort needed to win a living wage, and was a man of horse sense, drive, and huge confidence in the experience as a negotiator that he had gained as a trade union leader. He made it plain that he intended to apply his socialist convictions to foreign policy:

> Machiavelli in diplomacy is buried. It is a question of producing a real harmony between the growing aspirations of the whole of the masses of the people of the world and a higher standard of life. It is in this that diplomacy can fulfil its proper function.[2]

But British strength was apparent, not real, and these high hopes were soon frustrated. In Britain, the exchequer was empty and people were prostrate to a degree unimagined by countries that had been out of the war-zone for over two years. A final spurt of British energy had been devoted to switching all effort from Europe to a supposedly long war with Japan, and had suddenly had to be switched back again. Then came a body-blow—abrupt American cancellation of Lend-Lease at the end of the Japanese war. With no time to re-organize and no latitude for bargaining, the British Cabinet was obliged to negotiate a loan from the United States on most stringent terms, including one virtually impossible condition —a promise of early return to sterling convertibility. Some terse sentences later uttered by Attlee are a reminder of the parlous state of the nation;

> We had to have a loan. Without it it would have been impossible to exist, certainly without hardships on a scale no one had a right to ask of the British people at the end of a long war. The Americans thought we'd over-stated the case. We had not . . . You can criticize the loan and the arrangements surrounding it— and we fought inch by inch throughout the negotiations—but the fact remains that we could not do without it. The critics could shout. We had to run things.[3]

British troubles did not end at home. Crowds of starving people were roaming round a wrecked Europe, and had to be fed. All over the world were prisoners to be collected, troops to be re-patriated, mines to be swept, ships recovered from war service, before there was a chance of getting British civilian employment and Britain's export industries back on to an earning basis. The first job for the Cabinet was to organize British economic survival at a tolerable living standard, and the next to save Europe from famine and anarchy. By comparison with scenes near home, conditions in the Middle East looked comfortable, and that is why, after the Second World War as after the first, Egyptian and other claims to attention were fobbed off until more pressing matters had been dealt with.

Prostration might merely have retarded a new British deal for the Middle East. Another handicap—worry about the peace aims of Soviet Russia—blocked it altogether. From the time when the Soviet armies overran Eastern Europe early in 1945, it became clear to the men at the top in both Britain and America that the Russians were bent on setting up puppet governments of their own choosing in Poland and the Balkans, and ignoring the Declaration on Liberated Europe that had been extracted from them at Yalta. As soon as the fighting was over these anxieties increased because of differences over Germany—over reparations in particular. The Russians were determined to strip the Germans of assets from one side while the British and Americans were pouring in food, shelter and the necessities of life from the other. This Soviet pressure was directed to erecting a ring of buffer zones round Russia, and some of it fell on the Middle East—on Persia for Communist control of Persian Azerbaijan, and on Turkey for a base on the Black Sea Straits. By January 1946 the outlook in the eastern Mediterranean was black enough to cause President Truman to write in confidence to Byrnes, his Secretary of State, that:

> There isn't a doubt in my mind that Russia intends an invasion of Turkey and the seizure of the Black Sea Straits . . . I'm tired of babying the Soviets.[4]

The private papers of statesmen are full of such allusions but their letters and diaries are not immediately confided to the public. In 1945 most people in Britain and America had no conception of the disquiet felt by their leaders. No one enlightened public opinion because statesmen felt bound to keep silence in order to be sure of getting the Soviet Union into the United Nations and keeping it there; they also hoped for better relations sometime and somewhere on Russia's vast periphery. By popular standards the Russians were still heroes and saviours who had done more than their share of the fighting in Europe; thus anyone who criticized Soviet interference in other people's home politics raised instant protest; it came from quarters as far removed in outlook as the Keep Left group of the British Labour Party, and American anti-colonialists who still thought British imperialism the worst of evils. To recapture the state of opinion, it is only necessary to remember the surprise created when at Fulton, Missouri, in March 1946

Winston Churchill made a speech calling for an Anglo-American alliance against the Soviet Union. No one knew that he had secured the approval of Truman and Byrnes before he spoke, and large numbers of people in Britain wrote him off as a confirmed diehard lunging at an old enemy.

Worry about Soviet intentions passed right over the heads of most people in the Middle East. Except in Turkey and Persia, where Russian pressure was experienced at first hand and where—in keeping with character—the Turks defied it and the Persians adroitly circumvented it, people were unaware of menace; Egyptians, Jews and Arabs were all engrossed in their own concerns. A few Iraqi politicians appreciated the uneasiness among their immediate neighbours, because there is some traffic in ideas between Iraq and Persia on account of religious links, and because Iraqis of Ottoman vintage always kept up with friends in Turkey. (Nuri Pasha was often to be seen talking world politics from an armchair in the club at Istanbul.) But younger Iraqis knew no Turkish, and their thoughts were bent, as were those of most young men in the Middle East, on one of two topics—how to get rid of the British troops that were still milling round their countries, and how to engineer a Palestine settlement of their choice. None of them could credit British reasons for delay because the scene that met their eyes—British camps, British troop movements, and British officials pressing France to evacuate Syria and Lebanon—suggested that British power to make changes was unimpaired.

Egypt was the most restive of the Arabic-speaking states and was made more so by the British Government's failure quickly to remove its troops out of the Nile Valley and into the Suez Canal Zone prescribed in the 1936 treaty. One reason for this ill-omened pause was the sheer volume of the installations to be moved, and another, shortage of materials with which to build some necessary accommodation on the Canal; but a third was complacency. As so often before, too little heed was paid to warnings of inevitable Egyptian reactions and to the unwisdom of continuing to fly Union Jacks over barracks in Cairo (the Royal Air Force in Iraq was, by contrast, always kept out of sight). The Egyptians were full of a new sense of importance. British war measures had turned their capital into the hub of the whole Middle East, and, once they had been caused to look beyond the narrow confines of the Nile Valley, they had assumed a leading role with alacrity. They took for granted Egyptian primacy in the Arab League which, after much inter-Arab debate about sovereign rights, had finally come into existence in 1945. They were confident that Great Britain could not do less for them than it was doing for Syria, and were non-plussed and uncomprehending when, in answer to their claims, they received a note from London in January 1946 saying that the pre-war treaty of alliance had proved its worth, and that its revision must wait. They had no idea that a British Cabinet ready to be as generous to Egypt as to India could not treat them equally because India—lying behind the natural glacis of the Himalayas—was relatively far removed from the areas of Soviet pressures, which the Middle East— with its vulnerable oil-fields and precious lines of communication— was not.

Unsettled weather is no time for jettisoning treaties and the Labour Government felt bound to hang on to those that Britain possessed in the Middle East. The pre-war treaties with Egypt and Iraq each had more than ten years to run, and ministers hoped to be able to make some arrangement that would afford Britain continuing military rights in Palestine. When, beginning in the spring of 1946, the British at length found time to deal with Egyptian and Arab aspirations, the maximum they felt able to offer was revision of the old arrangements.

Bevin, with his confidence in his persuasive powers and his egalitarian cast of mind, was sure that something could be contrived between "equal partners", and he set about the job with vigour. But he overrated the cards in his hand. He was working under two handicaps. One was the sense of inequality that most small powers suffer when dealing with great; "we would like you better", once said an Iraqi minister, "if you were not so strong an ally". For this attitude Bevin was prepared; what he did not foresee was the degree to which it was exacerbated by decades of British power, exercised with bland assurance and, especially in Egypt, with disregard for local susceptibilities. His second handicap was net loss of British bargaining power. Britain needed concessions that the local peoples did not want to accord—British bases or, at minimum, a British right to re-enter Middle Eastern territory in the event of danger. But post-war Britain had nothing to offer in compensation. It could not offer money, because Britain had become a heavy war-debtor to the area, owing Iraq upwards of £70 million and Egypt nearly £400 million; or goods, because the United Kingdom had barely turned over to peace production; or dollars with which to buy American goods. When, making gestures that were almost quixotic in view of the shortage and poverty in Britain, dollars were made available to Persia or Iraq, the recipients had no conception of the degree of British effort and sacrifice that had been necessary. Bevin could not even offer armaments in the quantities on which Middle Eastern leaders had their eye, both because the world was in a state in which Britain might need all it possessed, and because of the drawbacks of arming anyone who had ambitions to fight in Palestine.

Between March 1946 and January 1948, the British Government attempted treaty re-negotiation everywhere. And everywhere it failed except in Transjordan—the one country so small and poor that even the impoverished British exchequer could offer something worth having. Transjordan (till 1946 an Amirate, but thereafter a kingdom, and later re-christened Jordan) was in any case the patrimony of King Abdullah, by now the doyen of the diminishing band of old Ottoman hands who appreciated Great Britain. But the treaty that Abdullah signed in 1946 exposed him to bitter criticism by the Arab League, because it was of pre-war pattern and gave away a twenty-five year right to station British troops in his territory. What business had he, asked his Arab critics, to be opening the door to Britain just as the Syrians and Lebanese had at last succeeded in closing it on France?

With an Egyptian prime minister, Sidqi Pasha, Bevin succeeded in hammering out a compromise on the basis of complete evacuation of British troops by September 1949 subject to two conditions —one, that rights claimed by the Egyptian crown over the Sudan should be subject to Sudanese consent; the other, establishment of an Anglo-Egyptian alliance that would produce combined military arrangements in the event of war. But the Egyptians disavowed both the agreement and Sidqi Pasha. Their ostensible reason for doing so was the proviso about the Sudan, but their real reason was the endemic one. Egypt wanted evacuation without conditions; no prime minister could consent to a continuing British alliance and survive.

In January 1948 the Iraqi nationalists administered a rebuff of the same pattern after Iraqi statesmen had signed a treaty of alliance with Britain—the Portsmouth Treaty—that gave the British a modicum of military rights in Iraq. In Iraq, as in Egypt, there were secondary reasons for public rejection of the treaty—a famine, mishandled publicity for an agreement signed in England, the climax towards which events were moving in Palestine. The

Egyptian bargain never came near to success; the Iraqi one nearly succeeded, partly through the long-standing difference of attitude to Britain, and partly because Iraq's geographical location renders some Iraqis more aware than other Arabs of the nature of Soviet foreign policy. But the end-product was identical in the two countries because the angry young men of the nineteen-twenties were now in middle-age, and neither they, nor anyone younger than they, would consider an agreement that fell short of evacuation and full independence.

The motive power behind the Foreign Office search for bases came from the Imperial General Staff. In 1946 its eye was on the disparity of strength between the Red Army and the Western forces in Europe, as well as on the Russian troops that were still in occupation of north Persia (the final withdrawal of Soviet troops from Persia took place on May 9). When, at the beginning of May, the British Chiefs of Staff consented to put political expediency before all else, and to offer evacuation to Egypt, they did so only because alternative Middle Eastern bases were available. By alternative bases, they meant not merely barracks and landing-grounds and the apparatus of G.H.Q., but storage and repair facilities of the kind available in Egypt; among their requirements were a good port, ample water supplies and a local labour corps. When the offer to evacuate Egypt was made, the two alternative sites they envisaged were Palestine as a whole, with its port, pipeline and refinery at Haifa, and—as a dump for heavier equipment that might be handier if stored in Africa than in Britain—a railway halt in Kenya called McKinnon Road. Where G.H.Q. was to go was still unsettled when the Egyptian treaty fell through. The Royal Air Force would have been content with Cyprus, but the army naturally favoured the mainland. But in 1946, Palestine was intended to be the main substitute for Suez; Libya, even if it were to become available, had not Palestine's natural or industrial assets. The soldiers therefore started on the enormous job of shifting square miles of war stores from Egypt to Palestine and Kenya.

The move began in spite of the fact that Palestine was already a scene of rebellion owing to British refusal to allow unlimited Jewish immigration; it was on July 22, 1946, that Jewish extremists blew up British military headquarters in the King David Hotel. But British army commanders are inured to unpopularity; they are ready to face an inordinate amount of local opposition and creation of inconvenience before they admit that a base is too hot to hold.

The movement of troops and goods entailed by this Palestine-cum-Kenya scheme continued until the date in September 1947 when the British Colonial Secretary announced that Britain was abandoning the Palestine Mandate.

But before then, new conditions at home and in Europe had begun to affect British Cabinet judgements of what was feasible. By the end of 1946, world commodity prices were rising to a height that gravely reduced the purchasing power of the American loan that had been negotiated on such exacting terms in 1945, and ministers—Dalton at the Exchequer and Cripps at the Board of Trade—were demanding changes of plan. Notably, they were asking for less feeding of Germany and less expenditure on troops in political outposts abroad:

> Week by week and day by day [later said Bevin of Dalton] he had to come to the Cabinet to report on the dollar position. It was not his fault. It was not anybody's fault. It was the fault of events, and it became perfectly clear with the rise in prices that sooner or later an enormous change in our whole position would have to be faced.[5]

In the Middle East, the first of several enormous changes was Bevin's capitulation to Treasury pressure for military economies in Greece and Turkey. The best available account of the process whereby this radical decision was reached, and communicated to the United States, is given in Dalton's memoirs, which suggest that the move was a sudden and a reluctant one. After a pause that was due to Bevin's sense of timing—he wanted to make sure that the Americans would stop the gap—the facts were stated in Washington and the United States was asked

> to make the longest, broadest and most meaningful step in the nation's history, out beyond the established frontiers of its influence.[6]

This step was: to take over the burden of financial and military support for the resistance of two eastern Mediterranean countries to Soviet pressure. Secretary of the Navy Forrestal records that the United States Cabinet received the demand with consternation:

> . . . Marshall said that this dumped in our lap another most serious problem—that it was tantamount to British abdication from the Middle East with obvious implications as to their successor.[7]

But the timing was good, and the Americans responded with the celebrated Truman Doctrine of March 12, 1947. The date was a red-letter day. Its importance was underrated only by Britons who were still unaware of their country's loss of money and resources, and therefore of power, as a result of the war. It is a turning-point in British Middle Eastern history, for after it, as General Marshall at once foresaw, responsibility for Middle Eastern defence against Russia was a shared, as opposed to a single-handed task.

Simultaneously, a second enormous change was taking place on the eastern side of the area. By rights, the independence of India should have reduced Britain's sense of responsibility for policing the classic passage through the Middle East. But habits die hard, and the British passage to India is also the Soviet passage to Africa. In 1947, relations with the Soviet Union were growing so bad in Europe that the British Imperial General Staff thought of the change as an amputation.

No money; no India; dwindling security in Palestine. Yet the British Cabinet's burden of anxiety was slightly allayed because, in the course of 1947, the truth about relations with Russia had become common knowledge. The revelation came from the Russians themselves through their coercion of Hungary, Rumania and Bulgaria, their creation of the Cominform, their refusal to let eastern Europe benefit by the Marshall Plan, and their share in organizing the Prague coup of February 1948. These events drove home even to left-wing critics of Bevin's "Tory policy" the Government's reasons for wanting American support and Middle Eastern bases.

So that a relatively united home front faced the next and worst post war crisis—the siege of Berlin. The first inkling of trouble was given when, on March 5, 1948, the American military governor in Germany sent home a prescient and alarming telegram about

> a subtle change in the Soviet attitude in Berlin which I cannot define but which now gives me a feeling that it [war] may come with dramatic suddenness. I cannot support this change in my own thinking with any data or outward evidence in relationships other than to describe it as a new tenseness in every Soviet individual with whom we have official relations.[8]

This message coincided with the zenith of British embarrassment in Palestine. It also coincided with the start of the European

Recovery Programme under the Marshall Plan, with its basic requirement of a steady flow of oil from the Middle East to Europe. Seen from London, the importance of defending the Middle East had not diminished with reduction of the British stake in India. It was as important as ever.

The British military planners at Middle East Headquarters knew that, in the event of war over Berlin, troops and equipment would be short in western Europe, and the Middle East was likely to be a secondary theatre. If these forecasts were correct, they could expect no reinforcements. They therefore made what dispositions they could under their own steam. Of the local governments, Jordan was the only sure ally; during 1947-8 they greatly improved the armament of the Arab Legion, which was, in their view, till then only of desert police standard, and strengthened its complement of British officers. They acted without time or thought for the Zionist view of this move.

They were also anxious to do work on Iraqi airfields and get flying experience there. It was largely under pressure from them that the Foreign Office pushed ahead with arrangements for a new Iraqi treaty in the autumn of 1947, regardless of a scene in Palestine that was the opposite of propitious. For the plan of the time was—in the event of war—to sabotage Abadan refinery and, if need be, also the oilfields of the Persian Gulf region, and for as long as possible to use Iraqi airfields to fly strikes into south Russia, and to delay Russian ground troops in the Persian mountains. In the longer run there was to be no attempt to hold more than the line from the Taurus mountains in Turkey to Aqaba on the Red Sea.

Although the British continued to deny the Egyptians and Arabs all their dearest wishes—evacuation, arms, satisfaction in Palestine, —and although there were now, as there had not been before the war, other powers in sight to whom to turn, a surprisingly large number of people in the Middle East kept up their habit of dealing with London. Though the British relationship to them had altered in that Britain was now a debtor instead of a creditor, old habits die hard and they still overrated British strength and capacity. The British therefore conceived the illusion that the goodwill they sought could be promoted by offering economic and technical aid to peoples desiring "development". Bevin deserves credit for propounding aid schemes that were by far the earliest to be offered in the Middle East but he disposed neither of the money nor the men to implement them. He opened a British Middle East Office in Cairo that gave excellent technical advice whenever consulted, but it was far too small to make any mark of consequence on the huge problems of the area. Moreover, British Government aid was often suspect as coming from a body that was, by local standards, too fond of asking for a *quid pro quo*; offers, even when selfless, were mistrusted because they were interpreted as sweeteners to the British quest for bases. There were psychological reasons, as well as quantitative ones, why many people in the Middle East preferred the United States to Britain as a source of aid with their development. British consultant and commercial firms, on the other hand, were freely used; when hired on the local government's own terms, and on the basis of an ordinary professional or commercial contract, their presence was unconnected with dominance, and their familiarity with local conditions was valued. For instance, a firm of British engineering consultants—Sir Alexander Gibb and Partners—advised Persia on municipal water supplies all through the British quarrel with Musaddiq over oil, and served Egypt as consultant on the Aswan dam no matter where the money for it was coming from, or what the relations between the British and Egyptian Governments.

A paradox of the years just after the war is that Britain and the United States, though they were working shoulder to shoulder in Europe, were often at loggerheads in the Middle East. Though their interests in the region were common interests (as was demonstrated when Truman took over responsibility for Greece and Turkey in 1947) the two powers differed in their method of approach to young nations; they also differed profoundly over Palestine. Their quarrel on this subject was complicated by the existence of disagreement about Palestine within both countries, and particularly within government circles in the United States. The White House, where several of President Truman's closest advisers were Zionists, was often out of tune with officials of the State Department and with Forrestal, now Secretary for Defense, for all of these worried about the repercussions of Arab animosity on oil supplies for Europe. Truman got the better of this American argument. He made an initial effort to work with the British, but thereafter lost patience with them. Tempers rose on both sides. Bevin, at the British end, grew angry at Truman's recommendations that Jews be poured into Palestine as if the matter were merely one of cash and carry, and had no political implications. He resented the degree to which White House policy was influenced by the Jewish vote in New York, and by the pro-Zionist bias of many important American newspapers. Finally, he was upset by Truman's tendency to behave as if Americans were the only people who were moved by the plight of Jewry. Truman, at the American end, thought Bevin so obstinate that he was led to back the Zionist contention that Palestine was the only acceptable asylum for Jews who wanted to leave Europe. To the British, Americans seemed blind to the burden this policy placed on the power that had to carry it out.

The transit of power in the Middle East had begun, but neither the Americans, who were receiving it, nor the British, who were shedding it, as yet appreciated the magnitude of the change. The Americans therefore saw no harm in belabouring Britain, while the British reckoned that they could manage the Palestine situation on their own. Both powers judged that there was room for the luxury of a quarrel at a point where no Soviet pressure was being applied. These assumptions may have been faulty; yet they were not disastrous, because Palestine and its future were matters of life and death neither to Britain nor to the United States. Throughout the quarrel, Bevin and Truman each knew that the other was sound as a bell on all contemporary questions of real moment to either country—the arrest of Communism, the British standard of living, the survival of the British Commonwealth, the siege of Berlin.

The plight of European Jewry in the Second World War had greatly exacerbated the British problem in Palestine, but had not altered its shape. Its hard core was, as ever, the question of numbers, a question made more poignant than before on account of the toll of Jewish life that Hitler had taken, and the longing of the survivors, now mostly in camps for displaced persons, to turn their backs on Europe. Some of the D.P.s wanted to go to Palestine, others to the New World, but the pressure on Palestine had, for a political reason, become more acute than before the war. As a result of the 1939 White Paper and of British restrictions on Jewish immigration during the war, Zionist leaders had abandoned faith—even hope—in the British Government as a source of succour, and had transferred their effort to Washington. At first, they sought to bring American pressure to bear on the British Government, but later, sensing that the balance of power was changing, they began to seek and organize direct American support for mass immigration to Palestine. By 1945, they had abandoned as out of date Weizmann's dignified conception of negotiation by stages and were, as he put it, relying

> on methods never known or encouraged among Zionists before the war. These methods were referred to by different names: "resistance", "defence", "activism". But . . . one feature was common to all of them: the conviction of the need for fighting against British authority in Palestine—or anywhere else, for that matter.[9]

This campaign, which began—as has already been described—before the end of the war, and lasted until the end of the mandate, was conducted with money collected chiefly in America. It was not a continuous success story; in the summer of 1946 even extremist leaders became sufficiently depressed to decide to aim not for the whole of Palestine (as the Biltmore resolutions of 1942 had done) but for part only of the territory. But the Zionists never wavered from their ultimate goal—complete control of immigration obtained through the establishment of a Jewish state. Since the Palestine Arabs would not hear of partition, and since they too had mustered fresh outside support, from the Arab League and from other Asian countries of importance to Britain, the British cup of trouble overflowed.

There are plenty of blow-by-blow accounts of the struggle in Palestine between the end of the war and the end of the mandate— a dreary record of terrorism, repression, fruitless negotiation and discussion at cross purposes. The part of the tale that is relevant here is what the British hoped to bring about by their decisions. As the Government wriggled this way and that in the toils of a problem that had not altered, except in degree, it was accused of taking sides by two communities battling for survival; by everyone except the Arabs, it was thought to be taking the Arab side. But when its acts are examined in the context of all Britain's problems of the time, most of them turn out to be based not on pro-Arab but on British policy. They are firmly rooted in home opinion, in Britain's financial and strategic lot, and in the wage packets of British and European workers who seldom if ever gave Palestine a thought.

British intentions were different at the three different stages into which the last years of the mandate can be divided. In the first period, which ended with reference of the problem to the United Nations in February 1947, the British were in control of events. Their soldiers were in a position to cordon and search the territory;

their politicians could time negotiations as they wished, and choose whom to see. Bevin was in the chair, and the latitude for British manœuvre looked ample enough to cause him to make his injudicious remark in the House of Commons that he would "stake my political future" on solving the problem of Palestine. But the look of latitude was illusory; there were no choices available other than those already discarded.

During the war, the Coalition Government had studied a ministerial plan for the partition of Palestine, and had rated it the least disadvantageous of the possible solutions (as most people came to do if they considered the problem with no immediate responsibility for executing a decision); but the Cabinet pigeonholed the idea because, records Lord Alanbrooke, the Chiefs of Staff were

> unanimously against any announcement before the end of the war.[10]

The Labour Government, after a quick initial survey in 1945, rejected partition for the well-worn reason that to impose it would require the use of force—an expedient that the British public would dislike at any time, and would not tolerate at the end of a long war. Bevin, in his search for an acceptable alternative, tried every device; he consulted the Americans, in the hope that they would be able to induce the Zionists to compromise, and he worked without them when they began to call Britain inhuman for refusing to shoulder, unaided, in Palestine, the whole political consequences of succouring European Jewry. Sometimes he tried working *tête-à-tête* with the Jews; sometimes with the Arabs. At moments he thought he was succeeding; he once told the House of Commons that after a meeting with Zionist leaders in the autumn of 1946, "I thought I had the right approach at last". But he was over-optimistic. No amount of negotiation could break a deadlock in which the Jews would not accept British control of numbers, and the British would not enforce the partition that would allow of Jewish control, because they would not apply force to the Arabs, who refused to accept partition of any kind. When Bevin tackled the Palestine Arabs, they disbelieved his suggestions that they might do better at British than at other hands; to them, his theory was a smokescreen for British determination to retain dominance.

In such a fix, British minds were bound to roam over every possible expedient; Bevin himself favoured a unitary state, requiring a British umpire, not merely because this arrangement would suit British defence plans, but because he thought it a mistake to create two states neither of which would be viable. Attlee became more and more drawn to getting out of a territory that brought Britain many more drawbacks than advantages; Colonial Office men hoped for a scheme of provincial autonomy that would preserve some of the admirable administrative work of thirty years; the War Office wanted Palestine as a base and was hard at work ferrying its stores into the territory; the Foreign Office, whose representatives in Arab capitals were reporting risk to defence plans and oil supplies if the Arabs were disregarded, was strongly against parti-tion. By the beginning of 1947, even Bevin had to admit that he had underrated the possibilities of negotiation between two com-munities bent on incompatible ends and each of which enjoyed enough support from abroad to be deaf to persuasion. In February 1947, and on the ground that it was imperative to cause outsiders brimming with vicarious advice to see the practical difficulties, the British Government referred its problem to the United Nations.

Thus began the second stage of Britain's operations—a stage at which the British had surrendered the political initiative, but still retained the practical responsibility for policing and administering Palestine. This combination did not work well. When the British Government first passed its problem to the United Nations, it did not envisage surrender of the mandate; it merely asked how its mandate "can be administered . . . or amended". But its loss of power to run matters was soon reflected in an increase of Jewish resistance to its authority, and by September it had changed its mind and announced that it was giving up the mandate. Few could believe their ears, both because such a decision was out of keeping with the long-standing pattern of British defence policy, and because the British were credited with an infinite capacity for stick-ing things out. The decision to quit was a sudden one; it was an-nounced at the United Nations on September 26, 1947, and military headquarters in the Canal Zone learnt almost overnight that their ferrying of goods to Palestine must stop. But it was based on several new and solid motives—political, financial and human—and, cumulatively, these make an impressive list.

One was the force of public opinion at home. The British public had taken Palestine in its stride for years, and had looked on "disturbances" and "violence" there much as it had viewed "the trouble" in Ireland—as an unpleasant experience that was part of the white man's burden, rather than as a symptom that, unless relieved, was bound to recur. But on August 1, 1947, its attitude changed, and the cause of the change was the hanging of two young sergeants whom Jewish terrorists executed as a reprisal. All home comment on that deed is different in tone from that on earlier terrorist acts, though many of these caused greater loss of life— for instance, the blowing up of the King David Hotel. Picture papers front-paged photographs of the hanged men, disgust was expressed at the placing of booby traps on their bodies, liberal opinion was exercised over small outbursts of anti-semitism in several British towns. At a most unsuitable moment, the event quickened anti-American feeling, for the excesses which the Zionists had perpetrated in advertising campaigns for funds in America had included remarks which stirred even the stolid British to anger. On August 1, the *Daily Mail* appealed to the feelings of "American women whose dollars helped to buy the rope".

The cost of Palestine to the home taxpayer also played its part, for financial crisis in Britain had reached another peak. In mid-August 1947, after just one month's fulfilment of the promise to the United States to get back to "normalcy" by making sterling convertible, the British Government had to go, hat in hand, to the Americans and ask to be freed from the obligation; the rush of conversions in order to be able to spend in countries which could promise early deliveries had caused an unbearable drain on sterling. The bill for Palestine between January 1945 and November 1947 was £100 million—a poor return for money in a year in which the British were finding it financially necessary to ration bread at home and to make troop withdrawals from all over southern Europe.

Another thought that weighed with the Cabinet in general, and Attlee in particular, was the example of India. There, two hostile communities had been confronted with the urgency of a time limit, and left to sort things out for themselves; though the price of settlement had been terrible—death dealt to more than two million people among the fleeing minorities on either side of the border— the storm had passed, and life had resumed its normal course; the experiment as a whole was therefore accounted successful. The Indian Independence Bill had become law in July, 1947.

Another date worth mention is August 28, when Egypt had failed to get the Security Council to declare the Anglo-Egyptian treaty of 1936 invalid. This treaty, which contained a clause rendering it valid until 1956, therefore remained in force and a British base of a certain size—though of a much smaller size than that to which it had grown—was still, in law, available on the Suez Canal.

There is a human reason to add to these dated entries. The Palestine problem, with its roots in irreconcilable promises and its regular crop of emotional complications, had often landed the British in false positions. For instance, the Labour Party was against the White Paper of 1939, which it held to be unfair to the Jews, and remained so; from the time that it took office, it improved on the immigration provisions of that paper; yet by Jewish standards it favoured the Arabs. Equally, Bevin was a humane man; he showed more compassion for the lot of the individual foreigner than any other British Foreign Secretary. Yet, over Palestine, Truman was able to play him into the position of a British monster confronted by an American saviour. Finally—another human impulse—the whole British Cabinet thought that it was time that others tried their hand at the problem and got blamed for doing their best.

At the third and final stage of decline—that is, for the remaining months of the mandate—not only were the British without control of diplomatic events; they lost control of the military situation also as, area by area, they evacuated Palestine. For at least two months before they left, the two communities were already fighting an undeclared war.

The British entered their valley of the shadow as soon as the United Nations Assembly, by a narrow majority, voted for partition in November 1947. The British Government had long shirked this solution because of the problem of enforcing it, and was not minded to enforce it single-handed on behalf of someone else. It fell back on the letter of the original British promise to guard the interests of both communities, and said that Britain would take no action that was not agreeable to both Jew and Arab. But once partition was decreed, this form of neutrality became impossible. For to help execute the U.N. resolution was to do what the Jews wanted and the Arabs did not, and was to favour the Jews; on the other hand, to do nothing was to impede execution of the decision, and to favour the Arabs. The British chose to do nothing.

This British decision was not taken for love of the Arabs. As so often happened in Palestine, it was made in the context of wider British interests. Whereas the Jews in the Jewish areas were on tiptoe to take over the reins of government, the Arabs in the Arab areas were a gaggle of contestants for leadership, all of them against partition and none with any thought of planning a successor régime. To hand over to any one of them would have been to make an invidious British choice; there was no surer way of incensing Arab governments whose goodwill was important to Britain on grounds both of defence and of oil.

No one shows at his best when losing his footing. In the early months of 1948, British policy was reduced to a clutter of expedients some of which puzzled and angered the United Nations. This body, which was itself now chopping and changing course over Palestine as it encountered the familiar snags of enforcing partition, was taken aback by British refusal to hand over to a neutral central authority until two weeks before the British departure. British insistence on retaining sole responsibility for law and order without the capacity to preserve either (except in a few barbed-wire enclosures and along narrow exit routes for its own forces) increased the scope for lawlessness. But the reason for apparent obstinacy was a British reason. The British clung to sole control—they even refused to let U.N. personnel delimit the frontiers for which the Assembly had voted—out of fear that U.N. officials would be set upon by angry Arabs, and that the departing British soldiers—the only troops available—would be called back from the coast to carry out a rescue operation that would entail an Anglo-Arab battle. The logic may have been sound, but the effect on the warring tribes in Palestine, and on world opinion, was deplorable.

In retrospect, the British method of abandoning the mandate would have been less undignified and reprehensible had the Government taken a few risks with the Arabs; as things were, it consigned to chaos a territory that it had taken on as "a sacred trust for civilization". But there were other reasons why it acted as it did.

One reason was muddle of the kind that springs from clashes between the vested interests of government departments. Such clashes are an ingredient of the policy of all nations more often than their nationals care to admit. In the winter of 1947–8, three British departments were shedding responsibility for Palestine—the Colonial Office, the War Office, the Foreign Office. The first wanted to save some of its handiwork from ruin; the second wanted to extricate its men and material; the third, to keep up the British position in the rest of the Arab world. None of the three wanted to be responsible for the life and limb of United Nations representatives. All their conflicting desiderata could not be reconciled at Cabinet level; and so, in their confusion at loss of the control they were accustomed to exercise, they took individual decisions and made individual statements that did not dovetail with other British acts, and that did not add up to a policy.

There was, however, one branch of British planning that was purposeful and coherent; this was military planning. News of the worsening situation in Berlin had begun to circulate in March 1948. In the two months between this date and the end of the mandate on May 15, the British forces in Palestine had orders to concentrate on avoiding further British loss of life, and to extract from Palestine as much as possible of the large quantities of war material that were stored there; all might be needed in Europe. The soldiers were to get away with as little friction as possible, leaving each district to whichever community was locally the better placed. The policy was succinctly put by the British general who evacuated Haifa:

> I have no desire whatever to involve my troops in these clashes [between Arab and Jew]. All I want is to secure the routes and sectors that I need to complete the British evacuation of Palestine . . .[11]

What can a departing army do the moment its instructions to get out unscathed start transcending its capacity to keep order anywhere except on its own thin line of march?

Critics of the British Government sometimes alleged that it deliberately organized the chaos it created because it wanted a fight, and wanted an Arab victory. But anyone who thought so had lost all sense of the place of Palestine in the British scale of values of 1948. An Arab win would have saddled Great Britain with at least two unthinkable consequences—accountability to the world for a new Jewish dispersion, and alienation of the United States at a moment when American goodwill was a matter of life and death to Great Britain not only financially, but in Germany.

Another suggestion, also unfounded, is that the British organized chaos in order that they might be able to stay on in Palestine. Quite the other way, their aim was to be rid of an incubus that was queering their relations with important allies:

> I do want to emphasize [said Bevin in March 1948] that we have to get into a position to enable us to get out of Palestine. That is the fundamental point of British policy.[12]

Balfour had been dead for eighteen years, but Lloyd George died only in 1945, three years too early to hear this obituary, or to know why his brain-child had become so great a British liability.

For the British, once the Palestine war was over and Israel had been recognized, memories of discomfiture in Palestine were soon crowded out by events of far greater significance to Britain's future. These were the Berlin air lift, the European Recovery Programme, the birth of N.A.T.O. and—in the Far East—communist victory in China and the Korean war.

But for Arabs, some of whom could see from their windows the busy scene of consolidation in Israel, thoughts about defeat in Palestine were bitter and constant, and precipitated action in pursuit of ideas and emotions that had been fermenting for years. Antipathy to régimes that had bungled a war, resentment at the selfishness of a class entrenched in power, determination to be rid of the British who were ostensibly friends of that class—all these grievances were linked by a process of reasoning that may not have been logical, but that was generally accepted. (Egyptians, for instance, sometimes allege that the British wanted to preserve the Egyptian monarchy; Nasser said so in July 1962. But this is incorrect; in fact, as soon as the Egyptian revolution of 1952 broke out, the British Embassy informed Neguib that, provided his movement could keep order, British interests were unaffected, and the British had no reason or wish to save King Farouk.)

Between 1949 and 1952, Arab social and political discontents led to domestic upheavals. In Syria, a succession of military coups gave control to army dictators allied to radical politicians; in Jordan, King Abdullah—friend to Britain—was murdered in a mosque in Jerusalem after he had taken over the Arab rump of Palestine; in Egypt, a major social revolution completely changed the seat of power. The opening round of the Egyptian revolution in January 1952, christened "Black Saturday", took the form of anti-foreign riots and the methodical burning of foreign property in the centre of Cairo. Six months later, after King Farouk had resisted efforts to clean up his government, the army refused to serve him further, deposed him, and installed in his place a military *junta* under a figurehead general, Mohammed Neguib, and a much younger dynamo, Gamal Abdel Nasser.

This new wave of nationalist and socialist emotion was by no means all due to chagrin about Palestine; it had older and deeper causes that were described in Chapter 5, and it swept with especial violence one country unaffected by the Palestine issue—Persia. In Persia, the outward form it took was an onslaught on the Anglo-Iranian Oil Company, and because a Persian hero, Musaddiq, fought a duel with that company, the world saw the spectacle only as a contest between David and Goliath, and derived from it the satisfaction that human nature gets when a giant is worsted; in the excitement, many people missed the wider significance of the revolt. As has already been explained, dislike of foreigners, and a special dislike of foreign exploitation of oil, had long consumed the Persians, both rich and poor. These emotions had been exacerbated by the wound caused to their self-respect when their country was occupied by the belligerents in 1941. When mortification that had been simmering for years came to a head in 1951 it was vented on the British oil company largely because by now there was only one big and vulnerable foreign target within range. (Soviet oil negotiators had been similarly attacked when Musaddiq first launched his anti-foreign campaign in 1944.) By selecting a foreign target, a conglomeration of different Persian discontents could be made to cohere. The following analysis cannot be bettered:

> The nationalist movement in this phase was anti-corruption and xenophobic, and was eventually formulated in terms of Islam. It began as a movement against the Anglo-Iranian Oil Company and although it was anti-foreign in form in the early period, it was a reflection in the main of the discontent with the ruling classes, of the disequilibrium in political, social and economic affairs inside Persia, and of the fear that dictatorship would be reimposed with foreign support. In other words, the nature of political power was still the fundamental problem. This is not to say that there was no grievance against the company or that the company had always been wise. Nevertheless, the company was in some measure made the scapegoat for internal failures. Once, however, the distrust and discontent felt towards the government had been focused on the company, it was but a short step to accuse the company of that very exploitation which the people had suffered at the hands of their own government for centuries.[18]

So Persians murdered a prime minister, Ali Razmara, who had the courage to tell them that underdeveloped countries cannot do without foreigners; mobs grew delirious over photo-montages showing

Razmara stooping to kiss the Union Jack, and nationalists responded indiscriminately to speeches of mullahs and communists. When Musaddiq proved to lack capacity to organize a state of new pattern, admiration for him did not die; he had been a champion of the national will, and a consistent one, and feelings about him were put into cold store until needed.

In 1947, when the British announced that they were leaving Palestine, no one in the Middle East believed them. The contrast in 1951 was great. When the A.I.O.C. retired from Persia, everyone deduced that British power was on the wane. Asians were helped to this conclusion when they saw the British cruiser sent to Abadan take no action beyond ferrying British citizens to safety; it had orders merely to stand by unless British lives were in danger. The Labour Government (in power until October 1951) decided against armed intervention less, it seems, out of the classic fear of a corresponding Russian move in the north than for reasons of home opinion, and out of anxiety not to jeopardize the unity in which the great bulk of the United Nations Organization was handling the Korean war.

British power was diminishing; what was to take its place? The Middle Eastern nationalists who asked themselves this question were on the whole anti-communist; if Soviet help was to be sought, they wanted it not for its own sake, but as a counterweight to un-avoidable Western help. Some countries—notably Persia after Musaddiq fell—turned readily to the big, rich, anti-colonial Western alternative to Britain—the United States.

In the course of this debate about the succession, some Middle Eastern countries took the opportunity to open breaches in their own sectors of the British front. In Saudi Arabia, where old King Ibn Saud was ailing (he died in 1953) nationalists less sagacious and tolerant than he made an expansionist thrust in the direction of the British protected Sheikhdoms in the Persian Gulf; in August 1952 a Saudi expedition seized the oasis of Buraimi, which lies about 100 miles nearer the coast than the maximum line that Ibn Saud had claimed in 1935. As Saudis are rich and able to win support by their wealth, and as the desert tribes who used the oasis were poor, this incident was long-drawn-out and led to an era of coolness between Britain and Saudi Arabia.

The nation to draw liveliest inspiration from the Persian example was Egypt. In October 1951, the last of the Wafd governments to hold office sought and won acclamation by unilaterally denouncing the 1936 Anglo-Egyptian treaty. From this moment, successive Egyptian governments began to encourage sabotage and guerrilla warfare against the British in the Canal Zone. After the revolution, the new men continued the campaign. "As long as there is a single foreign soldier on Egyptian territory," said Neguib, "let every Egyptian consider himself on the battlefield", and Nasser—at the time still second-in-command—:

> Not formal war. That would be suicidal. It will be a guerrilla war. Grenades will be thrown in the night. British soldiers will be stabbed stealthily. There will be such terror that, we hope, it will become far too expensive for the British to maintain their citizens in occupation of our country.[14]

He was as good as his word. By 1954, the Egyptians had deprived the base of Egyptian labour, had obliged the British military to enclose themselves within walls and barbed wire, had forced 80,000 men to spend much of their time on their own protection and had caused the British to interfere unduly with Egyptian civilian life; on one occasion, British soldiers razed part of an Egyptian village; the purpose was to preserve the Canal Zone water supply from sabotage, but a government's policy is out of joint if it has to instruct its embassy to explain away such an act in a foreign country. In Britain, more and more people grew doubtful of the value of a base at the mercy of a hostile government; one right wing newspaper commissioned a retired British general to visit the Zone and to be frank with its readers. His answer, never published because the Anglo-Egyptian agreement of October 1954 forestalled it, was that a British military base on the Suez Canal was now self-defeating and a liability.

British and American defence requirements were identical in the Middle East. Once the Palestine quarrel was out of the way, the American concept of a northern tier of anti-communist states enunciated by Dulles in 1953, and consisting of Greece, Turkey and Iran, seemed suitable for dovetail with the older and more conservative British concept of area defence based on Suez with outlying airfields in Jordan and Iraq. But Anglo-American co-operation, so well-knit at all points of Soviet pressure, was patchy in an area where the danger was less; friction often developed at points where the imperial partner was losing stamina, and the anti-imperialist partner was reluctant to take on the succession. When the two allies chose to use their influence jointly, they were usually able to make their influence felt. For instance, in company with France, they issued in 1950 a Tripartite Declaration on Palestine, intended to damp down disputes on its borders by rationing arms and freezing armistice lines all round Israel's periphery; this flimsy document served its purpose off and on for five years; for the last time, and a short time, the mere word of Western powers spoken in unison took effect in the jungle of Middle Eastern politics. Another joint venture was the effort both powers made to save the Palestinian Arab refugees from hunger and disease, though their efforts at resettlement were vain.

Yet another piece of Anglo-American co-operation produced, in 1954, a settlement of the dispute between the Persians and the A.I.O.C. At first the Americans had denied the British their support, and had been critical of an oil company which, in American eyes, was paying the price of old-fashioned, condescending and over-paternalistic behaviour. But later, the United States government became alarmed lest Musaddiq's lack of realism should plunge Persia into anarchy, and American negotiators combined with British emissaries to secure the compromise solution of the dispute that established a multinational consortium of oil companies in which A.I.O.C. was scaled down to a 40 per cent share.

In Egypt, by contrast, joint Anglo-American effort was vain. In the course of Western anxiety over Korea the two powers tried to entice the Egyptians into a Middle East Defence Organization (M.E.D.O.); this was to be a substitute for Great Britain's treaty, and was to include Turkey as a specimen of a small independent and trusting Moslem power. But by Egyptian standards the proposal was merely an international gloss on an old British design, and was not to be thought of. The Egyptians were uninterested in Korea, or in Soviet expansion. As their Foreign Minister explained to Bevin in 1950:

Our foreign policy is a very limited one, and can almost be resolved in these two questions now under discussion, the question of evacuation and that of the unity of Egypt and the Sudan under the Egyptian crown.[15]

Although the ratio of American to British power and influence in the Middle East was changing, the United States thought (and continued to think until the Suez crisis of 1956) that any military arrangement in the area south of the "northern tier" should be led by Great Britain. According to Eden, President Eisenhower agreed as late as January 1953 that it was "essential to maintain the base in Egypt", though many American soldiers and diplomats made no secret of their view that British adherence to old gambits in young and nationalist countries was out of date. After the failure of the M.E.D.O. proposal, the Americans left the British to negotiate a new Suez base agreement single-handed. The British Government, now under Churchill and Eden, was glad to act alone, but as negotiations proceeded, a combination of the mediocre cards Britain held, and of criticism from Americans who had made friends among the young officers who were running Egypt, produced some undisguised ill-feeling between the British and the American embassies in Cairo. These jars between allies can be overstressed, but they did not escape the Egyptians, and diminished British stature in their eyes without adding to that of the United States.

When Eden took over the Foreign Office in 1951, he was confronted with what he called in his memoirs a "lowering prospect". Yet from the standpoint of securing a defence arrangement with Egypt he was soon at one great advantage over his predecessors. Once Egypt's reformist colonels and wing-commanders came to power in 1952, Great Britain was quit of the implication that it dealt only with effete kings and self-interested pashas; it was also negotiating with a government that kept order, and used its mind, in contrast to political parties each utilizing the mob to turn out the other as soon as there was any hint of coming to terms with Britain on a basis of mutual concessions. At first this second gain was not obvious. The officers' *junta* appeared to be torn by faction—Neguib versus Nasser—and to be widely opposed inside Egypt; for these and other reasons, the British Government dawdled over negotiation with a body which it thought to be of doubtful stability. The main British misgiving was about Egyptian intentions towards the Sudan; this Egypt seemed to wish to rush into an association that was closer than most Sudanese desired. The Churchill Government also dallied because it needed time in which to bring round its own right-wing supporters to the need for a new policy. The Suez Canal had long held a special place in British esteem; Eden had once called it "the swing door of the British Empire", and—to the Conservatives who were soon christened the Suez group—it was as sacred as British soil. Members of the group called for much party cosseting, for a body of Conservative opinion, of unknown size, was against following the precedent set by Labour in India, Burma and Palestine, and at Abadan, and "scuttling" from the Canal Zone.

The advantage of dealing with a broadly-based dictatorship as opposed to the old competing parties first became plain over the Sudan. Neguib himself was half Sudanese, and much more sensitive to Sudanese opinion than most Egyptians. Under his influence, the *junta* dropped the popular slogan about "the unity of the Nile Valley" and instead called for its "independence and freedom"; the Egyptian Government later agreed with the British that the Sudanese must be free to choose their future, and an Anglo-Egyptian agreement on the Sudan was signed on February 12, 1953. One big obstacle to better relations was out of the way.

But the process of reaching agreement on the Canal Zone took a further year. Both sides wanted a settlement—Nasser for reasons of popularizing the revolutionary régime. Yet he was governing by committee and had difficulty in persuading the *junta* to agree to a British right of re-entry in time of danger, and to accept attack on Turkey as one of the conditions in which the right should apply. Simultaneously, Antony Head, the responsible British minister, had to contend with opposition from the Suez group at a moment when British tempers were roused to high pitch by Egypt's guerrilla war against the British base.

The debate that took place in the House of Commons when an Anglo-Egyptian agreement was at last initialled in July 1954 reveals why a Conservative cabinet agreed to this largest "enormous change" in British Middle Eastern policy. First, the hydrogen bomb had been fully tested, and had—in Churchill's words—made "forecasts which were well founded up to a year ago absolutely obsolete". Secondly, now that Turkey was a member of N.A.T.O., the area in which British troops were likely to be deployed was no longer the same. Thirdly, British military forces were overstretched, and the biggest need of the time was a larger strategic reserve at home. But, apart from the first reason, the main inducement to compromise was that local nationalism had rendered a base on Egyptian soil untenable; facilities that soldiers rated essential—labour, water, and access—were attainable only in a friendly Egypt, and Egyptian friendship was unattainable so long as the British continued to occupy Egyptian soil.

For a proud and great nation to take a step which looks as though she is being forced by duress to do something which she has

been shouted at to do for a long time and to do it deliberately
is always unpalatable to national pride,[16]

said Head to the critics who were accusing him of "digging the
grave of British greatness". Certainly, agreement had been secured
at a price, but a price worth paying if it purchased an agreement
that would win over a new brand of nationalist government, and if
it caused the most important of the Middle Eastern states to adopt
military plans that amounted to siding with the West in the cold
war. At the end of 1954—the year of agreement with both Egypt
and Persia—prospects that the Middle East would continue to look
West for friends were reasonable; some people thought them
bright.

M

8

THE FRAGMENTATION OF POWER: 1955–6

APART from giving an occasional jolt to Persia, the Soviet
Union had scarcely shown its head in the Middle East since
1917. Rebuffed in 1945–6 by both the Turks and the
Persians, it had retired within its shell. Part of the reason for its
long silence seems to have been worry lest pan-Arab nationalism
should awaken a unity movement among the six Soviet Moslem
republics that adjoin the Middle East; in any case the Soviet Government was fully occupied on other parts of Russia's circumference.
Except in Persia, the Soviets had not nourished communist parties
of any importance; and on the occasions when they had dabbled in
the Palestine affair, they had done so not for love of Jew or Arab,
but in order to weaken a British foothold and exploit an Anglo-
American quarrel.

Britain and America had therefore spent much time and money
on building an elaborate defence structure that sometimes looked
like an end in itself. American aid programmes were paid for out
of funds voted to arrest the spread of communism, on which much
British effort was also expended. Yet when the realm of "aid"
included not merely technical military instruction but teaching
villages how to spray D.D.T. or grow their own sugar-beet, the
men who ran the work were to be pardoned if they allowed
historical fact to slip from their minds. Everyone, including politicians, at times behaved as if Russia had never before put pressure
on the Middle East, and as if immunity from this pressure was
not a mere interlude but would last for ever.

The Middle East immediately adjoins Russia's soft underbelly.
A resumption of Soviet attention to it at some date was a foregone
conclusion. Students of the Soviet political programme within the
Union report, in retrospect, that a renewal of interest in the Middle
East began in periodicals, encyclopædias and teaching schedules in
the course of 1954. The point that is relevant to this book is whether
British or Anglo-American policy could have minimized or post-
poned the tremendous splash with which, in September 1955, the
Soviet Union—dressed in the shining armour of salvation from
Western dominance—vaulted over the Western barriers and into

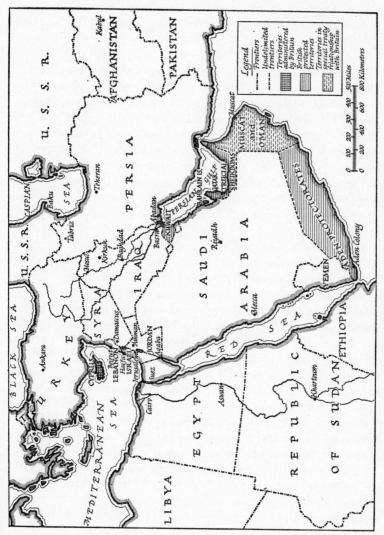

THE MIDDLE EAST IN 1956

Egypt and Syria. The occasion was an arms deal by Nasser with Czechoslovakia, or, as he later acknowledged, with the Soviet Union. The bargain was struck at Egypt's request, and the point to be surveyed is how far Western policy prompted the Egyptian invitation.

The British, once they had reached the Canal Zone agreement with Nasser in October 1954, hoped to be friends with everyone in a westward-facing Middle East. An American precedent suggested that this objective was attainable since the United States, which got on better with Nasser than did any other Western power, had during 1954 signed military aid agreements with Pakistan and Iraq. But Britain's path to the same relationship was obstructed by two snags—the bad old British name, connoting dominance to the people of every Middle Eastern state, and a problem of timing, which can be explained only by an excursion into the thick of Arab politics.

To outward appearances, the agreement that Nasser had secured on British evacuation placed him on the top of his world. But in fact his position was still precarious. He had eliminated Neguib from public life, but was on many counts ill placed. By reaching an agreement with Britain that fell short of the instant, complete break that years of propaganda had led Egyptians to expect, he had by popular standards been insufficiently nationalist; he was obliged to defend himself against charges of having given away too much, and, a week after the signature, was narrowly missed by an assassin during a mass meeting at Alexandria. In foreign policy, Egypt's outlook was also bleak. Nasser had alienated the Sudan by eliminating Neguib, and had antagonized Syria and Saudi Arabia by disbanding the young officers' chief rival for popular favour, the Moslem Brotherhood. The serious thinkers within the *junta* knew that Egypt's military strength was negligible, and that the twenty months that the British needed for withdrawal were a blessed respite in which to make good their revolution; they also reckoned that the only suitable source of the arms they needed was the Western world.

At the end of 1954, therefore, Nasser was casting about for a policy in which two points were fixed—that he needed the gift of time in which to accustom the Egyptian people to the idea that a country in Egypt's position must depend on foreigners, and that Egypt must have status and dignity, which by his standards meant no links with foreign military pacts. Admittedly he had just signed an agreement with Britain, but that was the end of an old chapter; there must be no new pacts except with Arab brothers.

Nuri Pasha, Prime Minister of Iraq, thought otherwise. He too was a realist—far more realistic than Egyptian public opinion allowed Nasser to be—about Arab military capacity; Iraq lived nearer than did Egypt to Turkey, Persia and Russia. Nuri had in 1954 signed an arms agreement with the United States, and he liked the shape of a pact of friendship and security reached in 1954 between Turkey and Pakistan. He was firmly in the Iraqi saddle thanks to rigged elections in 1954, but thought that he had rigged them in a good cause—that of stability. For the Iraqi Government disposed of ample funds thanks to oil royalties, and had under-taken an impressive development programme that called for a steady run of work undisturbed by lightning Cabinet changes (of which the Iraqi average over fifteen years had been two per year). Given stability, Nuri hoped to create enough employment on development work to cause prosperity to mature faster than social discontent and revolution. In order to work this programme, he ran a police state; at the same time, he belonged to an ex-Ottoman generation that saw no indignity in alliance with European powers; on both counts he was out of touch with the angry young men who admired Nasser for getting rid of the British.

This difference of opinion was an inter-Arab difference, and in the second half of 1954 Nuri and Nasser—both advocates of Arab unity—tried to resolve it. But they were not of the same generation or temperament, and they seem to have talked at cross purposes. Nuri got the Egyptians to agree that Iraq was "in special circum-stances due to its proximity to the U.S.S.R. and its common frontier with Persia", but in Egyptian estimation, though not in Nuri's view,

> Iraq derives a guarantee more than adequate from the [Arab] Collective Security pact, and from the fact that the Arabs are regarded as a cohesive block which does not reject co-operation with the West if Arab freedom and security are respected.[1]

By Nuri's standards, this was military makebelieve, and he said so; whereat (according to accounts of the talk later published in both countries) Nasser told him: "You are free to do what you like." Nuri interpreted this sibylline remark as "full agreement", but it was full agreement to differ, for Nuri signed a pact with Turkey.

The dealings of the two rivals with Turkey were an indication of the difference in their outlook. Nasser was quite ready to receive friendly visits from the governor of Ankara and Turkish journalists, but refused one from Menderes, the Turkish Prime Minister. Nuri, by contrast, not only received Menderes in January 1955 but sped him on his way round other Arab capitals. In a word, both Egypt and Iraq were ready to deal with the West and its friends, but Nasser, for internal reasons, wanted to move slowly, while Nuri, for external ones, wanted to move fast.

In this criss-cross of Arab aims and manœuvres, the British Government had to thrash out a decision about timing. Its choice lay between taking an initiative that would please the Turks and Nuri, and doing nothing, which would suit Nasser. With much evidence in his brief-case, Eden travelled east at the end of February to attend the opening meeting of the new regional defence pact for South East Asia—S.E.A.T.O. On the way, he called in Cairo; he did not take to Nasser, and dismissed Egypt's request for delay as unrealistic; he remarks in his memoirs that "I was familiar with this plea; it is never the right time for some". The S.E.A.T.O. meeting was invigorating; with his mind full of regional pacts and the existence of a gap between Pakistan (which belonged to S.E.A.T.O.) and Turkey (which belonged to N.A.T.O.), Eden called in Baghdad on his way home, and saw Nuri—not only a realist but a friend of thirty years' standing. On arrival home Eden told the House of Commons that

> I found in the Middle East a general acceptance of the need to organize a safe shield of defence to protect the area from aggression from without.[2]

He did not mention the time factor.

While Eden was in Asia a new and unconnected development had complicated the scene by sharpening Egypt's temper. On the borders of Palestine, the Tripartite Agreement of 1950 and the services of a United Nations Observer Corps had not eliminated raids and counter-raids. On February 28, 1955, Ben-Gurion, newly appointed to Israel's defence ministry, decided to teach Egyptian raiders a lesson, and staged a military attack on Egypt's military frontier post at Gaza. The success of this Israeli adventure directed Egypt's attention afresh to its military weakness, and caused Nasser to reflect much more angrily than before that Iraq had jumped the

queue for aid before he had had time to get the Egyptians into a fit
state of mind to accept it.

Throughout March, Britain had a clear choice before it. Like
the little red beacons that mark obstructions to low-flying aircraft,
red lights were winking all over the Middle East. Diplomats in
private, and certain newspapers in public, posed and discussed the
British dilemma:

> There are two courses open to him [Eden]. One . . . is to leave
> Middle Eastern security arrangements to develop on local initia-
> tive, in the knowledge that no government there would dream
> of turning in any direction but westward for help with arma-
> ments. The advantages of this course are that arrangements spon-
> taneously made tend to be firmer than sponsored ones, and less
> open to the accusation that they are Western imperialism in
> disguise. The alternative course is to add Britain's signature to
> the Turco-Iraqi Pact, and by doing so to impart to that pact the
> strength the Turks desire—a strength that they believe will
> attract Arab waverers into its orbit.
>
> Perhaps they are right, but the course they want has a draw-
> back. It would furnish a wide range of would-be neutral parties
> in the Arab states and Iran with an argument that Britain is
> back at old tricks in new guise. It would be likely, therefore,
> to divide the educated élite of every country in the Middle East
> into two groups—one priding itself on realism about security,
> and the other preening itself on seeing through Western
> machinations. Pacts so built have rickety foundations, and it
> might be best to let matters ride for long enough to enable the
> Egyptians and Arabs to sort out their muddled thoughts.[3]

This long quotation from a contemporary newspaper is reprinted
to show that the disadvantages of splitting the Arabs were discernible in March 1955. Why were they ignored and why did Eden, who
had always seen the virtues of harnessing Arab unity at times of
threat to Britain's Middle East interests, now decide to break up
that unity and to wean one Arab state—Iraq—from the others?

At the moment of British decision whether or not to join the
Turco-Iraqi Pact, the chief arguments for joining it came from the
defence departments. Though the soldiers had said that a big, com-
pact base was vulnerable and out of date, the Air Ministry thought
differently about landing-grounds. The Anglo-Iraqi Treaty of 1930,
which gave Britain rights at two Iraqi air bases, was shortly to

expire, and the Air Ministry looked with consternation at a map of the Middle East that would have no sure staging post between Cyprus and Aden or Bahrain. The Air Force said that it needed desert flying practice, and intermediary landing-grounds for short-range fighters on their way east and—above all—rights on Iraq airfields for servicing aircraft and for the radar warning system needed on the eastern flank of N.A.T.O. To join the Turco-Iraqi Pact would be to reach an arrangement with Iraq that would be equivalent to renewing the old treaty.

If forced to choose between Iraq and Egypt, politicians, led by Eden, preferred the staunch Turks and the friendly, stable Nuri to the two-headed Nasser, who, though he was scrupulously executing the Canal Zone agreement with one face, was broadcasting subversive anti-British propaganda in Arabic and Swahili with the other. Lastly, the Suez group, twisting the lion's tail from the back benches, was hoping to make it roar again, and favoured taking some initiative. Eden therefore took the plunge and joined the Turco-Iraqi Pact on April 4, 1955—the day before he became Prime Minister; thus enlarged, it became the Baghdad Pact. He had the satisfaction of noting that the pact worried the Russians; when Bulganin and Khrushchev visited London a year later, one of their conditions for co-operation was that it be repealed.

But, in signing it, the evidence that Eden discarded was also important: the age-old home truth that Egypt was the pivot of any Middle Eastern policy, the success Nasser had had in rallying the other Arab states against Nuri over Turkey, and the known reaction to new foreign pacts of the bulk of the Arab peoples. The British Cabinet was carried away by Air Ministry planners, a confident Nuri, and the optimistic Turks, and decided that, in spite of recent experiences in Egypt, there were places in the Arab world where military requirements outweighed the drawback of alienating nationalists.

In Britain, the House of Commons accepted the pact without a division. The one concern of questioners was lest it should harm Israel. Eden reassured them:

I take the view that when this agreement comes to be studied, it will be seen that from the point of view of Israel it is likely to be a desirable development because this is the first time an Arab state is looking in other directions than simply towards Israel.[4]

The flaw in this judgement becomes clear if it is set against the argument that Nuri expounded to the Iraqi Parliament in praise of the Turco-Iraqi Pact:

> I explained to the Egyptians that we have two foes; the first is Israel and the second is communism. As regards the first, Iraq's policy is to seek the assistance of as many Moslem combines as possible... I always placed first the Zionist danger and the need to secure the support of the world in order to eliminate that danger.[5]

Nuri could not say less and please his Iraqi hearers. Thus Eden's statement was true of Nuri, but not of the bulk of the people of Iraq.

Towards the end of April 1955, Nasser left Egypt for his first trip outside the Middle East, and attended the conference of Afro-Asian states at Bandung. Here he found himself seated with the Big Five—with Nehru, Chou En-lai, Sukarno and U Nu. He had been doubtful about going, for fear that Israel might be present, but in the course of the meeting, he grasped its usefulness. "Here I learned and realized," he later told an Indian journalist, "that the only wise policy for us would be positive neutrality and non-alignment." Bandung was a turning-point. It was also a source of inspiration about new trading patterns, for in the course of conversations with Chou En-lai, Nasser arranged to sell China some of Egypt's cotton surplus. He also confided Egypt's main perplexity—his difficulty in acquiring the modern arms that he needed chiefly in order to please his army supporters, though also of course to fortify his frontier with Israel. Chou En-lai inquired why he did not buy arms from Eastern block countries.

But though Egypt was attacking the Baghdad Pact, and Britain for joining it, and the United States for supporting it, Nasser did not seal his arms deal with the Czechs for another five months. He continued to prefer Western arms if he could get them, and to negotiate with the British and American ambassadors for them. The British Government, in the teeth of some acid Parliamentary questioning, sold him a little—including two destroyers (with two ditto to Israel), 32 centurion tanks, and surplus material from the Suez base; the Americans reached agreement on types and costs but not on how the goods were to be paid for. Both the Western allies were handicapped by the problem of keeping a balance on the borders of Israel, and the United States also by a problem of payment. For Nasser could not be given arms free under the American Mutual Security Act, because he would not accept the stipulation in that act that he must accept a "military assistance advisory group". The United States did not want payment in Egyptian cotton, and Egypt had no dollars to spare. This was the deadlock from which, having warned the British and American ambassadors from June onwards of his predicament, and the only way out of it, Nasser escaped by making the arms deal with the Czechs announced on September 27, 1955.

The whole elaborate structure of Anglo-American defence policy was altered by this coup. It nullified the western arrangement for an arms balance between the Arabs and Israeli; it converted western aid from a weapon in western hands into a bargaining counter for Egyptian or Arab use in the profitable process of taking aid from both sides of the iron curtain and, above all, it confirmed all but a few Arabs in the view that Nasser was a new Saladin. Others had talked; here was the man who acted, and who had given Middle Eastern states dignity and equality at last.

Britain and America, though put out of countenance by this great change in their power and status, had no choice but to grin and bear the Soviet blow. Egypt was an independent country with the right to buy and sell where it chose; they could not blame it for turning to another source to get the arms that they had been unwilling to provide. During the autumn of 1955, Eden and Dulles agreed that it would be disastrous were Egypt to become a habitual Soviet customer; rueful but resigned, they encouraged one another to go on helping Nasser; they continued to sell him arms and began to consider lending him money to start work on his twentieth-century pyramid, the Aswan High Dam. Both men consoled themselves, and the British and American publics, with speeches explaining that all would come right if only there were a settlement of the Arab-Israel dispute. This was true, but was only half the truth. The British were lulled by a half-truth into underrating the other half—the extent to which Nasser's attraction for all Arab peoples, and some Arab governments, was not only that of a champion against Israel but that of a hero who had ended British dominance over his country.

The one important card left in the western hand was America's great superiority over the Soviet Union in the matter of generosity about aid. At a loss for new ideas as to how to settle the Palestine dispute (which now handicapped United States policy as heavily as it had done British policy for a generation), the British and American Governments therefore decided to switch their attention to Aswan. By helping with the high dam they hoped to give Nasser cause to concentrate on the most formidable of Egypt's many domestic problems—how to keep Egyptian production abreast of an alarming increase in the population.

Nasser, if he could have had his choice, would have borrowed the whole sum he needed for the dam from a source untainted by politics, the World Bank. But Bank officials who had surveyed his scheme and estimated that it would cost $1,350 million thought that funds of these huge dimensions must come from several sources, as well as by stages. Three parties interested in social stability therefore decided jointly to lend the money for the first stage—the U.S. Government, the British Government and the World Bank. Their loan was to be subject to some conditions; notably, it was to be contingent on agreement with the Sudan about shares in the Nile waters; if these conditions were satisfied, the proportions suggestion were $56 million, $14 million and $200 million for the Americans, the British and the World Bank respectively. Other lenders had been circling round Nasser, and his favourable reception of this proposition early in 1956 amounted to a Western victory in an international competition to be the first to pay.

But neither Eden nor Dulles liked to think that footing bills was the only piece of constructive policy open to them in the Middle East. One possible course was to grasp the Soviet nettle and suggest a four-power attempt to solve some Middle Eastern problem or other, so depriving borrowers of the chance to solicit competitive bids from rival lenders. But the very idea of a combined operation was anathema to many Americans, and when the Soviet Union merely generalized amiably about what ought to happen, Eden and Dulles saw good reason to continue upon the old pattern. They decided that the best way to counteract Soviet influence at the centre of the Middle East would be to increase Western influence on its periphery. Dulles, architect of the northern tier, and Eden, architect of the Baghdad Pact, favoured extending the pact. The French (who had always hated the pact, which they saw as a symbol of the British power that had ousted France from the Levant) were just as mistrustful of Nasser as the British and Americans, for he was encouraging the Arab side in the Algerian war. But the French remedy for offsetting his influence was all their own; it was to arm Israel.

Except to pessimists who reckoned that the Baghdad Pact had provoked the Russians into changing their Middle Eastern policy, the pact looked healthy and successful in the autumn of 1955. The Turks had done some recruiting and secured two new members, Pakistan and Persia; the Turkish foreign minister had without difficulty talked over the Shah (who was anxious to secure enough arms to please his army), and the plunge had been taken in spite of opposition from the many Persians who thought the move was bound to induce new and unpleasant Soviet pressure. The Western bait of aid and armaments attracted attention, and in November, young King Hussein of Jordan made some inquiries about joining because he was interested in improving Jordan's defences against Israel.

In November 1955 Eden's Foreign Minister, Macmillan, attended a meeting of the Pact Powers in Baghdad. Here the Turks, brimming with the success of their recruiting, urged him to use Britain's influence with Jordan to tip the balance with King Hussein. Macmillan liked the Turks; they were robust and optimistic and so was he. He had never seen the scowls Turkey had long met from Syrians, and was now, as a member of a Western alliance, getting from many Jordanians also—black looks to which Turks are impervious. Despite some British misgivings, Macmillan decided to try the Turkish plan. He dispatched General Templer, Chief of the Imperial General Staff, to rope in another Arab member.

The disastrous Templer mission to Jordan in December 1955 exposed the degree to which Arab unity and Arab nationalism must now be taken into account in any successful Middle Eastern policy. The visit caused outbreaks of rioting that were only quelled when a new Prime Minister announced that no pacts with foreigners were contemplated. The Templer incident was proof that the force of public opinion in the Middle East, though it might be volatile, was henceforth powerful, and that its impulses were all against the policy of a few sedate politicians who thought a pact with the West a price worth paying for stability.

In Britain, people who had favoured the pact for the negative reason that it was better than nothing now began to admit its drawbacks; for instance *The Times* in May 1956 judged that:

The misfortune is that this particular pact has thrown other parts of the Middle East into reaction against Britain. This reaction was set off though not initiated by Macmillan's ill-advised dispatch of General Templer to Jordan. But the main reason why Nasser is able to use the Baghdad Pact to rally [the Arabs] is . . . because of the failure to settle the Arab-Israel dispute. . . .[6]

But pacts once sealed cannot easily be unmade; they have led to obligations to allies who cannot be let down.

Naturally Nasser was violently opposed to the Templer mission, which he saw as a new assault on Arab unity; he made capital out of its failure, as did Moscow radio. He had nothing to say against adherence by Pakistan and Persia to the pact; they were free to do as they chose; but he saw a similar step by Jordan as the business of all Arab states. Thus he was not feeling tractable when, in March 1956, he prepared to receive Selwyn Lloyd, the new British Foreign Secretary. Lloyd had a long agenda for discussion with the Egyptians. It included Britain's contribution to the Aswan Dam plans; the final stages of British military withdrawal from the Canal Zone; a new crisis in Arab relations with Israel and the unfriendliness of Cairo radio, particularly in its Swahili broadcasts to East Africa. Also, according to *The Times*, "one of the purposes may be to reassure Egypt that other countries will not join the [Baghdad]Pact ". As since the Templer experience, it was out of the question to ask other Arabs to join, this was a cheap concession for Britain to make. But it was not made.

Seen through Western eyes, the tale of events in 1956 is like the narrative in a Greek myth; disaster follows disaster, because the gods seem bent sometimes on causing accidents, and sometimes on exacting retribution for the very completeness of British dominance in former years. By a piece of ill-luck, the night of Selwyn Lloyd's first meeting with Nasser was the night on which both men heard from Jordan that King Hussein had dismissed the prop and commander of Jordan's army, Glubb Pasha, after twenty-six years of service. King Hussein's act was a piece of domestic policy; he had a much-criticized throne to consider; as he says in his memoirs:

With communism filtering into the Middle East and Cairo branding Jordan an "imperialist power", there was no alternative, Glubb had to go.[7]

He was dismissed largely in order that Hussein might satisfy the desire of Jordanians to command their own army—the most powerful single force in their country. Hussein's relations with Nasser were at the time so bad that he can have been influenced little if at all by some gibes about Glubb on Cairo radio. But the manner of the dismissal was unforgivably abrupt, and in the context of Egyptian radio attacks on every remnant of British influence in the Middle East, many British inevitably drew the conclusion that Nasser had undermined Glubb. The impression was heightened when Lloyd went on to Bahrain, where he was greeted with anti-British riots encouraged by Cairo radio. Eden's strong feelings against Nasser date not from the arms deal with the Soviet block but from Jordan's brusque dismissal of a loyal henchman, who was at the same time one of the last landmarks of British service rendered to Arab states. Eden's sense of affront was heightened when the Suez group, which at once pressed him to renounce all idea of lending for the Aswan Dam scheme, hinted that he had backed the wrong horse when he had put faith in Nasser as the future guardian of the Suez Canal.

According to Nasser, the main request he made to Lloyd during their frigid interviews was that "no more Arabs" should be asked to join the Baghdad Pact. Lloyd (remembering that the text of the pact contained a standing invitation to "any member of the Arab League") demurred, and said he must consult others before answering. His dilemma was one common in diplomacy; a sop to an adversary may displease an ally. Britain, again according to Nasser, never replied to his request, and on March 24, 1956, he took action to extract an answer. He sent, on a Saturday, for the correspondents of the London *Observer* and *Sunday Times*. This interview given to two first-class journalists is required reading for any student of Anglo-Egyptian relations; it sets out the whole position as Egypt saw it:

> From the *Sunday Times*: The only defence [in the cold war] is something that makes a people proof against any kind of external pressure no matter whence it comes, and that defence is nationalism.

> From the *Observer*: There was a brief honeymoon and then Britain plunged into the Baghdad Pact plan which she knew in advance was in our opinion a threat to our vital interests. It was also against the genuine desires of the Arabs. Any policy in this area must recognize nationalism . . . Arabs are not now able to accept themselves as a tail to British policy . . . I believe

that by attempting to keep this area as a sphere of influence Britain will lose her real interests.[8]

To Eden, whose temper was already prickly on account of adverse comment from Conservative back-benchers, this method of communication was a further irritant. On the Sunday (as the Egyptians were quick to note) the Foreign Office rapped out a declaration of faith in the Baghdad Pact. In April, the United States (which had not joined the Pact despite the pleadings of the Middle Eastern members) supported the British line by becoming a member of the Pact's economic and anti-subversion committees, and by establishing a military liaison group at its head-quarters. During the summer of 1956, therefore, British, American and Iraqi heads were often close together, devoting thought to the problem of how far Nasser was turning communist (all three underrated his neutralism), and to whether they could frustrate any attempt he might make to join hands with the pro-Russian faction in Syria. For a brief while, the Middle Eastern policies of Britain and the United States were more closely aligned than they had been for years; the only difference between them was that whereas the American purpose was to check communism, part of the British purpose was simultaneously to preserve some of Britain's former power and authority; the British were therefore keener than the Americans on arresting the spread of Nasser's influence, no matter whether or not it was pro-communist.

The stages by which the British and American Governments came to the conclusion that they must refuse Nasser the loan for the Aswan Dam belong as much to American as to British history. No lender enjoys dealing with a borrower who keeps flaunting his ability to turn elsewhere, but American disenjoyment of the experience was if anything bigger than Britain's because the contemplated American contribution was so much bigger than the British share. As time went on, therefore, Dulles became if anything angrier than Eden. Had Nasser been better acquainted with the non-Arab world, he might have realized that it was imprudent to run the risk of over-taxing the forbearance of a righteous but short-tempered American; for Dulles was a character reminiscent of Stevenson's Lord Justice, Weir of Hermiston:

That part of our nature which goes out (too often with false coin) to acquire glory or love seemed in him to be omitted . . . a great lawyer and . . . upright as the day . . . on he went up the great bare staircase of his duty, uncheered and undepressed.[9]

A presidential election in the United States was due in the autumn of 1956, and Senator McCarthy, though past his prime at home, was still in full cry about foreign policy, and branding as "stark immorality" the spending of American money abroad on any country that was taking help from Russia. In Congress, the Zionist lobby was opposed to helping Nasser, and a group of congressmen from the southern states was inquiring why America should subsidize cotton-growing by a foreign competitor. Conservative criticism in Britain was a shadow by comparison with this range of argument, but was in the same vein. The two biggest contributions to Dulles's annoyance, however, seem to have been Egypt's recognition of Communist China in May, and a story that Nasser circulated in July; this was a tale of much better offers for the dam from the Soviet Union—offers that simultaneous evidence from Moscow suggested had not been made. The Senate Appropriations Committee in Washington instructed Dulles not to lend money for the dam without reference back to it. Nasser, suddenly sensing the risk of losing both of two suitors, instructed his ambassador in Washington, who was in Egypt, to hurry back to his post and negotiate acceptance of the Western offer. The ambassador did so, but too late.

There were thus human and political reasons inside both the United States and Britain for calling off the Aswan Dam loan. They capped and transcended the financial grounds for doubts that were worrying all three intending lenders—uncertainty whether Egypt, which was mortgaging its cotton crop in order to pay for armaments, would be able to service so large a loan. Anglo-Saxon refusal to lend was justifiable; diplomacy's job was to decide how to render refusal bearable, and not too humiliating to the Egyptian borrower. According to Eden's autobiography, "I would have preferred to play this long and not have forced the issue." But Dulles played it short and withdrew the offer abruptly. The British followed suit next day, and—as the deal was a package one—the World Bank contribution automatically fell to the ground. Nasser heard the news over the radio while on a flight back from Yugoslavia. The date was July 19, 1956. Exactly a month earlier, amidst ceremony and exchanges of medals, the last British troops had left the Canal Zone.

.   .   .   .   .

The Suez Canal belonged to Egypt, but successive Egyptian Governments had felt powerless to extract income from it. The Khedive Ismail had sold his shares in the company in 1875, and his right to 15 per cent of its profits in 1880, and, soon after, Egypt had ceased to be its own master. By the time Egyptian national spirit rallied, the noiseless efficiency of the Suez Canal Company had become such a boon to the world that the Canal's name stood for service rather than gain. (Only a handful of shareholders had enjoyed the latter.) For decades, Egypt drew no direct income at all from the Canal's operation. In 1937, the Egyptian Government accepted a paltry but regular £300,000 per annum, and in 1949 a new agreement, related to the new Egyptian company law, associated the Egyptian Government with the company, appointed five Egyptian directors to the board, and accorded Egypt 7 per cent of the profits.

The main deterrent that prevented Egyptian nationalists from following the example of the states producing oil, or carrying it in transit by pipeline, and pressing a concessionaire for more money, was the British occupation; given the presence of so much power to apply pressure, Egyptians deduced that a fuss would be a failure. Other factors in their acceptance of the company's arrangements were a kind of awe for the service the Canal rendered to international shipping, and the thought that the company's concession had not long to run. Egypt was due to come into its rich inheritance in 1968.

Nasser's revolutionary Government had done more than any of its predecessors to extract benefits from the company. He and his colleagues talked freely in private of their desiderata—replacement of the pashas on the board by representatives of the young officers' movement, and a seat or two on its inner *Comité de Direction*; observation by the company of the Egyptian company law, which called for 40 per cent of Egyptian directors and 70 per cent of Egyptian employees; investment of a proportion of the company's reserves in Egypt; access for the Egyptian Treasury to some of the hard currencies earned by the company; and relaxation of the company's strict rule that pilots must have had ten years' experience on the high seas—a stipulation that cut out most Egyptians. In 1956 the company met one of these desires by agreeing to invest $60 million of its reserves in Egyptian development projects; simultaneously, the Egyptians showed the way their minds were working by raising some difficulties about visas for foreign pilots. Both parties knew that the end was in sight, and seemed to be looking forward to several years of pressure from one side and response from the other.

The Suez Canal Company's concession covered the operation of the Canal; the question of right of passage was governed by another and quite different agreement—the international Suez Canal Convention of 1888. This instrument guaranteed free and equal rights of passage in peace or war to the ships of all nations. It laid down that the Egyptian Government was to "take the necessary measures for ensuring the execution of the said Treaty", and charged the "Agents in Egypt of the signatory powers" to watch over the process.

While the British governed Egypt, Britain therefore safeguarded this right of passage. Thereafter, custom and the presence of British troops enabled the British Government to go on doing so, or to think that it was doing so. In fact, power passed out of British hands once the British garrisons left Cairo, as was proved when, after the Palestine war, the Egyptian Government refused the right of passage to Israeli ships. Nevertheless, British public opinion continued to take British good guardianship for granted; every village in Britain contained men familiar with the Canal Zone, and with keeping guard below the dun-coloured hills round Suez— "the white cliffs of Dover browned off", as the troops called them. The Suez group was not the only element in the British population that thought of the Canal as British soil.

On July 26, 1956—four years after King Farouk had sailed away into exile—Nasser was due to make a great anniversary-of-the-revolution speech in Alexandria. Everyone knew that he would retort to Western cancellation of the Aswan Dam loan; foreign embassies had their tape-recorders ready. The surprise he sprang was not so much his statement of nationalization as the speed, aplomb and success with which he carried out overnight seizure of the Suez Canal Company's installations, and set Egyptians to do its work. The Canal office in the Egyptian ministry charged with studying eventual take-over was very small; no one could have imagined that such a feat of organization was possible. By next morning, Egyptians were at all the controls.

This turn of the tables affected every nation whose ships used the Canal; for instance, to whom were masters to pay dues? But it particularly affected Britain, the prime user, and France, for the management of the Suez Canal Company had always been in French hands. In Britain in particular, sentiment, national pride, imperial interests and the ghost of total responsibility for guardianship caused mental and political turmoil. Everyone was reminded of Abadan.

From now on, constant reference will be made to the volume of Eden's autobiography called *Full Circle*—a book interesting for its omissions as well as its information. In it the choices before the British Government at the end of July 1956 are clearly set out. The immediate thought was the security of Europe's oil supplies: the long-term one was permanently to safeguard the interests of the users of the Canal. The choices were two: to strike at Nasser on behalf of the sanctity of a contract that lasted until 1968, or to negotiate in company with other users for suitable control of a nationalized Canal. The first course, followed in hot blood, would have suited the mood of a large section of British opinion; it would also have suited the French. But the Chiefs of Staff said that it was impossible; in spite of years of military outlay in the Middle East, no fire-brigade could be provided at short notice now that the nearest military bases were on islands, and British tanks could no longer rumble straight out on to foreign roads. The best they could do, without a land-base on the spot, was to prepare for an eventual operation, and this they at once received orders to do in conjunction with the French military authorities.

In spite of Nasser's "thumb on our windpipe", therefore, negotiation began, and in concert with Dulles, Eden summoned a conference of maritime powers. At this meeting, the British aims were two: to make sure that Egypt did not get away with unilateral denunciation of a concession, and to make good the international character of the Canal laid down in the 1888 convention. Neither was achieved. After a month during which Nasser had successfully operated the Canal in spite of worldwide anticipation that he would fail to do so, eighteen maritime nations sent him a proposal that an international body (of which Egypt was of course to be a prominent member) should manage and develop the Canal. This proposition was not of a shape to tempt Nasser, and the men who bore it to Cairo knew as much; Nasser held the cards, could reject compromise, and did so.

This conference and errand occupied the Canal users until September. Meanwhile, Anglo-French troop movements continued. A force based chiefly on Malta, but also on Cyprus for its parachute and aircraft components, was mounted during August and September. Its scale was determined by prognosis of the very worst— an opposed landing, help to the Egyptians from Russian pilots and tank experts, and a degree of chaos that might entail not only seizure of the Canal but the temporary occupation of Egypt. (The French included Middle Eastern political experts in their team.) But as the weeks went by these elaborate pre-conceptions grew more and more inapposite because delay was altering foreign thoughts about what Nasser had done, and weakening support for strong measures. The unexpected technical skill and determination of the Egyptians excited admiration. Canal users were not a tight-knit group, as the major oil companies had been after Abadan; they included some states, such as Greece or India, who were unaffected by the problems of denounced concessions, as well as some who were anti-colonial and opposed to arbitrary behaviour by great powers. The tempers of users also cooled as they reflected on the colossal inconvenience of sailing round by the Cape to get from the Persian Gulf to the Mediterranean. A tide of opinion led by India began to move in the direction of a compromise solution short of international control.

Eden saw British authority, and control of a British artery slipping from his grasp. To his fury, Dulles veered this way and that, sometimes working for international management, but sometimes seeming blind to the dangers of weakening the British stand. Eden took special exception to a "damaging statement" by Dulles on October 2, when at a Press conference about Anglo-American differences over a Canal Users' Association, Dulles joined the ranks of the anti-colonials and said that

> there is in Asia and Africa the so-called problem of colonialism. Now there the United States plays a somewhat independent role.[10]

If this was an oblique allusion to the fact that the United States would not support Britain and France in the use of force, Eden did not take it that way. The Americans made more than one equivocal reference to the use of force, but several times American statesmen made their meaning plain. According to Eden's memoirs, Eisenhower wrote to him on September 3 that "American public opinion flatly rejected force", and Dulles told Selwyn Lloyd in New York in October that "he was with Britain on every point except the use of force".

The British Government was pelted with advice from other quarters—with French encouragement, Soviet discouragement, Indian pleas for compromise and a predictable range of opinions from its embassies in the Arab states and Israel. Nuri Pasha (who, by an accident, happened to be dining at 10 Downing Street on the night of Nasser's nationalization speech) shared in the first burst of indignation, and was as keen as anyone for Britain to strike at Nasser while tempers were high; but on reflection Nuri stipulated —according to his biographer, Lord Birdwood—that any action against Egypt must be subject to three conditions: that Israel should not be involved in it; that there should be no French co-operation, and that all suggestion of Western "grab" of the Canal should be avoided. Eden seemed to think the Soviet attitude manageable; when he looked back on the conversations that he had held with Bulganin and Khrushchev on the Middle East in the previous April, he reckoned that

> later events showed that the Russians . . . understood our position pretty well. When troubles came, their opening moves were prudent.[11]

But this "prudence" evaporated. When Britain and France (as much to forestall appeal to the United Nations by others than out of faith in its supposedly slow mechanism) referred the problem of Canal management to the Security Council, the Soviet Union vetoed the operative part of the compromise resolution to which Britain was ready to subscribe. The date was October 13, an*' matters were back at deadlock.

These were the conditions in which, on October 16, Eden went into secret conclave with the French, who were in their turn harnessed to Israel. When planning policy in this company, Britain had much less room for manœuvre than either of its companions. Both of these had more acute reason than the British to hate Nasser —France, because Nasser was encouraging the Algerian war that was beginning to eat at its vitals, and Israel because Nasser's raiders were a day-to-day threat to its home security. France and Israel could afford one-track thinking; Britain, beset by extraneous interests, could not. For the British had to look at any plan of action against Nasser in the light of Commonwealth opinion— particularly Nehru's pacifist opinion; they had also to think of the effect on their faithful ally, Nuri Pasha. Thus, if there were

to be action against Nasser, France did not care how this was contrived, and Israel set only one limiting condition—that the Israel
army should be given time to achieve a clear military victory before
anyone else interfered. Britain, by contrast, could only contemplate
the use of force in a much narrower context. To use force, Eden
needed first, conditions in which Britain could condemn or threaten
both Egypt and Israel (this for Nuri's sake) and secondly, conditions in which British forces could act to save world shipping from
interference caused by cross-fire (this for the sake of Nehru and of
American opinion). Eden prepared for these contingencies in ruthless company.

Perhaps no one will ever know exactly by what process Eden and
Selwyn Lloyd reached agreement with their French counterparts,
Mollet and Pineau. The British and French archives of 1956, when
they become available to the public in the twenty-first century, may
not furnish the evidence, for the four men ceased to confide in
their officials. Neither Eden nor Lloyd had enough sense of the
past to recall how disastrous to British fortunes in the Middle East
had been Lloyd George's excursions into the region without consulting his professional advisers—his *tête-à-tête* with Clemenceau
about Palestine, and his breakfasts with Mark Sykes about Zionism.
Like hounds with a nose for a single scent, Eden and Lloyd followed
the course of making Nasser pay; they forgot or discarded American
warnings, Nuri's conditions, the importance of consulting the
British dominions, and the worth of opinions from Britain's
embassies in the Middle East.

Though history cannot yet follow their train of thought, conjecture has done so. Detective works of good quality have been
published in both Britain and France—Wint and Calvocoressi's
Middle East Crisis, Merry and Serge Bromberger's *The Secrets of
Suez*, and two studies by Erskine Childers, a succinct one in *The
Spectator* of October 30, 1959, and a longer one in his *The Road
to Suez*. All this evidence, when compounded, suggests that a
plan which some saw as a contingency plan, and others as a firm
plan with a time-table, went wrong over a hitch in timing. Childers,
who is the Inspector Maigret in the case, works backwards from the
Anglo-French ultimatum issued to Egypt and Israel on October 30.
This document proclaimed that shipping through the Canal must be
preserved from interruption; it therefore ordered both aggressor
and victim of aggression to get back ten miles from the Canal. It
also requested Egypt to accept temporary Anglo-French occupation

of some "key positions on the Canal". It requested answers within twelve hours. Failing compliance by one or both governments,

> United Kingdom and French forces will intervene in whatever strength may be necessary to secure compliance.[12]

At the moment of issue, the peculiar feature of this injunction was that it ordered Israeli forces to withdraw from a position they had not yet reached. Childers argues that an ultimatum that did not fit the facts had been prepared, as a contingency measure, for use in different circumstances, and that a last minute change of timing had made it inappropriate. He contends that the ultimatum made sense in one context only: if the Israeli army had reached the Canal, if cross-fire were endangering shipping, and if, because the Americans were engaged in a Presidential election, the United Nations machinery were temporarily paralysed. All these events in conjunction could have happened on November 6, for which date, argues Childers, the ultimatum must have been prepared. Before it, the Israelis could have achieved their "clean victory" and on it, the British could have upbraided both sides and avoided the embarrassment of taking action on the side of Israel.

The fortuitous event that threw out this time-table was revolution in Hungary. Soviet intervention to quell the Hungarians precipitated an Israeli decision, communicated to France but taken without notice to Eden, to advance Israel's intended attack on Egypt by several days in order to strike while world attention was riveted on the Hungarian crisis. The Childers conjecture is that the French were indifferent to this change; their politicians and generals were so sore about Algeria that they wanted to strike at Nasser come what might. When Israel attacked on October 29, Mollet crossed to London and, determined to push plans to a conclusion, had no compunction in playing false with both his partners. The Security Council was sitting on account of Hungary, and he was afraid that Eden's nerve might crack; Mollet pinned down his man by telling Eden that the Israelis were closer to the Canal than was the case, and that the ultimatum must be launched, now or never. Simultaneously he deprived the Israelis of their clean victory.

Here conjecture ends. Mollet and Eden were in conclave for some hours on the morning of October 30, 1956, and after their colloquy they issued their ultimatum, addressed to both Egypt and Israel. Mollet was satisfied. The Israelis called the news "a bombshell". Eden had taken action that did not fulfil some essential conditions for future British influence in the Middle East. He did worse. The Security Council discussed the Israeli aggression on the same day; giving way to French insistence on solidarity, Eden instructed the British representative in New York to join France in vetoing two resolutions calling on all United Nations members to refrain from using force or the threat of force in Egypt. On that afternoon in New York, Britain and France played themselves into a minority of two; the United States, the Soviet Union and even Australia voted against them.

In the whirl of this diplomatic agitation, the quandary into which the Cabinet's sudden orders plunged Britain's military planners often escapes comment. "The limiting factor," later explained the Commander-in-Chief of the combined Anglo-French expedition to Suez, "was clearly the Commando and armour located at Malta." Parachutists were not enough, and before action (other than inconclusive naval and air bombardment) could be taken in support of the ultimatum, this armour had to steam 936 miles, taking six days. Deeds that stood a chance of taking the world's breath away if done quickly, stood none by Day Six. In the interval, as soon as the ultimatum had been accepted by Israel and rejected by Egypt, the British spent five days on the holding operation of bombing targets in Egypt. They expended all this effort on a military adversary so weak that the Israel army had reckoned to win a clean victory in forty-eight hours, and nothing short of a sudden change of timing can have brought them to use plans intended for a quite different set of circumstances. Inevitably, five days' bombing of Egyptian targets caused all Arabs to deduce that the British had sided with Israel, and gave all other critics time in which to compose and co-ordinate their strictures.

Diplomatic and military plans must be judged by the degree to which they stand up to contemporary conditions, including unexpected conditions. A plan that is thrown out of joint by a change of date is faulty, and no plan is a good plan if it produces three of the worst mistakes a government can make—miscalculation of world opinion, bad military timing, and choice of an inconvenient ally. When the Anglo-French landing craft finally chugged ashore on November 5–6, these three handicaps had between them wrecked all chance of presenting the Anglo-French forces as knight-errants making the Suez Canal safe for the world. In the meantime, Egypt had seen which way the wind of international opinion was blowing, and had used the one conclusive weapon at its disposal; it had sunk ships in the Canal, and blocked it.

The rest of the tale of British action is soon told—military clockwork, negligible British casualties, the order to halt when only half of the blocked Canal had been occupied. One reason for the order, given on the day of the landing, was a volume of international and domestic pressure to desist that was not merely moral and diplomatic, but financial. A decisive reason for going into reverse was a disastrous run on the pound sterling that threatened the whole fabric of confidence in Britain that underpins the sterling area. No Chancellor of the Exchequer could afford to ignore the danger signals, or fail to recommend saving the pound by reversing the policy. The adventure was a failure; most members of the British Cabinet recognized it to be so; they decided to yield to the United Nations; Eden collapsed.

No matter whether Eden is judged to have been carried away by an obsession, or duped by France, or merely mistaken in his judgements, the consequences of his decisions to the remainder of British power and influence in the Middle East were great, and detrimental. Defence plans were deprived of the access to Suez that he himself had so painstakingly negotiated with Egypt. Even Arabs who disliked Nasser were alienated, while Arab friends were put out of countenance; poor Nuri became in most Arab eyes not merely Britain's toady but Britain's dupe and found himself obliged to propose Britain's ejection from the Baghdad Pact. Jordan dismissed the few British officers still serving with its forces, and abrogated the Anglo-Jordanian Treaty. As for oil, its transit was stopped not only by Nasser's blockships in the Suez Canal, but by the Arab states that controlled the trans-desert pipelines. The Syrians blew up the pumping stations on the lines from Iraq, and the Saudi Government forbade pumping to British-held terminals, or into British ships. (Ironically, the first multiple Arab action taken to apply the oil sanction that had often been discussed was precipitated by British action, and directed at Great Britain.) The Soviet Government, which on November 5 brandished rockets at London, was enabled to drive all thought of Hungary out of Arab minds, and momentarily to assume in Arab eyes the role of a saviour who had brought about the British cease fire order of the next day, and the Anglo-French withdrawal. The President of the United States was made a gift of an anti-imperialist cause carrying no risk of electoral embarrassment. Not even Israel was pleased; by its standards Mollet and Eden had robbed it of its chance of bringing Nasser down for ever.

The best that can be said of an adventure that brought these disastrous consequences is that Eden sought a comprehensible end in an incomprehensible way. An understanding reviewer of his memoirs (Martin Wight in *International Affairs* for July 1960) points out that he was in a classic dilemma and likens him to Brutus " 'by awful virtue urg'd' to the last extremity in defence of principle", yet running the risk of senselessly seeking to restore conditions past restoration.

In whatever light his act is seen, the methods he used prompt examination of the system that enabled him to go ahead. Even if he kept his officials in the dark, how did he induce a whole British Cabinet to follow his lead? His Defence Minister, Monckton, resigned while force was being accumulated in Cyprus, but immediately accepted another and less exacting post. At the moment of crux, only two junior ministers resigned in protest; the rest acquiesced. One deduction to be drawn from the course of events is that the power of a British Prime Minister is very great. Eden himself says in *Full Circle* that "in fact his authority is stronger" than that of *primus inter pares*. Above all, he chooses his ministers. He can work individually with one or several of them and present the Cabinet with some composite policy containing points agreed with each, but the sum of which no one of them would have chosen. Inertia, and unwillingness to disturb a card house by extracting one card, does the rest.

Another conclusion is that party loyalty is powerful; men who disapprove of a stroke of policy may think it a duty to remain in power on account of other work in progress. A third reflection is that decisions which involve a number of government departments, and which are taken in Cabinet committee, set in motion so many separate arms of a great machine that the effort to stop them all is more than any one minister, except the Prime Minister, can manage.

Personalities played their part in the decisions whereby the British Cabinet slid into the Suez quandary, and adopted a stately trot out of it led by the Chancellor of the Exchequer. As yet, there is only one authoritative account of personal participation in these doings; this appears in Eden's memoirs, and historians must be content with a single written source.

The title Eden chose—*Full Circle*—helps to reveal the way his mind worked. His long tenure of the Foreign Secretaryship had had many peak moments, but to him the most exalting happened in 1938. At the beginning of that year, deeply perturbed by Neville Chamberlain's rebuff of Roosevelt's suggestion for a joint stand against Hitler and Mussolini, Eden resigned rather than go on appeasing the latter. In 1956 he seems to have reasoned that, as Hitler later proved impervious to appeasement, it was his duty to be firm with Egypt's dictator for breaking a covenant. The note he had struck in 1938 echoed in other ears than his own, including Churchill's:

> But now on this night of February 20, 1938, and on this occasion only, sleep deserted me [wrote Churchill in 1948]. From midnight till dawn I lay in my bed consumed by emotions of sorrow and fear. There seemed one strong young figure standing up against long, dismal, drawling tides of drift and surrender, of wrong measurements and feeble impulses. My conduct of affairs would have been different from his in various ways; but he seemed to me at this moment to embody the life-hope of the British nation, the grand old British race that had done so much for men, and yet had some more to give.[13]

No man, however little vain, could forbear to flush with pride and resolve at memory of such a tribute from a master. The strong young figure felt bound to remain strong in riper years. Yet his circle is far from perfect, for the analogies he drew do not bear close scrutiny—neither that of Hitler with Nasser, nor that of the principles that prompted resistance to appeasement in 1938 with all the reasons that caused him to wish to topple Nasser. Indeed, the closest likeness to that year is one that he cannot have wished to underline—Neville Chamberlain's disastrous propensity, repeated by Eden in mid-October 1956, to dispense with the professional advice of the Foreign Service.

Memoirs make patchy history, but at their best they give a portrait of a man in the round—mind, flesh and blood, warts and all. The Eden memoirs are not of this satisfying quality; they portray only a mind, and a mind dwelling on a personal record and a conscience. So long as that mind is engaged in diplomatic work—negotiating, patching and reconciling in a quarrelsome world, it is in its element and moves with distinction. Handling Russia in Germany, or the European Defence Community, negotiating with Egypt over the Sudan and the evacuation, with America and Persia over the oil agreement, dealing with Korea, the Formosa Strait and—above all—with settlement in Indo-China, a masterly diplomat is seen at work. In 1953, the record breaks off for six months of grave illness; Eden had the gruelling experience of hearing a famous surgeon ask if he wanted the truth, and then telling him that "I would never recover unless I had a third operation". He underwent this ordeal and carried on. He bore burdens that would have been heavy for a man in the pink of health; he was handicapped by the additional nervous strain of finding Dulles exceedingly difficult; yet he did well in nearly every job that he tackled.

There follows the Prime-Ministership, beginning in April 1955. It happens to coincide with complications in the Middle East—till lately a British preserve, but a preserve no longer. The Eden that operates in these new conditions shows impaired judgement. There could be more than one reason for the waning capacity revealed in Book III of *Full Circle*—for instance the strain of following a great predecessor, or the discomfort of the wrong job for his temperament, or exhaustion after too much work during convalescence. Whatever the cause, former qualities shade off. Above all, Eden's capacity for seeing the other man's point of view diminishes, and he becomes readier and readier to describe foreign actions simply as misunderstandings of his own thought, or as baulks to his action. He sees Dulles as moved by spite, instead of as a man hard-pressed by Congress; he never mentions that Nasser ran the Suez Canal without a hitch to world shipping— a piece of information essential to an understanding of the world-wide diminution of support for international management; for lack of that key fact, a process that was *laisser faire* becomes, at Eden's hands, malevolence towards Britain.

When facts are omitted from a personal record produced within five years of events still fresh in mind (or still worse, when the facts that are given contradict one another), the soundness of a man's judgement is bound to be questioned. Eden's angle of vision is often so personal that he sees only what he wants to see. For instance, in spite of his admissions of American warnings against the use of force, he writes of the day on which the ultimatum was dispatched that we had no reason at this moment to suppose that the United States would oppose us at the United Nations upon almost every point.[14]

Again, after the attack, he states that "not a mouse moved in Arab lands". In fact, every Arab state, including even Iraq, took action in support of Nasser. All the wrecked pumping stations, closed pipelines, denounced treaties, lost bases and broken diplomatic relations seem to have meant nothing to the man who destroyed them.

Nevertheless his account of events must not be underrated, for it mirrors some constant thoughts that governed British Middle Eastern policy—for better, for worse—all the way through the period described in this book. It displays the habit of authority, the resentment at the intrusion of power greater than Britain's, the underestimation of local nationalism and the distaste for Egypt that coloured British action all along. Eden's urge to move without American interference is implicit throughout his account of Suez; his views on other points are explicit. Take Arab nationalism; by his standards, it "began to appear in its full shape" in a speech by Nasser of August 1956; those who have taken the trouble to read this book know that nationalism was easily discernible from the end of the Second World War, and that Nasser's brand had been patent ever since he successfully rallied the rest of the Arabs against Nuri and the Baghdad Pact at the beginning of 1955. As for Egypt, Eden gives it the old familiar rating; seizure of the Canal was "intolerable", but

this was still more so when the single nation that set out to dominate the Canal was Egypt.[15]

Few people in Britain remembered who was the ground-landlord, but this very British line of thought was spiced, in Eden's case, with an additional and exotic flavour. He had read Oriental Languages at Oxford—a subject with a syllabus that then ended in the Middle Ages. His main language was Persian, but study of Arabic (in which he recalls "an agreeable Arab historian of the early Caliphs") caused him to venerate the pure glories of Damascus and Baghdad and disdain the later hybrid caliphs of Egypt.

Eden carried the British Cabinet with him in deciding to attack, and had approximately half the British people behind him in thinking his thoughts and in approving what he did to further them. Those British citizens who shared his view did so not entirely on account of his theoretical reason for attacking Egypt—defence of the sanctity of agreements—but by reason of emotions built up during a series of British retreats and withdrawals. "Scuttle" from India had been accepted because the successor states paid Britain the compliment of staying within the Commonwealth; Palestine had been an inessential British interest, and Abadan one for which there were substitutes. But an accumulation of emotions long pent up burst forth as soon as alien hands touched that sacred cow, the Suez Canal.

Half Britain was with Eden, but the other half was against him. The resultant public uproar was greater even than on the last occasion when a British Government had flouted international rules—the outcry over the Hoare-Laval plan in 1935. Argument raged back and forth; families were divided as hotly as over the Irish question. Indignation was so great as to bring Eden's career to an end. But the instincts of the opposition were, unbeknown to many of its members, closer to the true state of power and politics in the Arab world than was the policy to which the Eden Cabinet consented.

9

AFTERMATH AND GLEANINGS

AFTER days so full of excitement, gunfire, telegrams and anger, the sequel cannot fail to be an anti-climax.

The Suez adventure put an end to British influence in all the more important countries of the Arab world except Iraq, and there the respite was short. At all points (except in Baghdad while Nuri Pasha's régime survived, and in the deep south made up of the Aden dependencies and the Arab principalities of the Persian Gulf) Britain's hold on events ceased, and remained at zero while the free world gasped at so radical a departure from British principle and practice. Asians and Africans were dumbfounded not so much at the act of dropping bombs on Nasser, for many victims of Egypt's radio invective felt that he had asked for trouble, but at British exercise of the veto at the United Nations on an injunction to cease fire.

But the doldrums do not last for ever. Sooner than anyone would have prophesied, chinks appeared through which, for a while, a modicum of British influence could be exerted. But the nature of that influence was altered because the power behind it was permanently impaired. From the time of Suez, Britain's dealings with Middle Eastern states assumed the shape and nature of its relations with uncommitted states in other parts of the world—for instance, with Spain, or the states of Latin America. The orb of regional power was shattered so thoroughly that no single aspirant to dominance has since been able to put it together again. The fag-end of British history that remains to be told is the story of an inconclusive struggle for the fragments.

The months immediately following the Suez crisis produced some galling demonstrations of Britain's changed status. For instance, British salvage vessels held ready in Cyprus at once began clearing Nasser's blockships from the Suez Canal, only to be told by the United Nations team on the job that their services were unwelcome to the sovereign power—Egypt—and that they must go. They went. Again, in March 1957, when the Jordanian throne was threatened by a radical group of politicians and colonels encouraged from Egypt and Syria, its fall was averted partly by King Hussein's personal coolness, but largely thanks to an American demonstration of support that included the dispatch of vessels of the Sixth Fleet to cruise off Beirut. A former British protégé had changed protectors, and thereafter drew the major grant-in-aid that enables Jordan to make ends meet not from Britain, but from the United States.

Yet American progress towards establishing a new brand of Western influence in the Arab world was beset by obstacles. For one thing, the Russians were at the height of their renown, not only as reputed saviours during the Suez crisis, but as a nation that had not only proved a match for the West, but had outstripped the United States in scientific attainment; 1957 was the year of the Sputnik. For another, President Eisenhower, in order to acquire greater powers to produce a fire-brigade in the event of a communist conflagration in the Middle East, was obliged to seek special sanction from Congress for swifter and more liberal use of American funds, and if need be American armed forces, than was possible under existing legislation. In order to win consent in Washington, he had to specify that these emergency facilities would be used only when Middle Eastern states asked for help "to combat international communism"; the phrase was attractive to American ears, but suspect to most Middle Eastern ones because it was reminiscent of the well-worn British technique of seeking allies in the cold war. In the end, only the President of Lebanon at once subscribed to this so-called "Eisenhower Doctrine"; the Shah, to the consternation of Persians who preferred neutralism, later concluded a bi-lateral agreement within its framework; elsewhere kings who would have been glad to make sure of its benefits were too wary of Arab public opinion to say so outright.

Much as Nasser would have liked to assume a dominant role, and to become leader of a neutralist block of all the Arab states, he proved unable to attract general Arab support. Some heads of state disliked his tendency to treat them as subordinates, others mistrusted his sudden and abusive radio outbursts. But the root cause of his inability to assume a commanding lead was the degree to which his appeal to peoples over the heads of their governments had given birth, in every Arab state, to a faction of "Nasserites" who were often encouraged by Egypt to undermine the authority of their own government. Sufferers from this Egyptian technique—

King Hussein, President Chamoun of Lebanon, King Saud, Iraqi ministers who did not share Nuri's self-confidence—were rendered uncertain how they stood with their own citizens, and opposed Nasser because of the atmosphere of insecurity that he created.

Nations in this state of uncertainty cannot avoid exploitation from outside, particularly exploitation by great powers in a state of armed peace with one another. For some time after the Suez crisis, therefore, it seemed that the United States and the Soviet Union would be able to pick up Arab sides, as in a game. Syria, and possibly also Egypt, seemed likely to be drawn towards the Soviet side, while the rulers of Lebanon, Jordan and Saudi Arabia— all hostile to communism—seemed virtually bound to lean on the United States.

If Arab inclinations had been stable, and if Arab alignments had assumed this neat pattern, the British might have had no further chance to take part in the affairs of the Levant. But owing to Arab doubts and quarrels, the pattern remained fluid, and, during 1957 resolved itself into a struggle between communists and anti-communists (each with their great-power supporters) for the soul and body of Syria. An unfriendly Syria is always an Iraqi bugbear because the oil pipelines from northern Iraq cross Syrian territory on their way to the Mediterranean; the royalist régime in Iraq was therefore as opposed as anyone to Soviet influence in Damascus, and so joined the fray. It was by the side-door of support for its Iraqi ally that Britain in 1957 unobtrusively resumed a minor role in anti-communist planning. Yet the attempt to capture Syria's allegiance was not a success from the standpoint of any one of the three great powers that took a hand in it. In February 1958, the Syrians finally evaded the Soviet embrace, but the rescuer that they called on to snatch them from the jaws of communism was not President Eisenhower. It was President Nasser.

Nasser's establishment in February 1958 of the United Arab Republic of Egypt and Syria drove a neutralist wedge into the heart of the Arab world. To some extent his innovation thwarted the Soviet Union, which had hoped to gain Middle Eastern influence through the medium of Syrian communism; during a short war of words which Nasser waged with Khrushchev, he told the Russians roundly that their action at the time of Suez had been a piece of bluff. But the foreign power to suffer the sharpest setback from the establishment of the U.A.R. turned out, in the not-so-long run, to be Great Britain. For the extension of Nasser's absolute power to

o

Syria's eastern frontier helped to precipitate the downfall of the pro-British régime in Iraq.

The conservative régime run by Nuri Pasha and the Iraqi royal house had, it will be remembered, grown increasingly out of touch with the bulk of Iraqi opinion during the years of Nasser's drive against foreign alliances and the Baghdad Pact, and against Nuri for impairing Arab unity. Many Iraqis shared Nasser's opinion on these topics, and disliked Nuri's fidelity to the British alliance; almost all deplored his inclination to rate the Baghdad Pact above inter-Arab defence arrangements, and despaired of any change in the conservative pattern of Iraqi society so long as "the Palace" and "the Pasha" ran the state. Until the Suez crisis, Nuri's régime stood a chance of survival. Its authoritarian home policy was conceived (as Nasser was later freely to acknowledge about Egypt's authoritarian home policy) in order to secure the continuity of management that is essential to quick development of a backward state. Nuri's objective was to spend the oil royalties with enough speed and acumen to keep social discontent at bay. But, from the moment of Suez, his prospects of executing this grand design became slender. For one of the results of Eden's policy was to render Nuri more unpopular than ever in Iraq; long known as Britain's crony, he was now branded also as the dupe of an ally that had fought alongside Israel. His retention of power during and after the Suez adventure was a tribute to his police force; it lasted only for twenty months.

On July 14, 1958, public antipathy to his régime erupted. The immediate cause of the explosion was a split in the army on receipt of orders to move troops to the Syrian frontier, lately become a frontier with Nasser. A rebellious regiment *en route* through Baghdad murdered the men the country held chiefly responsible for unpopular policies—the ex-Regent who had held on for too long to the young king's elbow, and Nuri Pasha. King Feisal II and the British alliance were consumed in the holocaust: the statue of Feisal I was dragged in the dust. In those July days, the British Government lost one of its most loyal and consistent Arab friends; it also reaped the last sad harvest of its Baghdad Pact and Suez policies—both insufficiently attuned, as Nuri himself was in his old age insufficiently attuned, to modern Arab thinking, and both too old-fashioned to capture Arab admiration.

The Iraqi revolution plunged all the anti-communist and anti-Nasser régimes in the neighbourhood into consternation. In

Lebanon, where intermittent civil war had been in progress for months, President Chamoun invoked the Eisenhower doctrine, and, though much criticized at home for "internationalization" of a domestic conflict, got an immediate response from American marines and the Sixth Fleet. In Jordan, King Hussein, who was in grave danger of the same fate as his Iraqi cousin, also asked for American or British forces:

> We needed some help—not so much physical as moral help. A token force would be enough—something to take off some of the load at least for a short while. . . . I had purposely allowed the British and Americans to decide which country should send troops and the answer came swiftly. . . .[1]

London and Washington agreed that the burden of criticism for foreign landings was better shared, and to keep company with the massive American landing in Lebanon, British paratroops were flown into Jordan from Cyprus.

And so it happened that, within two years of the British lapse from Arab grace over Suez, a British force took the old familiar road to the rescue of an Arab state. But any likeness to old times was superficial; to imagine that this action belonged to the old brand of intervention that governed the long-term course of Middle Eastern politics was to overrate its nature. As a remedy for shock, the Anglo-American landings were a success; they preserved stability in the Middle East as a whole. But that lavish display of Western military efficiency in no way increased British or American influence on the long-term course of inter-Arab relations:

> The West could scarcely have bettered this parade of its talents for the benefit of a wondering Orient. . . . But the Western gesture had been to some extent made in a vacuum: it did not affect or impinge upon the real issues in the Arab world. The deeper currents flowed unchanged and unchecked round the tiny islets which the West was maintaining as closely guarded reserves for two chiefs of state. Around and about them, disorderly Arab tides eddied and swirled, wholly unaffected.[2]

When the British paratroops left Jordan in October 1958, British influence in the Middle East was at a lower ebb than at any moment described in this book. Britain had no diplomatic relations with Egypt, and none, therefore, with Syria; none with Saudi Arabia on account of frontier disputes to be described, and none worth mentioning with Iraq. For although the British Government, with a degree of haste that seemed indecent, established relations with the Iraqi regicides as a necessary insurance for Western oil interests in Iraq, the relationship was one of mistrust on both sides.

Yet though the Iraqi revolution at first sight held such promise for Nuri's adversaries—Nasser and the Soviet Union—it benefited neither to the extent that they anticipated. Instead, it served to emphasize the political axiom that, in countries torn by internal dissension, foreign powers that try to meddle incur as many liabilities as assets. For the outsider cannot avoid identification with one faction, and so earns the dislike of all the rest. Britain experienced this drawback in Nuri's Iraq, the United States and the Soviet Union in the harassed Syria of 1947; it is invariably and always the lot of any outside power that tries to influence Persia, and, intermittently, it has been the fate of Nasser in almost every Arab state.

The Iraqi revolution ushered in an era of Arab dissension and backbiting, plotting and counterplotting, and patterns of friendship and enmity that changed so fast that outside wooers desisted from the wooing, and all three drew back. Never had the members of the Arab League been more divided. A scene of political turmoil was relieved only by the common sense with which Arab civil services, and Arab business communities, left politics to a warring few, and handled economics in a watertight compartment; in their need to earn income, they kept international trade and traffic on the move, including the oil traffic. From 1958, all the great powers, Britain included, watched inter-Arab politics from the side-lines. Communist China, which had demonstrated that it too was interested in extending its influence by opening and heavily overstaffing an embassy in republican Iraq, modified its effort as soon as asked by the Iraqis to do so. Disengagement was the only profitable course.

Arabs like to think that, but for British and French acts of self-interest that go back to the Sykes-Picot Agreement, Arab unity would have blossomed from 1919. Profitless though it is to speculate about the might-have-been, even their best friends doubt their theory. At the time, their loyalties were to tribe, district and township; in the Arabian peninsula, Ibn Saud and the Sharif of Mecca were on bad terms; farther north, minorities of all kinds—Druses, Christian communities, Kurds and others—gave their allegiance to leading families; there was no cadre of army officers from which a Kemal or a Reza Khan might spring; towns were nervous of bedouin ascendancy; the desert mistrusted the town. In the light of experience that includes experiences of the nineteen-sixties, it seems logical to see the problem of Arab unity in another light altogether. However strong the ties of culture and emotion, political unity is a product of modern education, good communications and freedom from outside interference, not to mention the gift of time. None of these were available in 1919; all in conjunction were never present in the nineteen-fifties.

There was one exception to the British state of detachment. In the coastal belt of southern Arabia that consists of the Aden dependencies, the Sultanate of Muscat and Oman, and the small Arab principalities of the Persian Gulf, British dominance continued; unchallenged by great powers, it rendered the area a replica in miniature of the one-time British position in the Middle East as a whole.

Coastal Arabia has figured little in this narrative because, for three of the four decades described, it played no part in world affairs. It continued to be, as it had been for more than a century, part of the protective rind acquired for India, and for British and Indian security and trade. Under the shelter of the British protection that gave nearly two centuries of peace to the Indian Ocean, a chain of small principalities lived their life of poverty and domestic feud. Even the disturbing ideas sown during the Second World War largely passed them by. Social and political upheaval did not seriously strike them until the nineteen-fifties. Then, trouble erupted at a number of points as a result here, of sudden wealth from oil; there, at sight of the British putting up with insults from Musaddiq; everywhere, at sound of Nasser's radio programmes directed against colonialism and entanglement with foreigners.

It is impossible to generalize about the whole of this protected fringe because the territories that compose it bear a range of differing relationships to Britain. At one end of the scale is Aden—eighty square miles of colonial territory that in 1963 became part of an Arab Federation of South Arabia, but in which, by an arrangement of British devising, Britain nevertheless retained sovereignty. At the other end of the scale lies the Sultanate of Muscat and Oman—an independent state in treaty relations with various outside powers, but under promise to cede territory to no one without

British consent. In 1961 Kuwait, on the strength of its wealth and rapid development, also became fully independent; by an arrangement reached in amity and agreement, the British ended their protective role; Kuwait became an Amirate, and the Kuwaitis immediately joined the Arab League. In between these extremes lie two clusters of small sheikhdoms in varying forms of treaty relationship with Britain. The group situated within the Persian Gulf consists of Bahrain (which is an island) and eight family estates on the Arabian shore—Qatar, Abu Dhabi, Dubai, Sharjah and four even smaller holdings. Since some have oil resources, while others are merely hoping for them, an assortment of ruling families has hitherto preferred not to federate. All are British-protected, in that Britain long ago bound itself to look after their defence and foreign relations, but none are termed protectorates, and each runs its own domestic affairs. In the protectorates on the south side of the Arabian peninsula (the so-called Aden protectorates) the British connexion was for years the same in theory, but was in practice closer. Though each state nominated its own ruler, the choice was subject to recognition by the Governor of Aden; further, all were so poor that the British taxpayer virtually financed them. In contrast to the Persian Gulf sheikhs, some of these southern rulers fell in with the British view that a federation might safeguard their future, and began to form one in 1959.

Retention of British sovereignty at Aden was devised by the British government in 1963 as a means of retaining a base of the old imperial pattern, to replace vanished or vanishing strong points at Suez and in Kenya. An "amphibious joint service task force" stationed east of Suez was wanted for three reasons—as a staging post, acclimatization area and storage point half way to Singapore, and manned in the interests of global strategy; as a toe-hold from which "to protect our oil"; and as a springboard from which to fulfil pledges to Arab rulers, and other allies.

Assessment of the first requirement is a conundrum even for the experts whose job it is to pay and plan for each fresh nuclear missile or deterrent. Assessment of the second is less conjectural. Most of the experiences recounted in this book suggest that, in peace time, there are guarantees as good as or better than the presence of alien troops for ensuring the flow of Arab oil, and that the best is to offer the vendor state (who needs income just as badly as Britain needs oil) an assured market and a steady revenue. Despite the change of régime in Iraq in 1958, and the change of status in Kuwait in 1961, these were the factors that continued to govern the direction of the oil trade.

But supply, say some, is not Britain's only cause for concern about the safety of Persian Gulf oil; this last is important also for its effect on the British balance of international payments. Their anxiety is or was justified. For many years, there appeared in the invisible accounts of this balance a current item of some importance —the profit from British oil operations in the Gulf—as well as a sizeable capital item—large-scale investment in London by rulers wishing to hold savings in a place of safety for use if and when their oil was exhausted. (No figures can be given, as both items appear under more comprehensive heads.) But the contention, though valid in the nineteen-fifties, when profit margins on oil operations in the Middle East were big enough to constitute a credit item of significance, became unimportant in the nineteen-sixties owing to substantial reduction of those margins. Further, by the same date the flow of Arab investment into London was less assured. Some of the rich rulers in the Gulf had become aware that the danger to ward against was less the exhaustion of their oil than encroachment by Arab neighbours, and had realized that the best way to buy security for the future was to put their money to work not in London, but in other Arab states.

The best of Britain's reasons for continued involvement in the politics of an Arab peninsula is the British pledge to protect Arab sheikhdoms against encroachment. Yet there are snags to fulfilling a promise given in conditions very different from those of today.

When British protection was first offered by the British authorities in India, and first accepted by the Persian Gulf sheikhs, it was envisaged on the British side as a purely naval operation. The land frontiers of each sheikhdom lay in uncoveted deserts, and more than once as the years went by, British officials neglected chances to define them. They let matters slide either because the drawing of boundaries seemed unimportant in such sands, or else out of reluctance to stir up old feuds. By the time of Arab awakening to land values in the era of oil discovery, this omission had become difficult to repair; moreover, since the protecting power had undertaken to look after external relations, undelimited frontiers between Arabs had become a British liability.

Trouble followed as soon as the larger neighbours began to lay claim to all or part of some sheikhdoms as belonging to their own domain. From time to time, the Yemen staked claims on the borders of the Aden Protectorates; intermittently, Persia reiterated a claim to Bahrain. In 1952, as has already been mentioned, Saudi Arabian expansionists took advantage of old King Ibn Saud's incapacity during his last illness to take a step that he would never have countenanced, and to try conclusions with Great Britain in order to push the Saudi frontier eastwards towards the sea; they chose as their first objective the only place with which the Saudi family had any vestige of historical connexion, which was the oasis of Buraimi. In 1957, the same Saudis sought to create themselves a *Sudetenland* by assisting an uprising in Oman. In 1961, directly the Kuwaitis acquired full independence, the Iraqi head of state claimed Kuwait as part of Iraq.

From the British standpoint, the essential feature of these disputed claims was that they committed British troops to arresting expansion by Arab at the expense of Arab. If the sole objective was to preserve the *status quo*, British intervention at the request of one side was in every case a success. But what did Britain gain or lose by taking sides in Arabia?

On the asset side, a promise was honoured. When calls for help came, response was made, and British troops were more than once welcomed by some threatened ruler. But there were offsetting liabilities. British intervention always generated hostility in other Arab states, and often in states whose goodwill was even more important to Britain than that of the ruler in jeopardy. Further, even within the sheikhdom that got the help, many nationalists accepted it with reserve. They tolerated it largely because political or social conditions in the encroaching state were not sufficiently inviting to stir their instincts for Arab unity, or to cause them to want to exchange a free and profitable life under the British umbrella for the restrictions and hazards that prevail in some of the Arab League states. But these conditions are open to change, and so is the Arab mood. While the demand for British intervention lasts, there are grounds for maintaining the "perpetual" undertakings given in a climate of Victorian confidence about the future. Yet they call for thought, for they expose Britain to forseeable embarrassment. What if a ruler wants the help, and his people do not?

In the bottom of most hearts in the Gulf sheikhdoms, there is a hankering ultimately to belong to some larger unit than a principality that is in some cases little more than a family estate, or an oilfield. Therefore should conditions change, and either the Arab League reorganize itself in unity, or some strong and well-managed Arab state or federation of states seek to attract some or all of the coastal sheikhdoms into its orbit, their response might be cordial, and Britain would gain nothing by trying to prolong dependence on itself. It has lost nothing by acknowledging the independence of Kuwait.

By acceding, in 1961, to Kuwait's wish for full independence, the British seized a chance to reduce commitments that had in the course of time become awkward. At Aden in 1963, by contrast, they committed themselves more deeply than before to involvement in the affairs of Arabia. For they induced the citizens of Aden Colony to join an Arab Federation that is being groomed for ultimate independence, yet in the same agreement they retained their own sovereignty at Aden. They thus linked the labour force on which their Aden base must rely to an Arab group that is bound to develop familiar symptoms; experience in all other dependencies shows that dependent peoples grow more nationalist as Independence Day approaches. The British furnished the people of Aden with a loophole through which to quit the South Arabian Federation, but none through which to leave the British fold. Yet they linked them to a group that might, if central Arabia or Yemen were to outgrow its age of despotism, one day wish to add itself to some larger Arab federation. (A revolution in Yemen broke out in 1962.)

For a span of time that no one can predict, jobs and a building boom at the Aden base may hold nationalism in check, but such sweeteners have never yet proved lasting. As in the Canal Zone, the duration of that span is not in Britain's control; it hangs on Arab politics. And at the politics of the rest of Arabia the Arabs of Aden are bound forever to be looking over their shoulder.

Seen in retrospect, the marks that the British left on the Middle East as a result of forty years of dominance are less arresting than those they left behind them at other points in Asia and Africa. The great heritage of culture and administration that they left to India was not repeated, partly for lack of time, and partly because an autumn sowing of gifts and services was quickly overgrown by the nationalism of peoples wishing to revive civilizations of their own. Yet political and administrative training at British hands left a certain heritage; this is discernible when administration in the Middle Eastern countries which lived for a spell under British control or mandate is compared with that in Middle Eastern countries which did not; the marks are also to be seen in the many countries in which ex-Palestinian Arabs educated during the mandate are sought as employees in the upper reaches of professional and administrative work.

Nevertheless, the British hallmark was not deeply engraved. Parliaments, courts of justice and civil services on the British model soon began to wither for lack of roots everywhere except in Israel; there they survive less as a monument to the mandate than as evidence that Western institutions, to flourish readily, need the Western background of education and intellectual formation that so many of the Jews possessed.

Elsewhere, ruler after ruler dispensed with parliamentary democracy; some even required robed judges to take part in their triumphal parades. But, of the authoritarian heads of state, only Nasser felt sufficiently sure of his following to be candid about one major reason why he could not brook democratic checks and balances:

Political parties are banned in Egypt at the moment because I was determined that our measures to improve the great mass of the people should be put through without opposition or sabotage.[3]

In a word, development cannot be hastened without continuity.

There is another reason why the main countries of the Middle East were less receptive to British ideas than were Indians. In addition to a difference in cast of mind between the Indian and the Egyptian or Iraqi, there was a significant constitutional difference in the relationship Britain bore to each. In India the relationship was clear-cut; the British were masters. In Egypt and Iraq they were masters in fact but not in name; an element of make-believe was injected by the British into the so-called independence of both states. British preoccupation with the defence of an Empire to which neither of the two nations belonged created ambiguities that soured two peoples neither truly independent on the one hand, nor comfortably communing within the Commonwealth on the other. Memories of British dominance are noticeably warmer in territories with which the relationship with Britain was unequivocal, as it was in the Sudan.

The best kind of epitaph commemorates a life that was worth living. Britain, in its forty years of dominance in the Middle East, earned enough acquiescence, and at times admiration, to save the British skin in two world wars. It also afforded the local peoples a life-giving interlude of freedom from the disagreement and upheaval that was bound to follow the break-up of the Ottoman Empire—an interlude that, at the beginning of 1963, still continues in the Persian Gulf and south Arabia.

All told, there was less British dishonesty about policy than is often imagined. Successively, Kitchener and Grey, Lloyd George and Balfour, Churchill, Eden and Bevin pursued British ends according to their lights. Some of them underrated nationalism; all had to weigh considerations in the Middle East against British interests far and wide outside it; each worked in as much ignorance of the future as does the statesman of today when he contemplates the Arabia or the Persia of tomorrow. Each, having surveyed the whole range of British interests not only abroad but at home, acted as he thought was for the best. "Had I known the unknown," says the Koran, "I would have done more good."

FAMILY TREE OF BRITAIN'S HASHIMITE ALLIES

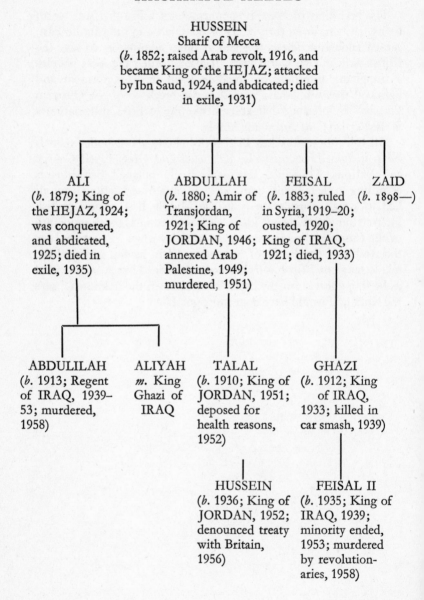

HUSSEIN
Sharif of Mecca
(*b.* 1852; raised Arab revolt, 1916, and
became King of the HEJAZ; attacked
by Ibn Saud, 1924, and abdicated; died
in exile, 1931)

ALI
(*b.* 1879; King of
the HEJAZ, 1924;
was conquered,
and abdicated,
1925; died in
exile, 1935)

ABDULLAH
(*b.* 1880; Amir of
Transjordan,
1921; King of
JORDAN, 1946;
annexed Arab
Palestine, 1949;
murdered, 1951)

FEISAL
(*b.* 1883; ruled
in Syria, 1919–20;
ousted, 1920;
King of IRAQ,
1921; died, 1933)

ZAID
(*b.* 1898—)

ABDULILAH
(*b.* 1913; Regent
of IRAQ, 1939–
53; murdered,
1958)

ALIYAH
m. King
Ghazi of
IRAQ

TALAL
(*b.* 1910; King of
JORDAN, 1951;
deposed for
health reasons,
1952)

GHAZI
(*b.* 1912; King
of IRAQ,
1933; killed in
car smash, 1939)

HUSSEIN
(*b.* 1936; King of
JORDAN, 1952;
denounced treaty
with Britain,
1956)

FEISAL II
(*b.* 1935; King of
IRAQ, 1939;
minority ended,
1953; murdered
by revolution-
aries, 1958)

REFERENCES

INTRODUCTION (pp. 11–21)

1. First report of the Committee of Imperial Defence; quoted in Lord Hankey. *The Supreme Command: 1914–1918*. London: Allen & Unwin. 1961. Vol. I. p. 46.
2. Alanbrooke, Lord. "Notes on my Life"; quoted in Arthur Bryant. *Triumph in the West*: Completing the Diaries of Field-Marshal Viscount Alanbrooke. London: Collins. 1959. p. 533.
3. Ewart, British ambassador to Prussia, 1791; quoted in J. Holland Rose. *William Pitt and National Revival*. London: Bell. 1912. p. 617.
4. Statement of P. & O. Superintendent to a Select Parliamentary Committee, 1858; quoted in H. L. Hoskyns. *British Routes to India*. London: Longmans, Green. 1928. p. 289.
5. Lytton to Cranbrook, 1878; quoted in E. Thompson and G. T. Garratt. *Rise and Fulfilment of British Rule in India*. London: Macmillan. 1934. p. 516.
6. White to Salisbury, 1885; quoted in C. L. Smith. *The Embassy of Sir William White at Constantinople*. London: O.U.P. 1957. p. 160.
7. Cecil, Lady G. *Life of Robert, Marquis of Salisbury*. London: Hodder & Stoughton. 1931. Vol. IV. pp. 139–40.
8. Robinson, R. and Gallagher, J. with Alice Denny. *Africa and the Victorians*. London: Macmillan. 1961. p. 289.
9. Grey to Lowther, July 1908. *British Documents on the Origin of the War*. London: H.M.S.O. 1928. Vol. V. p. 263.

1. ACCIDENT AND DESIGN IN WAR: 1914–18 (pp. 23–49)

1. Sykes Papers. Sledmere No. 1.
2. Wingate Papers. Box 236/2.
3. Grey to Cambon, May 16, 1916. Text of Sykes-Picot Agreement in J. C. Hurewitz. *Diplomacy in the Near and Middle East*. New York: Van Nostrand. 1956. Vol. II. p. 19.
4. Stein, L. *The Balfour Declaration*. London: Vallentine Mitchell. 1961. p. 223. The circumstances of Grey's proposal are described in Chapter 14 of this book.
5. *Arab Bulletin*. No. 77. January 1918.
6. Hankey, Lord. op. cit. Vol. II. p. 599.
7. Stein, L. op. cit. p. 309.
8. Amery, L. S. *My Political Life*. London: Hutchinson. 1953. Vol. II. p. 102.
9. Dugdale, Blanche. *Arthur James Balfour*. London: Hutchinson, 1936. Vol. II. p. 201.

10. Text in Sir A. T. Wilson. *Loyalties: Mesopotamia. 1917–1920*. London: O.U.P. 1930. Vol. I. pp. 237–8.
11. Stein, L. op. cit. p. 550.
12. Yale Papers. Report No. 7, December 12, 1917.

2. TOGETHER AT THE PEACE: 1919–22 (pp. 50–70)

1. *Documents on British Foreign Policy 1919–39*. London: H.M.S.O. Series I: Vol. IV. Document 242 of August 11, 1919. pp. 340–1.
2. Memorandum quoted in Winston Churchill. *The World Crisis : The Aftermath*. London: Thornton Butterworth. 1929. p. 361; New York: Scribners. 1929. pp. 381–2.
3. Yale Papers: Notes of interviews in London, September–October 1919. Interview with T. E. Lawrence of October 8, 1919.
4. Quoted in George Young. *Egypt*. London: Benn. 1927. p. 228.
5. Nicolson, Harold. *Curzon: The Last Phase*. London: Constable. 1934. p. 136.
6. Memorandum from Foreign Office to Secretary of State, Washington. Initialled C. of K. March 1, 1922. Text in *Foreign Relations of the United States*. 1927. Washington: U.S. Government Printing Office. Vol. III. p. 524.
7. Burgoyne, E. *Gertrude Bell: from her Personal Papers. 1914–26*. (Letter of September 5, 1920.) London: Benn. 1961. p. 162.
8. General Staff memorandum of December 1919; quoted in Winston Churchill. op. cit. p. 371 (London), p. 393 (New York).
9. Storrs, Ronald. *Orientations*. London: Nicholson & Watson. 1937. pp. 505–6.
10. Meinertzhagen, R. M. *Middle East Diary. 1917–1956*. London: Cresset Press. 1959. p. 26.
11. *Documents* etc. I:IV. op. cit. p. 592.
12. Cox, Percy. "Summary of Events in Iraq" published in *The Letters of Gertrude Bell*. Ed. Lady Bell. London: Benn. 1927. Vol. II. p. 528.
13. *The Sunday Times,* London, August 22, 1920. Printed in *The Letters of T. E. Lawrence*. Ed. David Garnett. London: Cape. 1938. pp. 315–7. Letters 123 to 136 in this collection put the same case.
14. Wavell, Lord. *Allenby in Egypt*. London: Harrap. 1943. p. 77.
15. Meinertzhagen, R. M. op. cit. p. 25.

3. THE YEARS OF GOOD MANAGEMENT: 1922–45
(pp. 71–94)

1. Private letter from C. J. Edmonds to the author, 1961.
2. *The Times*, London, November 30, 1922.
3. Quoted in A. J. Toynbee. *Survey of International Affairs*. 1925: Vol. I. London: O.U.P. for R.I.I.A. Appendix IV. p. 580.

4. Grobba to the Wilhelmstrasse (tr.), November 9, 1937. Text in *Les Archives Secrètes de la Wilhelmstrasse*. Paris: Plon. 1954. Vol. V. Book 2. pp. 19–20. The description of the Nazi attitude to Palestine on page 85 of the present book is based on this volume of the Wilhelmstrasse documents.

5. Hull, Cordell. *Memoirs*. London: Hodder & Stoughton. 1948, and New York: Macmillan Company. 1948. Vol. II. p. 1502.

6. *Fables de La Fontaine*. Book VI: Fable 8. "Le Vieillard et l'Ane".

7. *The Times*, London, May 30, 1941.

8. Text of the Biltmore Program in J. C. Hurewitz. op. cit. Vol. II. pp. 234–5.

4. THE ROLE OF OIL IN BRITISH GOVERNMENT POLICY (pp. 95–115)

1. Churchill to the House of Commons, June 7, 1914.

2. Baldwin to the House of Commons, March 26, 1929; appended to his statement is the full text of the Treasury letter of May 25, 1914. (Hansard: Cols. 2263–4).

3. Wilson, A. T. *South West Persia: Letters and Diary of a Young Political Officer*. London: Readers' Union for O.U.P. 1942. p. 290.

4. *Documents* etc. I:IV. op. cit. Document 265 of September 9, 1919. p. 374.

5. Letter in *The Times*, London, August 2, 1924.

6. Edmonds, C. J. *Kurds, Turks and Arabs*. London: O.U.P. 1957. p. 398.

7. Longrigg, S. *Oil in the Middle East*. London: O.U.P. for R.I.I.A. 2nd edition. 1960. p. 107.

8. Letter from Foreign Office to Embassy of the United States, March 4, 1932. Text in *Foreign Relations of the United States*. 1932. Washington: U.S. Government Printing Office. Vol. II. p. 9.

9. *Yearbook of the International Court of Justice: 1951–1952*. Chapter V: V. Anglo-Iranian Oil Company case (United Kingdom v. Iran). (Preliminary Objection.) pp. 85–6.

10. Churchill to the House of Commons, July 17, 1914.

11. Eden, Anthony. *Full Circle*. London: Cassell. 1960. p. 358; Boston: Houghton Mifflin. 1960. p. 401.

12. Eden, Anthony. op. cit. p. 465 (London), p. 520 (Boston).

5. THE SPECTRUM OF MIDDLE EAST RESISTANCE (pp. 116–130)

1. Lord Lloyd to the House of Lords. December 11, 1929.

2. Rondot, Pierre. In *Revue Générale de Droit International Public* for

July–December 1948; quoted in G. E. Kirk. *The Middle East in the War. Survey of International Affairs : 1939–46.* London: O.U.P. for R.I.I.A. 1952. p. 305.

3. Pannikar, K. M. *Asia and Western Dominance.* London: Allen & Unwin. 1953, and New York: John Day. 1954. p. 262.
4. Thompson, E. *A Farewell to India.* London: Benn, 1931. p. 85.
5. Translated as Appendix VII in G. Lenczowski. *Russia and the West in Iran.* New York: Cornell University Press. 1929. pp. 328–376.

6. THE DECLINE OF BRITISH NERVE (pp. 131–150)

1. *National Review.* February 1903. p. 989. This article, purporting to be extracted from a "History of the British Empire" published in A.D. 2031, gives an idea of what young men of its day thought about imperialism. It was anonymous, but was written by a Conservative, Cuthbert Medd – a young Fellow of All Souls who had died in 1902.
2. Buchan, John. *A Lodge in the Wilderness.* Edinburgh: Wm. Blackwood. 1906. p. 78.
3. Forster, E. M. *The Longest Journey.* pub. 1907. London: Edward Arnold. 1943 edition. p. 146.
4. Buchan, John. op. cit. Nelson edition. 1916. p. x.
5. Thornton, A. P. *The Imperial Idea and its Enemies : A study in British Power.* London: Macmillan. 1959. p. 81.
6. *The Round Table.* September 1928. p. 772.
7. Macdonald to Allenby, October 7, 1925. Text in Hurewitz. op. cit. p. 129.
8. *The Westminster Gazette,* July 28, 1924.
9. Cromer, Lord. *Ancient and Modern Imperialism.* London: Murray. 1910. p. 75.
10. Eden to the House of Commons, February 24, 1936. The report he summarized had been reproduced, partly verbatim and partly in summary, in the *Giornale d'Italia* of February 20, 1936.
11. Letter in *The Times,* London, December 12, 1935.
12. Murray, Gilbert. *From the League to the United Nations.* London: O.U.P. 1948. pp. 20 and 23.

7. THE YEARS OF IMPOTENCE 1945–54 (pp. 151–177)

1. R.I.I.A. Cairo Group. "The Importance of the Middle East." Paper I of *The Interests of the Commonwealth in the Middle East.* Preparatory papers for an unofficial Commonwealth Relations Conference, 1945. p. 1.
2. Bevin to an International Conference of Agricultural Producers, May 20, 1946.
3. Williams, Francis. *A Prime Minister Remembers : the War and Post-*

War Memoirs of the Rt. Hon. Earl Attlee. London: Heinemann. 1961. p. 134.

4. *Mr. President: The First Publication from the Personal Diaries, Private Letters, Papers and Revealing Interviews by Harry S. Truman.* ed. William Hillman. New York: Farrer, Strauss & Young. 1952. p. 23.

5. Bevin to the Labour Party Conference, Scarborough, May 20, 1948.

6. Dalton, Hugh. *High Tide and After.* London: Frederick Muller. 1962. The quotation is from a broadcast of March 14, 1947, by the American commentator Joseph Harsch, of which Dalton thought so well as to reproduce it at length.

7. *The Forrestal Diaries* (entry for February 25, 1947). ed. Walter Millis. London: Cassell. 1952. p. 242; New York: Viking Press. 1951. p. 245.

8. Quoted in *The Forrestal Diaries.* op. cit. pp. 367–8 (London), p. 387 (New York).

9. Weizmann, Chaim. *Trial and Error.* London: Hamish Hamilton. 1949. p. 543; Philadelphia: Jewish Publication Society of America. 1949. p. 442.

10. Alanbrooke, Lord. Diary for November 6, 1944; quoted in Arthur Bryant. *Triumph in the West.* op. cit. p. 321.

11. Quoted in Walid Khalidi. "The Fall of Haifa" in monthly *Middle East Forum.* Beirut: December 1959. p. 26.

12. Bevin to the House of Commons, March 23, 1948.

13. Lambton, Anne K. S. "The Impact of the West on Persia", in R.I.I.A. quarterly *International Affairs.* January 1957. p. 24.

14. Interview with Marguerite Higgins. *The New York Herald Tribune,* November 21, 1952.

15. *Egyptian Green Book* on Anglo-Egyptian conversations of 1950–51. Government Printing Press. Cairo: pp. 95–6.

16. Head to the House of Commons, July 28, 1954.

8. THE FRAGMENTATION OF POWERS: 1955–6
(pp. 178–206)

1. *Al Akbar.* Cairo: December 19, 1954. (Quoted in BBC Summary of World Broadcasts; Part IV, No. 529.)

2. Eden to the House of Commons, March 8, 1955.

3. *The Economist,* London, March 19, 1955. p. 979.

4. Eden in reply to Morrison, House of Commons, March 30, 1955.

5. Nuri Pasha to the Iraq Chamber of Deputies, February 2, 1955. (Summarized, with quotations, in BBC SWB, Part IV, No. 542.)

6. *The Times,* London, May 7, 1956.

7. King Hussein of Jordan. *Uneasy Lies the Head.* London: Heinemann 1962. p. 138; New York. Bernard Geis Associates. 1962. p. 138.

8. *The Sunday Times* and *The Observer*, London, March 25, 1956.
9. Stevenson, R. L. *Weir of Hermiston*. Tusitala edition. London: Heinemann. 1924. pp. 17 and 21.
10. Dulles at a Press conference in London, October 2, 1956. *Department of State Bulletin,* October 15, 1956. p. 577.
11. Eden, Anthony. *Full Circle*. op. cit. p. 358 (London), p. 401 (Boston).
12. Full text in *Documents on International Affairs, 1956.* London: O.U.P. for R.I.I.A. p. 261.
13. Churchill, Winston. *The Second World War*. Vol. I. London: Cassell. 1948. p. 201; Boston: Houghton Mifflin. 1948. pp. 257–8.
14. Eden, A. op. cit. p. 258 (London), p. 590 (Boston).
15. Eden, A. op. cit. p. 437 (London), p. 487 (Boston).

9. AFTERMATH AND GLEANINGS (pp. 207–219)

1. King Hussein of Jordan. op. cit. p. 204.
2. Rondot, Pierre. *The Changing Patterns in the Middle East*. (Tr.) London: Chatto & Windus. 1961. p. 14.
3. Nasser, President. Article based on conversations with David Wynne-Morgan. *The Sunday Times*, London, July 1, 1962.

BIBLIOGRAPHICAL NOTES

A. GENERAL BOOKS ON BRITISH POLICY

BULLARD, SIR READER. *Britain and the Middle East: from the earliest times to 1950.* London, 1951.

MARLOWE, JOHN. *Arab Nationalism and British Imperialism.* London, 1961.

KIRK, GEORGE E. *A Short History of the Middle East.* London, 1948.

ROYAL INSTITUTE OF INTERNATIONAL AFFAIRS (R.I.I.A.) *The Middle East: a political and economic Survey.* Third edition. London, 1958.

R.I.I.A. *Survey of International Affairs.*

The two special volumes in this series that are wholly devoted to the Middle East in the Second World War and after are listed as relevant to Chapters III and VII below. But useful sections on Middle Eastern history by Professor Arnold Toynbee and other hands are to be found in the annual volumes for:
1925 (Vol. I), 1928, 1930, 1934, 1936, 1937, 1938 (Vol. I), 1951, 1952, 1953, 1954, 1955–6, and 1957–8.

Two books on Asia, though dealing chiefly with India, are relevant to Middle Eastern disquiet and nationalism:

PANNIKAR, K. M. *Asia and Western Dominance.* London 1953; New York, 1954.

WINT, GUY. *The British in Asia.* London, 1947.

B. PUBLISHED DOCUMENTS

One collection, excellently annotated, deals exclusively with the Middle East:

HUREWITZ, J. C. *Diplomacy in the Near and Middle East.* Vol. I: 1534–1914; Vol. II: 1914–1956.

Volume II contains all or part of the text of many major British diplomatic documents in the period covered by this book.

See also:

British Documents on the Origins of the War: 1898–1914. ed. Gooch and Temperley. Vols. V, IX (Part II) and X. London, H.M.S.O.

Documents on British Foreign Policy: 1918–1939. ed. Woodward and Butler. First Series. London, H.M.S.O.

Volume IV is indispensable to study of the post-war settlement in the Middle East.

Important documents on Anglo-Arab relations during the First World War were published in three British White Papers issued for purposes of the Palestine Round Table Conference of 1939:

Cmd. 5957. *Correspondence between Sir Henry McMahon and the Sharif of Mecca.*

Cmd. 5964. *Statements made on behalf of His Majesty's Government during the year 1918 in regard to the future status of certain parts of the Ottoman Empire.*

Cmd. 5974. *Report of a Committee set up to consider certain correspondence between Sir Henry McMahon and the Sharif of Mecca in 1915 and 1916.*

See also:

Die Europäische Mächte un die Türkei während des Weltkrieges. ed. E. Adamov. German translation of Volume VI of documents from the Czarist archives published in Moscow in 1924. Dresden, 1932.

Foreign Relations of the United States. Washington, Government Printing Press: annually.

Documents relating to the Palestine Problem. London, Jewish Agency, 1945.

Les Archives Secrètes de la Wilhelmstrasse. Paris, 1954. Volume V: Livre II of this French translation of Nazi documents covers the Middle East in 1937–9.

R.I.I.A. *Documents on International Affairs.* London, annually.

The volume for 1956 is particularly useful on the Baghdad Pact and the Suez crisis.

C. UNPUBLISHED PAPERS

The Arab Bulletin: 1915–1919. Reports prepared by the Arab Bureau in Cairo. Available by permission of the Foreign Office Library, London.

The Arabian Report. Prepared weekly in London by Sir Mark Sykes for a short period in the second half of 1916. Available by permission of the Foreign Office Library, London.

The Papers of Lord Milner. Available by permission of the Librarian of New College, Oxford. Include material on Allenby's political embarrassments in Palestine and Syria, on British plans for Egypt, and on British military withdrawal from Persia in 1919–20.

The Sledmere Papers of Sir Mark Sykes. Available by permission of Sir Richard Sykes at Sledmere, East Yorkshire, or in microfilm at St. Antony's College, Oxford. Include material on British wartime negotiations with Arabs and Zionists, and on plans for the future of Asiatic Turkey.

The Papers of Sir Reginald Wingate. This huge collection, available by permission of the School of Oriental Studies, Durham University, includes material on the British negotiations with the Sharif of Mecca, and on relations with Egypt between 1916 and 1919.

The Yale Papers. Originals in the open archives of the State Department, Washington; parts available in microfilm at St Antony's College, Oxford. William Yale reported from Cairo (1917) and later from Palestine, Syria and Paris, chiefly on the desires of the Middle Eastern peoples.

D. WESTERN PERIODICALS SPECIALIZING IN MIDDLE EASTERN POLITICS

LONDON:

The BBC *Summary of World Broadcasts* (SWB). Daily digests of foreign broadcasts began in 1939. The issue of a separate section (Part IV) on the Arab World, Israel, Greece, Turkey and Persia began in April 1949. (A corresponding monitoring service is available in Washington.)

The Jewish Observer and Middle East Review. Weekly from 1952.

The Mid-East Mirror. A weekly digest of newspaper news and articles from 1949.

The Mizan Newsletter. A monthly review of Soviet writing on the Middle East. From 1959.

The Near East and India. Weekly from 1908; became *Great Britain and the East* from 1935. Outclassed after the Second World War.

The Royal Central Asian Journal. Quarterly.

PARIS:

Les Cahiers de l'Orient Contemporain. Quarterly from 1945. Give extracts from press and speeches.

Orient. Quarterly from 1957.

Revue du Monde Musulman. Nos. 1–66 from 1907 until 1926.

WASHINGTON:

The Middle East Journal. Quarterly from 1947.

ROME:
Oriente Moderno. Monthly from 1921.

LEIDEN:
Die Welt des Islams. Quarterly from 1913 to 1942; resumed publication 1951. Includes material in English.

E. SOURCE MATERIAL FOR CHAPTERS

INTRODUCTION

HOSKINS, H. L. *British Routes to India.* London, 1928.

ROBINSON, R. and GALLAGHER, J., with ALICE DENNY. *Africa and the Victorians: the official mind of Imperialism.* London, 1961.

and, on points of detail:

GREAVES, R. L. *Persia and the Defence of India: 1884–1892.* London, 1959.

MARLOWE, JOHN. *Anglo-Egyptian Relations: 1800–1953.* London, 1954.

SMITH, C. L. *The Embassy of Sir William White to Constantinople: 1886–1891.* London, 1957.

WILSON, SIR A. T. *The Persian Gulf.* London, 1928.

CHAPTER I. ACCIDENT AND DESIGN IN WAR: 1914–1918

In addition to official war histories, and to passages in the well-known memoirs and biographies of statesmen and soldiers involved, notably Asquith, Balfour, Beaverbrook, Churchill, Grey, Kitchener, T. E. Lawrence, Lloyd George, Robertson and Smuts, the following are of special interest:

AMERY, L. S. *My Political Life.* Vol. II. London, 1953.

BERTIE, LORD. *The Diary of Lord Bertie of Thame.* ed. Lady Algernon Gordon Lennox. London, 1924.

CAMBON, PAUL. *Correspondance 1870–1924.* Vol. III. Paris, 1946.

FYVEL, T. R. "Weizmann and the Balfour Declaration." In Weisgal, M. and Carmichael J. (ed). *Chaim Weizmann: a biography by several hands.* London, 1962.

HANKEY, LORD. *The Supreme Command: 1914–1918.* 2 vols. London, 1961.

LESLIE, SHANE. *Mark Sykes: his life and letters.* London, 1923.

SAMUEL, VISCOUNT. *Memoirs.* London, 1945.

SANDERS, LIMAN VON. *Five Years in Turkey* (trs) Annapolis, 1928.

STORRS, SIR RONALD. *Orientations*. London, 1937.

WEIZMANN, CHAIM. *Trial and Error*. Philadelphia and London, 1949.

WINGATE, SIR RONALD. *Wingate of the Sudan*. London, 1955.

A relatively full picture can be obtained by reading Lord Hankey's book in conjunction with four histories of policy :

GOTTLIEB, W. W. *Studies in Secret Diplomacy during the First World War*. London, 1957.

KEDOURIE, ELIE. *Britain and the Middle East: the vital years: 1914–1921*. London, 1956. The most perceptive book available on Anglo-Arab relations.

PINGAUD, A. *Histoire diplomatique de la France pendant la Grande Guerre*. Vols. I and III. Paris, 1940.

STEIN, LEONARD. *The Balfour Declaration*. London, 1961. This scholarly book is broader in scope than its title suggests and includes a valuable bibliography of unpublished Zionist papers.

On political aspects of the campaigns in the Middle East, see:

ARTHUR, SIR G. *Life of Lord Kitchener*. Vol. III. London, 1920.

BREMOND, E. *Le Hedjaz dans la Guerre Mondiale*. Paris, 1931.

CHIROL, SIR V. *The Egyptian Problem*. London, 1921.

ELGOOD, P. G. *Egypt and the Army*. London, 1924.

EVANS, R. A. *Brief outline of the Campaign in Mesopotamia*. London, 1926.

LIDDELL HART, B. H. *T. E. Lawrence in Arabia and After*. London, 1934.

WAVELL, A. P. *The Palestine Campaigns*. London, 1929.

WILSON, SIR A. T. *Loyalties: Mesopotamia: 1914–1917*. London, 1930.

For the British excursions into central Asia, see:

LENCZOWSKI, G. *Russia and the West in Iran*. Cornell, N.Y., 1949.

ULLMAN, R. H. *Intervention in the War: Anglo-Soviet Relations 1917–1921*. Vol. I. Princeton, N.J. and London, 1961. Vol. II of this good book is to follow.

CHAPTER II. TOGETHER AT THE PEACE: 1919–22

The best history of the Anglo-French quarrel over Turkey's Arab provinces is:

ZEINE, Z. N. *The Struggle for Arab Independence*. Beirut: 1960. Has a comprehensive bibliography.

See also:

ANTONIUS, G. *The Arab Awakening*. London, 1938.

CUMMING, H. H. *Franco-British Rivalry in the Post-War Near East*. London, 1938.

HOWARD, H. N. *The Partition of Turkey*. Oklahoma, 1931.

KHAIRALLAH, K. T. *Le Problème du Levant: les régions arabes libéreés*. Paris, 1919.

In addition to standard histories of the Peace Conference, the following are useful works by or about men who participated in the peace settlement:

CATROUX, GENERAL G. *Deux Missions en Moyen Orient: 1919–1922*. Paris, 1958.

CHURCHILL, WINSTON. *The World Crisis: the Aftermath*. London and New York, 1929.

GARNETT, DAVID (ed.) *The Letters of T. E. Lawrence*. (Part III: 1918–22.) London, 1938.

HOUSE, EDWARD M. and SEYMOUR, C. (ed.) *What Really Happened at Paris*. New York, 1921.

LLOYD GEORGE, D. *The Truth about the Peace Treaties*. 2 vols. London, 1938.

MARTET, JEAN. *Clemenceau Peint par Lui-même*. Paris, 1929. *Les Silences de M. Clemenceau*. Paris, 1930.
These verbatim accounts of the events of Clemenceau's life as told to his former secretary include comment on his tussle with Lloyd George over Mosul and Syria.

MEINERTZHAGEN, R. M. *Middle East Diary: 1917–1956*. London, 1959. *Army Diary: 1899–1929*. London, 1960.

NICOLSON, HAROLD. *Peacemaking, 1919*. London, 1933. *Curzon: The Last Phase*. London, 1934.

LYAUTEY, PIERRE. *Le Drame Oriental et le Rôle de la France*. Paris, 1923.

SAMNE, GEORGE. *Raymond Poincaré*. Paris, 1933.
Includes a few details of Anglo-French interviews with Syrian Arabs.

YOUNG, SIR HUBERT. *The Independent Arab*. London, 1933.

For the settlement in individual areas:

ABDULLAH, KING. *Memoirs*. London, 1950.

BELL, LADY (ed.) *The Letters of Gertrude Bell*. Vol. II. London, 1927.
Includes a sketch of events by Sir Percy Cox.

BURGOYNE, E. *Gertrude Bell: from her personal papers: 1914–1926.* London, 1961.

COOPER, DUFF (Lord Norwich). *Old Men Forget.* London, 1954.
He was in the Egyptian Department of the Foreign Office, and in the know, at the time of the Milner Mission.

GRAVES, P. *The Life of Sir Percy Cox.* London, 1941.

KEDOURIE, E. *Sa'ad Zaghlul and the British.* In *St. Antony's Papers No. 11.* London, 1961.

KIRKBRIDE, SIR A. "The National Government of Moab." In *A Crackle of Thorns.* London, 1956.

KISCH, F. H. *Palestine Diary.* London, 1938.

LUKE, SIR HARRY. *Cities and Men: an Autobiography.* Vol. II. London, 1953.

PHILBY, H. ST. J. *Forty Years in the Wilderness.* (Chapter V on "T. E. Lawrence and his critics".) London, 1957.

SPECIAL COMMISSION TO EGYPT (The Milner Mission). *Report.* Cmd. 1131. London, H.M.S.O., 1921.

SYMES, SIR STEWART. *Tour of Duty.* London, 1946.

WAVELL, FIELD-MARSHAL VISCOUNT. *Allenby in Egypt.* London, 1943.

WILSON, SIR A. T. *Mesopotamia: 1917–1920: A Clash of Loyalties.* London, 1931.

CHAPTER III.

THE YEARS OF GOOD MANAGEMENT: 1922–1945

Books on the years between the wars are best listed country by country, with the exception of:

MONROE, E. *The Mediterranean in Politics.* London, 1938.

SETON-WILLIAMS, M. V. *Britain and the Arab States: 1920–1948.*
Is marred by many slips and mis-spellings of names, but is conveniently arranged, and prints the text of many agreements and statements of policy.

By countries, useful books dealing *inter alia* with British policy are:

For Egypt: COLOMBE, M. *L'Evolution de l'Egypte: 1923–1950.* Paris, 1951.

LITTLE, TOM. *Egypt.* London, 1958.

LLOYD, LORD. *Egypt since Cromer.* 2 vols. London, 1933.

R.I.I.A. *Great Britain and Egypt: 1914–1951.* Information Papers No. 19. Second edition: 1952.

and:

MARLOWE, J. *Anglo-Egyptian Relations,* op. cit.; YOUNG, G. *Egypt.* op. cit.

For Iraq: IRELAND, P. W. *Iraq.* London, 1937.

KHADDURI, MAJID. *Independent Iraq: 1932–1958.* Second edition. London, 1960.

LONGRIGG, S. *Iraq: 1900–1950.* London, 1953.

and:

BELL, LADY. *Gertrude Bell.* op. cit.; BURGOYNE, E. *Gertrude Bell.* op. cit.

For Palestine and Transjordan: BENTWICH, N. *England in Palestine.* London, 1932.

ESCO FOUNDATION. *Palestine: a study of Jewish, Arab and British Policies.* New Haven, Conn., 1947.

HUREWITZ, J. C. *The Struggle for Palestine.* New York, 1950.

LUKE, SIR HARRY. *Cities and Men.* Vol. III. London, 1956.

MARLOWE, J. *The Seat of Pilate.* London, 1959.

PALESTINE ROYAL COMMISSION (The Peel Commission). *Report.* Cmd. 5479. London, H.M.S.O. 1937.

HANNA, P. S. *British Policy in Palestine.* Washington, 1942.

R.I.I.A. *Great Britain and Palestine.* Information Papers No. 20, 3rd edition, 1946.

and:

STORRS, SIR R. *Orientations.* op. cit.; WEISGAL, M. W. and CAR-MICHAEL, J. *Chaim Weizmann.* op. cit. WEIZMANN, CHAIM. *Trial and Error.* op. cit.

For policy during the Second World War, the indispensable book is:

KIRK, G. E. *The Middle East in the War: 1939–1946.* In the R.I.I.A. Survey series. London, 1952.

Also relevant are the war memoirs or histories by Alanbrooke (ed. Bryant), Catroux, Churchill, Cordell Hull, Casey, Chandos, de Gaulle, Harry Hopkins, Truman, Wavell and Weygand. See also:

WILSON, FIELD-MARSHAL LORD. *Eight Years Overseas: 1939–1947.* London, 1950.

and, for Persia, LENCZOWSKI, G. *Russia and the West in Iran.* op. cit.

CHAPTER IV.

THE ROLE OF OIL IN BRITISH GOVERNMENT POLICY

For the history of the Middle Eastern oil concessions, the best book is:

LONGRIGG, S. *Oil in the Middle East.* 2nd edition. London, 1961.

See also:

DELAISI, F. *Oil: its influence on politics* (tr) London, 1922.

FINNIE, D. H. *Desert Enterprise.* Harvard, 1958.

FORD, ALAN W. *The Anglo-Iranian Oil Dispute of 1951–2.* Berkeley, Cal. 1954.

SHWADRAN, B. *The Middle East, Oil and the Great Powers.* New York, 1955. London, 1956.
Includes the best bibliography available, covering government print and articles in periodicals.

For the Mosul dispute, the best book is:

EDMONDS, C. J. *Kurds, Turks and Arabs.* London, 1957.

For the early years, see also:

MINEAU, WAYNE. *The Go-Devils.* London, 1958.

WILSON, A. T. *South-West Persia: Letters and Diary of a young Political Officer: 1907–1914.* London, 1942.

For Anglo-American government dealings, see correspondence published from 1919 in *Foreign Relations of the United States,* op. cit.; and:

FEIS, HERBERT. *Petroleum and American Foreign Policy.* Stanford, Cal. 1944.
———————— *Seen from E.A. Three International Episodes.* New York, 1947.

HOSKINS, H. L. *Middle East Oil in United States Foreign Policy.* Public Affairs Bulletin No. 89. Washington, 1950.

U.S. CONGRESS. Senate. *Hearings of Special Committee Investigating the National Defense Program. Part 41. Petroleum arrangement with Saudi Arabia.* (80th Congress: March, October and November 1947 and January 1948.) Washington, 1948.

For general problems of nationalization, price, etc., involving governments:

HARTSHORN, J. *Oil Companies and Governments.* London, 1962.

LEEMAN, W. A. *The Price of Middle East Oil.* Cornell, N.Y. and London, 1961.

WHITE, GILLIAN. *The Nationalisation of Foreign Property*. London, 1961.

CHAPTER V. THE SPECTRUM OF MIDDLE EAST RESISTANCE

Until after the Second World War, the only well-known books in English on Arab and Egyptian nationalism were:

ADAMS, C. C. *Islam and Modernism in Egypt*. London, 1933.

ANTONIUS, GEORGE. *The Arab Awakening*. op. cit.

For the scene in Ottoman times, see:

La Verité sur la Question Syrienne. Stamboul, 1916.

ZEINE, Z. N. *Arab-Turkish Relations and the Emergence of Arab Nationalism*. Beirut, 1958.

Since 1945 nationalism in general, and the intellectual leadership exercised by Cairo over nationalists in the Arabic-speaking states, have become subjects of much study. See:

AHMED, J. M. *The Intellectual Origins of Egyptian Nationalism*. London, 1960.

GIBB, SIR H. A. R. *Modern Trends in Islam*. Chicago, 1947.

HAIM, SYLVIA. *Arab Nationalism: an Anthology*. Los Angeles and London, 1962.

HOURANI, ALBERT. *Arabic Thought in the Liberal Age*. London, 1962.
This important book provides clues to Arab inaction as well as to thought. Includes a good bibliography.

LAQUEUR, W. Z. *Communism and Nationalism in the Middle East*. New York and London, 1956.

———————— (ed.) *The Middle East in Transition*. London, 1958.
The essays in Part I of this book make the essential connexion between nationalist feeling and social awakening.

NASSER, PRESIDENT GAMAL ABDEL. *The Philosophy of the Revolution*. Cairo, 1954.

NURI PASHA AS-SAID. *Arab Independence and Unity*. Baghdad, 1943.
Passages are reprinted in HUREWITZ, J. C. *Diplomacy*, Vol. 2. op. cit.

SAFRAN, NADAV. *Egypt in search of Political Community*. Harvard, 1961.

SAYEGH, FAYEZ A. *Arab Unity: Hope and Fulfilment*. New York, 1958.

Studies of social disquiet include:

BERGER, MORROE. *The Arab World To-day*. New York, 1962.

FISHER, SYDNEY, N. (ed.) *Social Forces in the Middle East*. Cornell, N.Y., 1955.

WARRINER, DOREEN. *Land and Poverty in the Middle East*. London, 1948. *Land Reform and Development in the Middle East*. London, 1957.

On Persian nationalism, there is no good book in English, but useful essays are:

KAZEMZADEH, F. "Ideological crisis in Iran." In LAQUEUR, W. Z. *The Middle East in Transition*. op. cit.

LAMBTON, ANNE K. S. "The Impact of the West on Persia." In the R.I.I.A. quarterly *International Affairs*, January 1957.

Persian resentment at British management of the oil industry is reflected in:

ELWELL SUTTON, L. P. *Persian Oil: a study in Power Politics*. London, 1955.

On Jewish nationalism and resistance to Britain:

EBAN, A. "Tragedy and Triumph" (1939–1949). In WEISGAL, M. W. *Chaim Weizmann*, op. cit.

KOESTLER, A. *Promise and Fulfilment: Palestine 1917–1949*. London, 1949.

TAYLOR, ALAN R. *Prelude to Israel: an analysis of Zionist Diplomacy*. New York, 1959.

TREVOR, DAPHNE. *Under the White Paper*. Jerusalem, 1948.

and, for the growth of armed resistance:

BAUER, Y. "The Beginnings of the Palmach: 1940–41" in *Studies in History*. Hebrew University of Jerusalem, 1961.

BEGIN, M. *The Revolt*. London, 1951.

KIMCHE, JON and DAVID. *The Secret Roads*. London, 1954.

WATERS, P. M. *Haganah* (pamphlet). London, 1947.

WILSON, R. D. *Cordon and Search: with 6th Airborne Division in Palestine: 1945–1948*. Aldershot, 1949.

CHAPTER VI. THE DECLINE OF BRITISH NERVE

The best book on the wane of imperialism in the whole period covered by this chapter is:

THORNTON, A. P. *The Imperial Idea and its Enemies*. London, 1959.

See also:

FIELDHOUSE, D. K. "Imperialism: an historiographical Revision" in *The Economic Historical Review*. London. Second Series. Vol. XIV. No. 2, 1961.

and the file of *The Round Table*, which began publication in 1909.

On the motives for nineteenth-century imperialism:

BODELSEN, C. A. *Studies in mid-Victorian Imperialism.* Copenhagen, 1924. Reprinted London, 1960.

ROBINSON, R. and GALLAGHER, J. *Africa and the Victorians.* op. cit.

On economic motives:

BRAILSFORD, H. N. *The War of Steel and Gold.* London, 1914.

HOBSON, J. A. *Imperialism: a Study.* London, 1902.

LENIN, A. *Imperialism: the Highest State of Capitalism* (Russian edition, 1917) trs. New York, 1933.

STRACHEY, JOHN. *The End of Empire.* London, 1959.

On the bright side of imperialism:

HANCOCK, W. K. *Argument of Empire.* London, 1943.

MADARIAGA S. DE and BRAILSFORD, H. N. *"Can the League Cope with Imperialism?"* Discussion published by the Foreign Policy Association. New York, 1928.

ZIMMERN, ALFRED. *The Third British Empire.* London, 1926.

For development of the idea that colonial rivalry was dangerous to the world:

BARNES, LEONARD. *The Future of Colonies.* London, 1936.

SWANWICK, H. M. *Builders of Peace: ten years' history of the Union of Democratic Control.* London, 1926.

TAYLOR, A. J. P. *The Troublemakers: Dissent over Foreign Policy: 1792–1939.* London, 1957.

WINKLER, HENRY R. *The League of Nations Movement in Great Britain: 1914–1919.* Rutgers, 1952.

WOOLF, LEONARD. *Imperialism and Civilisation.* London, 1928.

CHAPTER VII. THE YEARS OF IMPOTENCE: 1945–1954

Parts of this chapter have already appeared in my essay on "Mr. Bevin's Arab policy" in *St. Antony's Papers No. 11* (London, 1961); this deals at greater length with the Middle Eastern policy of the Labour government.

The most detailed survey available is:

KIRK, GEORGE. *The Middle East: 1945–1950.* In the R.I.I.A. *Survey* series. London, 1954.

Of the political memoirs of the period, much the most useful is the diary kept by James D. Forrestal, United States Secretary for the Navy and later for Defense. See:

BYRNES, JAMES. *Speaking Frankly*. New York and London, 1947.

EDEN, ANTHONY. *Full Circle*. London and New York, 1960.

DALTON, HUGH. *High Tide and After*. London, 1962.

MILLIS, WALTER (ed.) *The Forrestal Diaries*. New York, 1951. London, 1952.

TRUMAN, H. S. *Memoirs*. Vol. II. *Years of Trial and Hope*. New York and London, 1956.

WILLIAMS, FRANCIS. *Ernest Bevin*. London, 1951.

——————————— *A Prime Minister Remembers: the war and post-war memoirs of the Rt. Hon. Earl Attlee*. London, 1961.

On the Anglo-Egyptian prelude to the 1954 treaty. See:

EDEN, ANTHONY. *Full Circle:* (Book One). op. cit.

EGYPTIAN GREEN BOOK. *Records of Conversations, Notes and Papers exchanged.* . . . March 1950–November 1951. Cairo: Government Printing Press, 1951.

GREAT BRITAIN. *Anglo-Egyptian Conversations on the Defence of the Suez Canal and of the Sudan*. Cmd. 8419. London, H.M.S.O. 1951.

LACOUTURE, J. and S. *Egypt in Transition* (trs). New York and London, 1958.

On British policy in the last years of the Palestine mandate:

CROSSMAN, R. H. S. *Palestine Mission*. London, 1946.

GRAVES, R. M. *Experiment in Anarchy*. London, 1949.

GLUBB, J. B. *A Soldier with the Arabs*. London, 1957.

KIMCHE, JON. *Seven Fallen Pillars*. Revised edition: London, 1953.

KIMCHE, JON and DAVID. *Both Sides of the Hill: Britain and the Palestine War*. London, 1960.

KIRKBRIDE, SIR A. "The Army of Deliverance." In *A Crackle of Thorns*. London, 1956.

MANUEL, FRANK E. *The realities of American-Palestine Relations*. Washington, 1949.

GREAT BRITAIN. *Palestine: Statement relating to Causes of Violence* . . . Cmd. 6873. London, H.M.S.O. 1946.

SACHER, HARRY. *Israel: the Establishment of a State*. London, 1952.

CHAPTER VIII. THE FRAGMENTATION OF POWER: 1955–1956

The quarrel between Egypt and Iraq over the Baghdad Pact, and Britain's part in it, is best followed in the Mid-East Mirror and BBC SWB (Part IV) for the winter of 1954–55. Important issues of the SWB are, for Egypt, Nos. 534, 535 and 537 (January 1955) and for Iraq, No. 542 of February 1955.

For the rival policies, see also:

BIRDWOOD, LORD. *Nuri as-Said.* London, 1959.

IONIDES, M. *Divide and Lose: the Arab revolt 1955–1958.* London, 1960.

WHEELOCK, K. *Nasser's New Egypt.* New York and London, 1960. Includes useful references.

For British policy throughout the period:

EDEN, ANTHONY. *Full Circle.* op. cit.
In conjunction with this book should be read two perceptive reviews by Martin Wight in the R.I.I.A. quarterly *International Affairs*, July 1960, and by Alastair Buchan in the London monthly *Twentieth Century*, March 1960.

For Anglo-American relations on Middle Eastern matters:

CAMPBELL, JOHN C. *Defense of the Middle East.* Revised Edition. New York, 1960.
This useful book has a well-annotated bibliography, chiefly of American books, that need not be duplicated here.

NICHOLAS, H. G. *Britain and the United States.* London, 1963.

POLK, W. R. "America in the Middle East: 1947–1958" in *St. Antony's Papers No. 11.* London, 1961.

For background information on the Suez Canal:

WATT, D. C. *Britain and the Suez Canal: the background.* London, R.I.I.A., 1956.

POYDENOT, HENRI. *Le Canal de Suez.* Presses Universitaires de France. Paris, 1955.

For critical appreciations of the Suez Crisis:

BROMBERGER, MERRY and SERGE. *The Secrets of Suez.* (trs.) London, 1957.

CHILDERS, ERSKINE B. "The Ultimatum" in *The Spectator*, October 30, 1959.

——————————— *The Road to Suez.* London, 1962.

HOURANI, ALBERT. "The Crisis of 1956." In *St. Antony's Papers No. 4.* London, 1958.

WINT, G. and CALVOCORESSI, P. *Middle East Crisis.* London, 1957.

For Soviet policy, see:

LAQUEUR, W. Z. *The Soviet Union and the Middle East.* New York, 1959.

———————— *The Middle East in Transition.* op. cit. Part II is devoted to the subject.

———————— "The 'National Bourgeoisie': A Soviet Dilemma in the Middle East" in R.I.I.A. quarterly *International Affairs,* July 1959.

WHEELER, GEOFFREY. "Russia and the Middle East" in *International Affairs,* July 1959.

———————— with DAVID MORRISON. "Russia and the Arab World" in R.I.I.A. monthly *The World Today,* July 1961.

See also two bibliographies on Soviet literature, with brief English descriptions of the material:

Soviet Middle East Studies: an analysis and bibliography. R.I.I.A. London.

Bibliography of recent Source Material on Soviet Central Asia and its Borderlands.
Issued twice yearly by the Central Asian Research Centre, London.

CHAPTER IX. AFTERMATH AND GLEANINGS

The best analysis of the degree to which power changed hands after the Suez crisis is:

RONDOT, PIERRE. *The Changing Patterns in the Middle East.* (trs.) London, 1961.

Also relevant are:

CARACTACUS (pseud). *Revolution in Iraq.* London, 1959.

HUSSEIN, KING. *Autobiography: Uneasy Lies the Head.* London and New York, 1962.

QUBAIN, FAHIM. *Crisis in Lebanon.* Washington, 1961.

For events in Aden and the Persian Gulf area:

KELLY, J. B. "The Legal and Historical Basis of the British position in the Persian Gulf" in *St. Antony's Papers No. 4.* London, 1958.

———————— "Sovereignty and Jurisdiction in Eastern Arabia" in R.I.I.A. Quarterly *International Affairs,* January 1959.

Sultanate and Imamate in Oman. Chatham House Memorandum. December 1959.

Eastern Arabian Frontiers (to be published). London, 1963.

KING, GILLIAN. *The Future of Aden and British Defence Policy in the Indian Ocean.* Chatham House Essays series. London, 1963.

Q

INDEX